The Photographic History
of The Civil War

In Ten Volumes

THEATRE OF
**SOUTHWESTERN
CAMPAIGNS**

SCALE OF MILES

0   25   50   75   100

THE CHURCH WHERE THE VETERAN ARMIES CLASHED

The shot-holes in the little Dunker church of Antietam, and the dead in Blue and Gray as they lay after the battle-smoke had lifted, mark the center of the bloodiest single day's fighting in the Civil War. Here the grand armies of the North and South faced one another on September 17, 1862. At sunrise the action began; by 4 o'clock in the afternoon it was over, and the dead and wounded numbered twenty-three thousand five hundred. The preponderance of the army under McClellan, with his eighty-seven thousand men, was offset by the presence of three great Confederate leaders whose names had already rung round the world—Lee, Jackson, and Longstreet—with numbers less than half those opposed to them. On the 18th the armies lay exhausted; and on the 19th Lee abandoned his invasion of the North.

The Photographic History
of The Civil War

Two Years of Grim War

Francis Trevelyan Miller
Editor in Chief

Contributors

WILLIAM H. TAFT
President of the United States

HENRY WYSHAM LANIER
Art Editor and Publisher

EBEN SWIFT
Lieutenant-Colonel, U. S. A.

FRENCH E. CHADWICK
Rear-Admiral, U. S. N.

GEORGE HAVEN PUTNAM
Major, U. S. V.

MARCUS J. WRIGHT
Brigadier-General, C. S. A.

HENRY W. ELSON
Professor of History, Ohio University

JAMES BARNES
Author of "David G. Farragut"

CASTLE BOOKS ★ NEW YORK

CONTENTS

Contents

Part IV

Part V

FOREWORD TO VOLUME II

IT is the central act in the great American war drama, and the one of highest suspense, that is presented by Volume II of THE PHOTOGRAPHIC HISTORY. Volume III will be found to cover the period between the first move against Lee by Grant (May, 1864), and Appomattox—a series of battles bitterly contested, but properly described in the volume-title as "DECISIVE," since it had then become only a question of time, with skill and bravery so conspicuous on either side, before the weight of Northern resources and organization would inevitably crush the impoverished Confederacy. But prior to the unifying under Grant of the Federal military force in May, 1864, and subsequent to McClellan's Peninsula Campaign (with which Volume I closes), the actions form a veritable "tug-of-war," a giant struggle of veteran armies, the result of which no contemporary observer could determine. This is the period covered by the present volume—the combats of matched armies, while Federal and Confederate hoped alike, each praying for the triumph of the cause to which he had pledged his soul and body.

Each of the remaining seven volumes of THE PHOTOGRAPHIC HISTORY—IV to X—deals with a special side of the conflict: cavalry, soldier life, the navy, forts and artillery, prisons and hospitals, with other important phases being separately treated.

CEDAR MOUNTAIN—POPE'S ADVANCE IS CHECKED

PICKETS ON RESERVE—ACROSS THIS WHEATFIELD
THE UNION CHARGE WAS SWEPT BACK BY
"STONEWALL" JACKSON

WHERE THE COMMANDER HEARD THE CANNONADING

The Hudson farmhouse, with its mossy shingles, vines, and aged locust trees, suggests anything but the storm-center of a nation at war. Yet it was here that General John Pope set up his headquarters while his eight thousand trained soldiers under General Banks sped toward Gordonsville, to strike the first blow of what the new general had promised would be a series of victories. As this picture was taken, the New York *Herald* wagon stands plainly in view to the left of the porch; the newspaper correspondents prepared to despatch big "stories." John Pope was the leader whose swift success in capturing New Madrid and

POPE'S HEADQUARTERS DURING THE BATTLE OF CEDAR MOUNTAIN

Island Number Ten in the Mississippi campaign formed a brilliant contrast, in the popular mind, to the failure of the Eastern armies in their attempt upon Richmond. Pope himself proclaimed, "I have come to you from the West, where we have always seen the backs of our enemies." So he set out for the front with "headquarters in the saddle." He could not know what the world later learned—that Robert E. Lee and "Stonewall" Jackson were generals before whose genius few opponents, however brave, could make headway. And so it was too late when Pope heard the cannonading from the Hudson house on the 9th of August.

A HALT ON THE DAY OF BATTLE

The 9th of August, 1862. A sultry day in old Virginia. The brook rippling toward the Rappahannock cools the hoofs of the battery horses at halt, tired with rushing their heavy guns south from Culpeper Court House. The cannoneers lolling on horseback and caisson-seats look as if they too like to rest in the shade. Some gaze at the lucky wagoners across the creek, at ease while their horses feed. Least war-like of all seems the queer wagon to the right. They stare at it, and the civilian beside it, and at his companion wielding the

FEDERAL ARTILLERY NEARING CEDAR MOUNTAIN

clumsy apparatus for that newly discovered art—photography.   Little do the actors in this quiet interlude imagine that by half-past two this afternoon the Federal batteries will plunge into range of a flaring crescent two miles long—"Stonewall" Jackson's guns; that those guns will roar destruction upon them for three hours without ceasing; and that before another sun rises, two thousand of Pope's army will lie dead and wounded beside thirteen hundred men in gray, upon the battle-ground of Cedar Mountain.

McDOWELL'S HEADQUARTERS

Manassas, July 8, 1862. General McDowell, who had been so unfortunate in the first great battle of the war, was made commander of the Third Corps of the newly created Army of Virginia under Pope. McDowell had his headquarters at Manassas. He moved southward during this month with Pope's army toward Gordonville. But Lee, by his brilliant and daring tactics, drove the Federal troops back until a three-days' battle was fought in the vicinity of the residence which the camera has preserved for us in this picture. McDowell once more had the chagrin of seeing a beaten army falling back on Washington.

A ROUGH–HEWN CAUSEWAY (See facing page)

THE ARMY'S HANDY MEN

The Federal army, under Pope, in its advance against Lee needed much more than well drilled regiments of soldiers. Indeed, during the forward march the engineer corps was the busiest division of the army. Artillery battalions and provision trains had to have bridges to cross the numerous streams flowing into the Potomac and the Chesapeake. Three pictures on this page and the preceding show us the men at their work in that summer of long ago. The polka-dot shirt of the foreman (page 14), the roughly hewn timbers cut from the banks, the improvised derrick, the piers built in the middle of the stream around which the water is now rippling, the quiet trees on the banks—all these features stand out as clearly as they did in August of 1862, as the engineer corps was working on the north fork of the Rappahannock, near Sulphur Springs. The pictures are of the same bridge from different points of view.

CROSSING THE RAPPAHANNOCK

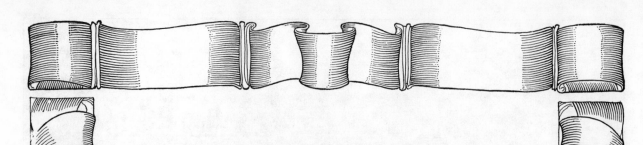

CEDAR MOUNTAIN

The Army of Virginia, under Pope, is now to bear the brunt of Lee's assault, while the Army of the Potomac is dismembered and sent back whence it came, to add in driblets to Pope's effective.—*Colonel Theodore A. Dodge, U.S.A., in "A Bird's-Eye View of the Civil War."*

GENERAL GEORGE B. McCLELLAN, with all his popularity at the beginning, had failed in his Peninsula campaign to fulfil the expectations of the great impatient public of the North. At the same time, while the Army of the Potomac had as yet won no great victories, the men of the West could triumphantly exhibit the trophies won at Donelson, at Pea Ridge, at Shiloh, and at Island No. 10. The North thereupon came to believe that the Western leaders were more able than those of the East. This belief was shared by the President and his Secretary of War and it led to the determination to call on the West for help.

The first to be called was General John Pope, who had won national fame by capturing New Madrid and Island No. 10 on the Mississippi River. In answer to a telegram from Secretary Stanton, Pope came to Washington in June, 1862. The secretary disclosed the plans on which he and President Lincoln had agreed, that a new army, to be known as the Army of Virginia, was to be created out of three corps, then under the respective commands of Generals McDowell, N. P. Banks, and John C. Fremont. These corps had been held from the Peninsula campaign for the purpose of protecting Washington.

Pope demurred and begged to be sent back to the West, on the ground that each of the three corps commanders was his senior in rank and that his being placed at their head would

A BREATHING SPELL

Federal Encampment at Blackburn's Ford on Bull Run, July 4, 1862. When McClellan went to the Peninsula in March of 1862 he had expected all of McDowell's Corps to be sent him as reënforcement before he made the final advance on Richmond. But the brilliant exploits of Jackson in the Shenandoah required the retention of all the troops in the vicinity of Washington. A new army, in fact, was created to make the campaign which Lincoln had originally wanted McClellan to carry out. The command was given to General John Pope, whose capture of Island No. 10 in the Mississippi had brought him into national importance. The corps of Banks, Frémont, and McDowell were consolidated to form this new army, called the "Army of Virginia." General Frémont refused to serve under his junior, and his force was given to Franz Sigel, who had won fame in 1861 in Missouri. This picture was taken about two weeks after the reorganization was completed. The soldiers are those of McDowell's Corps. They are on the old battle-field of Bull Run, enjoying the leisure of camp life, for no definite plans for the campaign have yet been formed.

WHERE JACKSON STRUCK

Cedar Mountain, Viewed from Pope's Headquarters. On the side of this mountain Jackson established the right of his battle line, when he discovered at noon of August 9th that he was in contact with a large part of Pope's army. He had started from Gordonsville, Pope's objective, to seize Culpeper Court House, but the combat took place in the valley here pictured, some five miles southwest of Culpeper, and by nightfall the fields and slopes were strewn with more than three thousand dead and wounded.

doubtless create a feeling against him. But his protests were of no avail and he assumed command of the Army of Virginia on the 26th of June. McDowell and Banks made no protest; but Fremont refused to serve under one whom he considered his junior, and resigned his position. His corps was assigned to General Franz Sigel.

The new commander, General Pope, on the 14th of July, issued an address to his army that was hardly in keeping with his modesty in desiring at first to decline the honor that was offered him. "I have come to you from the West," he proclaimed, "where we have always seen the backs of our enemies —from an army whose business it has been to seek the adversary and to beat him when found. . . . Meantime I desire you to dismiss from your minds certain phrases which I am sorry to find much in vogue among you. I hear constantly of . . . lines of retreat and bases of supplies. Let us discard such ideas. . . . Let us look before us and not behind."

The immediate object of General Pope was to make the capital secure, to make advances toward Richmond, and, if possible, to draw a portion of Lee's army away from McClellan. His first objective was Gordonsville. From this town, not far from the base of the Blue Ridge Mountains, there was a railroad connecting it with Richmond—a convenient means of furnishing men and supplies to the Confederate army. Pope decided to occupy the town and destroy the railroad. To this end he ordered Banks to Culpeper and thence to send all his cavalry to Gordonsville, capture the town and tear up ten or fifteen miles of the railroad in the direction of Richmond. But, as if a prelude to the series of defeats which General Pope was to suffer in the next six weeks, he failed in this initial movement. The sagacious Lee had divined his intention and had sent General "Stonewall" Jackson with his and General Ewell's divisions on July 13th, to occupy Gordonsville. Ewell arrived in advance of Jackson and held the town for the Confederates.

IN THE LINE OF FIRE

Where the Confederate General Winder was killed at Cedar Mountain. It was while directing the movements of four advance batteries that General Winder was struck by a shell, expiring in a few hours. Jackson reported: "It is difficult within the proper reserve of an official report to do justice to the merits of this accomplished officer. Urged by the medical director to take no part in the movements of the day because of the enfeebled state of his health, his ardent patriotism and military pride could bear no such restraint. Richly endowed with those qualities of mind and person which fit an officer for command and which attract the admiration and excite the enthusiasm of troops, he was rapidly rising to the front rank of his profession."

In the campaign we are describing Jackson was the most active and conspicuous figure on the Confederate side. He rested at Gordonsville for two weeks, recuperating his health and that of the army, which had been much impaired in the malarial district of the Peninsula. The fresh mountain air blowing down from the Blue Ridge soon brought back their wonted vigor. On July 27th A. P. Hill was ordered to join him, and the Confederate leader now had about twenty-five thousand men.

The movement on Gordonsville was exactly in accordance with Jackson's own ideas which he had urged upon Lee. Although believing McClellan to be in an impregnable position on the Peninsula, it was not less evident to him that the Union general would be unable to move further until his army had been reorganized and reenforced. This was the moment, he argued, to strike in another direction and carry the conflict into the Federal territory. An army of at least sixty thousand should march into Maryland and appear before the National Capital. President Davis could not be won over to the plan while McClellan was still in a position to be reenforced by sea, but Lee, seeing that McClellan remained inactive, had determined, by sending Jackson westward, to repeat the successful tactics of the previous spring in the Shenandoah valley. Such a move might result in the recall of McClellan.

And so it happened. No sooner had Halleck assumed command of all the Northern armies than the matter of McClellan's withdrawal was agitated and on August 3d the head of the Army of the Potomac, to his bitter disappointment, was ordered to join Pope on the Rappahannock. Halleck was much concerned as to how Lee would act during the Federal evacuation of the Peninsula, uncertain whether the Confederates would attempt to crush Pope before McClellan could reenforce him, or whether McClellan would be attacked as soon as he was out of his strong entrenchments at Harrison's Landing.

THE LEADER OF THE CHARGE

The Hero of the Federal Attack. General Samuel W. Crawford, here seen with his staff, at Cedar Mountain led a charge on the left flank of the Confederate forces that came near being disastrous for Jackson. At about six o'clock the brigade was in line. General Williams reported: "At this time this brigade occupied the interior line of a strip of woods. A field, varying from 250 to 500 yards in width, lay between it and the next strip of woods. In moving across this field the three right regiments and the six companies of the Third Wisconsin were received by a terrific fire of musketry. The Third Wisconsin especially fell under a partial flank fire under which Lieut.-Colonel Crane fell and the regiment was obliged to give way. Of the three remaining regiments which continued the charge (Twenty-eighth New York, Forty-sixth Pennsylvania, and Fifth Connecticut) every field-officer and every adjutant was killed or disabled. In the Twenty-eighth New York every company officer was killed or wounded; in the Forty-sixth Pennsylvania all but five; in the Fifth Connecticut all but eight." It was one of the most heroic combats of the war.

COL. ALFRED N. DUFFIÉ

A Leader of Cavalry. Colonel Alfred N. Duffié was in command of the First Rhode Island Cavalry, in the Cavalry Brigade of the Second Division of McDowell's (Third) Corps in Pope's Army of Virginia. The cavalry had been used pretty well during Pope's advance. On the 8th of August, the day before the battle of Cedar Mountain, the cavalry had proceeded south to the house of Dr. Slaughter. That night Duffié was on picket in advance of General Crawford's troops, which had come up during the day and pitched camp. The whole division came to his support on the next day. When the infantry fell back to the protection of the batteries, the cavalry was ordered to charge the advancing Confederates. "Officers and men behaved admirably, and I cannot speak too highly of the good conduct of all of the brigade," reported General Bayard. After the battle the cavalry covered the retreat of the artillery and ambulances. On August 18th, when the retreat behind the Rappahannoc was ordered, the cavalry again checked the Confederate advance. During the entire campaign the regiment of Colonel Duffié did yeoman's service

The latter of the two possibilities seemed the more probable, and Pope was therefore ordered to push his whole army toward Gordonsville, in the hope that Lee, compelled to strengthen Jackson, would be too weak to fall upon the retiring Army of the Potomac.

The Union army now occupied the great triangle formed roughly by the Rappahannock and the Rapidan rivers and the range of the Blue Ridge Mountains, with Culpeper Court House as the rallying point. Pope soon found that the capturing of New Madrid and Island No. 10 was easy in comparison with measuring swords with the Confederate generals in the East.

On August 6th Pope began his general advance upon Gordonsville. Banks already had a brigade at Culpeper Court House, and this was nearest to Jackson. The small settlement was the meeting place of four roads by means of which Pope's army of forty-seven thousand men would be united. Jackson, informed of the advance, immediately set his three divisions in motion for Culpeper, hoping to crush Banks, hold the town, and prevent the uniting of the Army of Virginia. His progress was slow. The remainder of Banks's corps reached Culpeper on the 8th. On the morning of the 9th Jackson finally got his troops over the Rapidan and the Robertson rivers. Two miles beyond the latter stream there rose from the plain the slope of Slaughter Mountain, whose ominous name is more often changed into Cedar. This "mountain" is an isolated foothill of the Blue Ridge, some twenty miles from the parent range, and a little north of the Rapidan. From its summit could be seen vast stretches of quiet farmlands which had borne their annual harvests since the days of the Cavaliers. Its gentle slopes were covered with forests, which merged at length into waving grain fields and pasture lands, dotted here and there with rural homes. It was here on the slope of Cedar Mountain that one of the most severe little battles of the war took place.

THE FIRST CLASH

Battlefield of Cedar Mountain, August 9, 1862. Here the Confederate army in its second advance on Washington first felt out the strength massed against it. After Lee's brilliant tactics had turned McClellan's Peninsula Campaign into a fiasco, the Confederate Government resolved to again take the offensive. Plans were formed for a general invasion of the North, the objective points ranging from Cincinnati eastward to the Federal capital and Philadelphia. Immediately after Washington got wind of this, Lincoln (on August 4th) issued a call for three hundred thousand men; and all haste was made to rush the forces of McClellan from the Peninsula and of Cox from West Virginia to the aid of the recently consolidated army under Pope. On August 9, 1862, the vanguards of "Stonewall" Jackson's army and of Pope's intercepting forces met at Cedar Mountain. Banks, with the Second Corps of the Federal army, about eight thousand strong, attacked Jackson's forces of some sixteen thousand. The charge was so furious that Jackson's left flank was broken and rolled up, the rear of the center fired upon, and the whole line thereby thrown into confusion. Banks, however, received no reenforcements, while Jackson received strong support. The Federal troops were driven back across the ground which they had swept clear earlier in the afternoon.

The Battle of Cedar Mountain, August 9, 1862. The lower picture was taken the day after the battle that had raged for a brief two hours on the previous evening. After an artillery fire that filled half the afternoon, the advanced Federal cavalry was pressed back on the infantry supporting the batteries. Banks underestimated the strength of the Confederates. Instead of sending to Pope for reenforcements, he ordered a charge on the approaching troops. The Confederates, still feeling their way, were unprepared for this movement and were thrown into confusion. But at the moment when the Federal charge was about to end in success, three brigades of A. P. Hill in reserve were called up. They forced the Federals to retrace their steps to the point where the fighting began. Here the Federal retreat, in turn, was halted by General Pope with reenforcements. The Confederates moving up their batteries, a short-range artillery fight was kept up until midnight. At daylight it was found that Ewell and Jackson had fallen back two miles farther up the mountain. Pope advanced to the former Confederate ground and rested, after burying the dead. The following morning the Confederates had disappeared. The loss to both armies was almost three thousand in killed, wounded and missing. The battle had accomplished nothing.

On the banks of Cedar Run, seven miles south of Culpeper and but one or two north of the mountain, Banks's cavalry were waiting to oppose Jackson's advance. Learning of this the latter halted and waited for an attack. He placed Ewell's batteries on the slope about two hundred feet above the valley and sent General Winder to take a strong position on the left. So admirably was Jackson's army stationed that it would have required a much larger force, approaching it from the plains, to dislodge it. And yet, General Banks made an attempt with an army scarcely one-third as large as that of Jackson.

General Pope had made glowing promises of certain success and he well knew that the whole North was eagerly watching and waiting for him to fulfil them. He must strike somewhere and do it soon—and here was his chance at Cedar Mountain. He sent Banks with nearly eight thousand men against this brilliant Southern commander with an army three times as large, holding a strong position on a mountain side.

Banks with his infantry left Culpeper Court House on the morning of August 9th and reached the Confederate stronghold in the afternoon. He approached the mountain through open fields in full range of the Confederate cannon, which presently opened with the roar of thunder. All heedless of danger the brave men ran up the slope as if to take the foe by storm, when suddenly they met a brigade of Ewell's division face to face and a brief, deadly encounter took place. In a few minutes the Confederate right flank began to waver and would no doubt have been routed but for the timely aid of another brigade and still another that rushed down the hill and opened fire on the Federal lines which extended along the eastern bank of Cedar Run.

Meanwhile the Union batteries had been wheeled into position and their deep roar answered that of the foe on the hill. For two or three hours the battle continued with the utmost fury. The ground was strewn with dead and dying

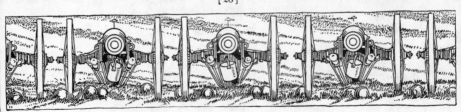

SURVIVORS OF THE FIGHTING TENTH

When Crawford's troops were driven back by A. P. Hill, he halted on the edge of a wheatfield, where he was reenforced by the Tenth Maine. For nearly half an hour it held its own, losing out of its 461 officers and men 173 in killed and wounded. A few days after the battle some survivors had a picture taken on the exact spot where they had so courageously fought. The remains of the cavalry horses can be seen in the trampled field of wheat. From left to right these men are: Lieutenant Littlefield, Lieutenant Whitney, Lieut.-Colonel Fillebrown, Captain Knowlton, and First-Sergeant Jordan, of Company C.

THE HOUSE WELL NAMED

Slaughter's house, overlooking the scene of carnage of Cedar Mountain, stood on the northern slope in the rear of the position taken by the Confederate troops under General Ewell. The brigades of Trimble and Hayes were drawn up near this house, at some distance from the brigade of Early. After the battle the whole of Jackson's army was drawn up on the slopes near it.

THE FUGITIVES

Virginia Negroes following Pope's soldiers in their retreat from Cedar mountain. From the beginning of the war Negroes had been a subject of debate. Even before Bull Run, on May 26, 1861, General B. F. Butler had declared that all fugitive slaves would be considered as contraband of war. Congress, however, decided in August that all slaves confiscated should be held subject to the decision of the United States courts. In April of 1862, General Hunter, at Hilton Head, South Carolina, declared that all slaves in his military department were "forever free," but a week later Lincoln annulled the proclamation. Hunter, however, raised a storm by organizing a regiment of fugitive slaves. It was only before Cedar Mountain—to be precise, on July 22, 1862—that "all National commanders were ordered

FOLLOWERS OF POPE'S RETREAT

to employ as many Negroes as could be used advantageously for military and naval purposes, paying them for their labor and keep-ing a record as to their ownership as a basis on which compensation could be made in proper cases." Ten days after the battle, Greeley published his famous letter to Lincoln, "The Prayer of Twenty Millions." On September 22, 1862, the Emancipation Proclamation was issued, and on January 1, 1863, the final proclamation was made that "Negroes would be received into the military and naval service of the United States Corps." This picture was taken about the time Greeley's letter was pub-lished--less than two weeks after the battle of Cedar Mountain had been fought.

and human blood was poured out like water. But the odds were too great and at length, as the shades of evening were settling over the gory field, Banks began to withdraw the remnant of his troops. But he left two thousand of his brave lads—one fourth of his whole army—dead or dying along the hillside, while the Confederate losses were in excess of thirteen hundred.

The dead and wounded of both armies lay mingled in masses over the whole battle-field. While the fighting continued, neither side could send aid or relief to the maimed soldiers, who suffered terribly from thirst and lack of attention as the sultry day gave place to a close, oppressive night.

General Pope had remained at Culpeper, but, hearing the continuous cannonading and knowing that a sharp engagement was going on, hastened to the battle-field in the afternoon with a fresh body of troops under General Ricketts, arriving just before dark. He instantly ordered Banks to withdraw his right wing so as to make room for Ricketts; but the Confederates, victorious as they had been, refused to continue the contest against the reenforcements and withdrew to the woods up the mountain side. Heavy shelling was kept up by the hard-worked artillerymen of both armies until nearly midnight, while the Federal troops rested on their arms in line of battle. For two days the armies faced each other across the valley. Then both quietly withdrew. Pope's first battle as leader of an Eastern army had resulted in neither victory nor defeat.

THE SECOND BATTLE AT BULL RUN

THE UNION RETREAT—SIGEL'S CORPS RECROSSING THE
RAPPAHANNOCK, AUGUST 19, 1862

THE RAILROAD AS AN

The Federals are clearing up the railroad, the Confederate damage to which compelled Pope to fall back in order to retard Lee's advance toward Washington. "Stonewall" Jackson, who knew every foot of the Manassas region, did not despatch Ewell's forces with Stuart's cavalry to fall upon Catlett's Station and Manassas Junction for nothing. At Manassas the Confederates captured a million dollars' worth of army reserve supplies, seriously crippling Pope's movements for the remainder of the campaign. Meanwhile Jackson, pressing forward, united with Ewell and threatened Pope's exposed flank. The purpose of the advance of Jackson to give battle to Pope

ELEMENT IN WARFARE

near Manassas and Bull Run was to prevent the concentration
of a heavy Federal force between his column and Longstreet's,
then more than a day's march distant. The crippling of his
railroad communication and the seizure of his stores were not
in themselves sufficient to do this. In the pictures we see the
work-trains of the Military Railroad removing the wreckage,
gathering up débris to be used in repairing the road and its
rolling-stock, and the tracks being relaid and guarded by the
soldiers. Before Pope could reestablish his railroad communication, Lee's clever maneuvers drew the Federals into the
disastrous battle of Second Bull Run.

AN IMPORTANT PART OF THE WAR GAME

A problem for the practical railroad man. It takes all kinds of people to make up a world and it takes all kinds of men to make up an army. In the volunteer forces that fought in the ranks of both North and South were men of every calling, every profession, mechanics, artisans, artificers, men familiar with machine-shop practice as well as the men of field and plow, and the thinking soldier whose hand was as ready with the pen as with the sword. Was an engine-driver needed, or a farrier or carpenter, the colonel of a regiment had but to shout. But so important did the lines of communication by railway become to both armies that separate com-

REPAIRING AFTER THE CONFEDERATE RAID ON POPE'S LINE OF MARCH

mands of practical engineers, trackmen, and wreckers had to be organized and maintained. Train-wrecking seems a cruel act of deliberate vandalism, yet it is part of warfare. When penetrating the enemy's country over unpatroled and ill-guarded routes, the engine-driver might expect any time to see just ahead of him, and too late to call for brakes, the misplaced rail or the broken culvert that would hurl him and his train, laden sometimes with human freight, into river-bed or deep abyss. War leads to strenuous life and deeds of daring, and upon no force was the labor and the danger harder than the men of the track and throttle.

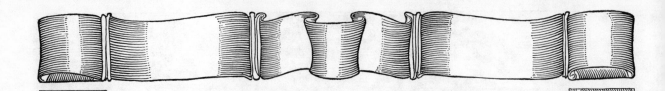

SECOND BATTLE OF BULL RUN

The battle was indeed one of which General Lee had good reason to be proud. It would be hard to find a better instance of that masterly comprehension of the actual condition of things which marks a great general than was exhibited in General Lee's allowing our formidable attack, in which more than half the Federal army was taking part, to be fully developed and to burst upon the exhausted troops of Stonewall Jackson, while Lee, relying upon the ability of that able soldier to maintain his position, was maturing and arranging for the great attack on our left flank by the powerful corps of Longstreet.—*John C. Ropes, in "The Army Under Pope."*

THE battle of Cedar Mountain was but a prelude to the far greater one that was to take place three weeks later on the banks of the little stream that had given its name, the year before, to the first important battle of the war; and here again the result to be registered was similar to that of the preceding year—a result that brought dismay to the people of the North and exultation to the adherents of the Southern cause. The three intervening weeks between the battles of Cedar Mountain and the Second Bull Run were spent in sparring, in marshaling the armed hosts, in heavy skirmishing and getting position for a final decisive struggle.

Two events of this period invite special attention. The respective heroes were J. E. B. Stuart, the daring Southern cavalry leader, and " Stonewall " Jackson. The victim in each case was General Pope. Before relating these incidents, however, we must take a general view of the field. General Pope's headquarters at this moment were at Culpeper, with a large part of his army, but he had left much of his personal baggage and many of his private papers at Catlett's, a station on the Orange and Alexandria Railroad between Culpeper and

THE UNHEEDED WARNING

Here we see Catlett's Station, on the Orange & Alexandria Railroad, which Stuart's cavalry seized in a night sortie on August 22, 1862. The damage done was not severe. Stuart was unable to burn the loaded wagon-trains surrounding the station and had to content himself with capturing horses, which he mounted with wounded Federal soldiers; he escaped at four the next morning, driven off by the approach of a superior force. Pope, at the time, was in possession of the fords of the Rappahannock, trying to check the Confederate advance toward the Shenandoah.

CATLETT'S STATION

At Manassas Junction, as it appeared in the upper picture on August 26, 1862, is one of the great neglected strategic points in the theater of the war. Twenty-five miles from Alexandria and thirty miles in a direct line from Washington, it was almost within long cannon-shot from any point in both the luckless battles of Bull Run. It was on the railway route connecting with Richmond, and at the junction of the railway running across the entrance to the Shenandoah Valley and beyond the Blue Ridge, through Manassas Gap. The Confederates knew its value,

Stuart's raid, however, so alarmed General Halleck that he immediately telegraphed Pope from Washington: "By no means expose your railroad communication with Alexandria. It is of the utmost importance in sending your supplies and reinforcements." Pope did not fall back upon his railroad communication, however, until after Jackson had seized Manassas Junction. and after the first battle of Bull Run built the fortifications which we see in the upper picture, to the left beyond the supply-cars on the railroad. Pope, after the battle of Cedar Mountain, should have covered it, extending his lines so as to protect it from Jackson's incursion through Thoroughfare Gap; instead he held the main force of his army opposing that of Lee.

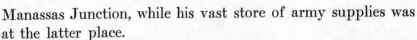

Manassas Junction, while his vast store of army supplies was at the latter place.

Pope's great source of uncertainty lay in the fact that he did not know whether Lee would move against him or would follow McClellan in the latter's retreat from the Peninsula; nor did he know when the reenforcements promised from McClellan's army would reach him. Meanwhile Lee had decided to let McClellan depart in peace and to advance against Pope, with the whole Confederate army. To this end Longstreet was ordered to the scene and with his corps he reached Gordonsville on August 13th.

A few days later the two Confederate generals, Lee and Longstreet, ascended to the top of Clark's Mountain, from which, through powerful field-glasses, they obtained a good view of Culpeper, about twelve miles away. They saw that Pope's position was weak and determined to attack him without delay. Lee ordered his army to cross the Rapidan. He also sent a courier to gallop across the country with an important dispatch to General Stuart, disclosing his plans. It was now that General Pope met fortune; he captured the courier and learned of Lee's plans. Pope knew that he was not in position to meet Lee's army at Culpeper, and he withdrew from that place and took up a strong position behind the Rappahannock. Lee had strained every nerve to get at his antagonist before the latter left Culpeper and before he could be reenforced by McClellan's army. But sudden rains changed the Rappahannock from a placid stream into a rushing torrent. The Confederates were delayed and meantime the reenforcements from the Peninsula began to reach Pope's army. General Reno with a part of Burnside's corps was on the ground by August 14th. One week later came Generals Kearny and Reynolds —both splendid leaders, both destined to give their lives for their country within a year—to join the Army of Virginia with some thousands of additional fighters from the Army of the Potomac.

WHERE THE THUNDERBOLT FELL

The havoc wrought by the Confederate attack of August 26th on the Federal supply depot at Manassas Junction is here graphically preserved.   When Jackson arrived at sunset of that day at Bristoe's Station, on the Orange & Alexandria Railroad, he knew that his daring movement would be reported to Pope's forces by the trains that escaped both north and south.   To save themselves, the troops that had already marched twenty-five miles had to make still further exertions.   Trimble volunteered to move on Manassas Junction; and, under command of Stuart, a small force moved northward through the woods.   At midnight it arrived within half a mile of the Junction.   The Federal force greeted it with artillery fire, but when the Confederates charged at the sound of the bugle the gunners abandoned the batteries to the assaulters.   Some three hundred of the small Federal garrison were captured, with the immense stores that filled the warehouses to overflowing.   The next morning Hill's and Taliaferro's divisions arrived to hold the position.   The half-starved troops were now in possession of all that was needed to make them an effective force.   Jackson was now in position to control the movements of the Federal army under Pope.

Lee was completely thwarted in his purpose of attacking Pope before his reenforcements arrived. But he was not idle. He sent the dauntless cavalry leader, J. E. B. Stuart, to make a raid around the Union army. Stuart did this effectively, and this was the first of the two notable events of these weeks of sparring. Crossing the Rappahannock at Waterloo Bridge with fifteen hundred mounted men as bold and dauntless as himself, Stuart dashed up the country, riding all day and all night. After the coming of night on the evening of the 22d, in the midst of a torrential rainstorm, while the darkness was so intense that every man was guided by the tread of his brother horsemen, Stuart pounced upon the Federals near Catlett's Station, overpowered the astonished guard, captured nearly two hundred prisoners, scattering the remainder of the troops stationed there far and wide in the darkness, and seized Pope's despatch-book with his plans and private papers. Stuart took also several hundred fine horses and burned a large number of wagons laden with supplies. Among his trophies was a fine uniform cloak and hat which were the personal property of General Pope. These were exchanged on the following day for General Stuart's plumed hat which a few days before had been left behind by that officer when surprised by Federal troops.

Stuart's bold raid proved a serious misfortune for the Union army. But Lee had far greater things in store. His next move was to send Jackson to Pope's rear with a large part of the Confederate army. Stealthily Jackson led his army westward, shielded by the woods, the thickets, and the low hills of the Blue Ridge. It was a quiet rural community through which he passed. The great majority of the simple country folk had never seen an army, though it is true that for many days the far-away boom of cannon had reached their ears from the valley of the Rapidan. Now here was a real army at their very doors. Nor was it a hostile army, for their sympathies were Southern. With baskets and armfuls of

A START TOO LONG DELAYED

Where the troops of General McClellan, waiting near the round-house at Alexandria, were hurried forward to the scene of action where Pope was struggling with Jackson and Ewell. Pope had counted upon the assistance of these reënforcements in making the forward movement by which he expected to hold Lee back. The old bogey of leaving the National Capital defenseless set up a vacillation in General Halleck's mind and the troops were held overlong at Alexandria. Had they been promptly forwarded, "Stonewall" Jackson's blow at Manassas Junction could not have been struck. At the news of that disaster the troops were hurriedly despatched down the railroad toward Manassas. But Pope was already in retreat in three columns toward that point, McDowell had failed to intercept the Confederate reënforcements coming through Thoroughfare Gap, and the situation had become critical. General Taylor, with his brigade of New Jersey troops, was the first of McClellan's forces to be moved forward to the aid of Pope. At Union

BRIGADIER–GENERAL
GEORGE W. TAYLOR

Mills, Colonel Scammon, commanding the First Brigade, driven back from Manassas Junction, was further pressed by the Confederates on the morning of August 27th. Later in the day General Taylor's brigade arrived by the Fairfax road and, crossing the railroad bridge, met the Confederates drawn up and waiting near Manassas Station. A severe artillery fire greeted the Federals as they emerged from the woods. As General Taylor had no artillery, he was obliged either to retire or charge. He chose the latter. When the Confederate cavalry threatened to surround his small force, however, Taylor fell back in good order across the bridge, where two Ohio regiments assisted in holding the Confederates in check. At this point, General Taylor, who had been wounded in the retreat, was borne past in a litter. Though suffering much, he appealed to the officers to prevent another Bull Run. The brigade retired in good order to Fairfax Court House, where General Taylor died of his wounds a short time afterward.

bread and pies and cakes they cheered as best they could the tattered and hungry men on the march.

General Lee in the meantime had kept Longstreet in front of Pope's army on the Rappahannock to make daily demonstrations and feints and thus to divert Pope's attention from Jackson's movements and lead him to believe that he was to be attacked in front. The trick was eminently successful. "Stonewall" Jackson suddenly, on August 26th, emerged from the Bull Run Mountains by way of the Thoroughfare Gap and marshaled his clans on the plains of Manassas, but a few miles from the site of the famous battle of the year before.

Pope had taken alarm. He was astonished to find Jackson in his rear, and he had to decide instantly between two courses—to abandon his communications with Fredericksburg on the one hand, or with Alexandria and Washington on the other. He decided to keep in touch with Washington at all hazards. Breaking his camp on the Rappahannock, he hastened with all speed to lead his forces toward Manassas Junction, where he had stored vast quantities of provisions and munitions of war. But he was too late to save them. Jackson had been joined by Stuart and his cavalry. On the evening of the 26th they were still some miles from Manassas and Trimble was sent ahead to make sure the capture before Pope's army could arrive. Through the darkness rode these same hardy men who had a few nights before made their bold raid on Catlett's Station. Before midnight they reached Manassas. They met little opposition. The guard was overpowered. The spoils of this capture were great, including three hundred prisoners, one hundred and seventy-five horses, ten locomotives, seven long trains of provisions, and vast stores and munitions of war.

Next morning the weary and hungry foot soldiers of Jackson's army came upon the scene and whatever else they did they feasted as only hungry men can. An eye-witness wrote, "To see a starving man eating lobster-salad and

AN UNREALIZED OPPORTUNITY

Here might have been won a Federal victory that would have precluded defeat at Second Bull Run. The corps of General Heintzelman, consisting of the divisions of Hooker and Kearny, was the next detachment of McClellan's forces to arrive to the aid of Pope. On the 28th of August, Heintzelman had pushed forward to Centreville, entering it soon after "Stonewall" Jackson's rear-guard had retired. Instead of pursuing, Heintzelman drew up his forces east of Cub Run, which we see in the picture. Jackson's forces, now in a precarious position, fell back toward Thoroughfare Gap to form a junction with Longstreet's Corps, which Lee had sent forward. The battle was commenced on the west somewhat feebly by Generals McDowell and Sigel. By nightfall the Confederate left had been driven back fully a mile.

MAJOR-GENERAL SAMUEL P. HEINTZELMAN AND STAFF

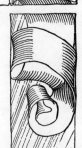

drinking Rhine wine, barefooted and in tatters, was curious; the whole thing was incredible."

The amazement at the North when the news of the capture of Manassas became known cannot be described. But the newspapers belittled it, declaring that it was merely a bold raid and that for any large force to get between Pope's army and Washington before Pope became aware of the attempt was simply impossible.

Jackson had done an astonishing thing. But his position was precarious, nevertheless. Pope was moving toward him with a far larger army, recently augmented by Heintzelman's corps from the Army of the Potomac, while Fitz John Porter with an additional force was not far off. It is true that Longstreet was hastening to the aid of Jackson, but he had to come by the same route which had brought Jackson— through Thoroughfare Gap—and Pope thought he saw a great opportunity. If he could only detain Longstreet at the gap, why should he not crush Jackson with his superior numbers? To this end he sent orders to Porter, to McDowell, and to Kearny and others whose forces were scattered about the country, to concentrate during the night of the 27th and move upon Jackson. McDowell sent Ricketts with a small force—too small—to prevent Longstreet from passing through Thoroughfare Gap, and hastened to join the main army against Jackson. But that able commander was not to be caught in a trap. He moved from Manassas Junction by three roads toward the old battle-field of Bull Run and by noon on the 28th the whole corps was once more united between Centreville and Sudley Spring. Late in the day he encountered King's division of McDowell's corps near the village of Groveton, and a sharp fight was opened and kept up till an hour after dark. The Confederates were left in possession of the field.

The following day, August 29th, was the first of the two days' battle, leaving out of account the fight of the evening

THE TWICE-WON FIELD

Sleeping on their arms on the night of August 29th, the Federal veterans were as confident of having won a victory as were the raw troops in the beginning of the first battle of Bull Run. But the next day's fighting was to tell the tale. General Ewell had been wounded in the knee by a minie ball in the severe fight at Groveton and was unable to lead his command; but for the impetuosity of this commander was substituted that of Longstreet, nicknamed 'the War-Horse," whose arrival in the midst of the previous day's en-

MAJOR-GENERAL R. S. EWELL

MAJOR-GENERAL JAMES LONGSTREET

gagement had cost the Federals dear   On the morning of the second day Longstreet's batteries opened the engagement.   When the general advance came, as the sun shone on the parallel lines of glittering bayonets, it was Longstreet's men bringing their muskets to "the ready" who first opened fire with a long flash of flame.   It was they who pressed most eagerly forward and, in the face of the Federal batteries, fell upon the troops of General McDowell at the left and drove them irresistibly back.   Although the right Federal wing, in command of General Heintzelman, had not given an inch, it was this turning of the left by Longstreet which put the whole Federal army in retreat, driving them across Bull Run.   The Confederates were left in possession of the field, where lay thousands of Federal dead and wounded, and Lee was free to advance his victorious troops into the North unmolested.

THE BATTLE-FIELD OF SECOND BULL RUN (MANASSAS), AUGUST 29-30, 1862

before and the desultory fighting of the preceding ten days. General Pope was still hopeful of crushing Jackson before the arrival of Longstreet, and on the morning of the 29th he ordered a general advance across Bull Run. As the noon hour approached a wild shout that arose from Jackson's men told too well of the arrival of Longstreet. Far away on the hills near Gainesville could be seen the marching columns of Longstreet, who had passed through the gap in safety and who was now rushing to the support of Jackson. The Confederate army was at last to be reunited. Jackson was greatly relieved. Pope had lost his opportunity of fighting the army of his opponent in sections.

The field was almost the same that the opposing forces had occupied a year and a month before when the first great battle of the war was fought. And many of them were the same men. Some who had engaged in that first conflict had gone home and had refused to reenlist; others had found soldiers' graves since then—but still others on both sides were here again, no longer the raw recruits that they were before, but, with their year of hard experience in the field, they were trained soldiers, equal to any in the world.

The two armies faced each other in a line nearly five miles long. There was heavy fighting here and there along the line from the early morning hours, but no general engagement until late in the afternoon. The Union right pressed hard against the Confederate left and by ten o'clock had forced it back more than a mile. But the Confederates, presently reenforced in that quarter, hurled heavy masses of infantry against the Union right and regained much that it had lost. Late in the afternoon fresh regiments under Kearny and Hooker charged the Confederate left, which was swept back and rolled in upon the center. But presently the Southern General Hood, with his famous Texan brigade, rushed forward in a wild, irresistible dash, pressed Kearny back, captured one gun, several flags and a hundred prisoners. Night then closed over

THE FIGHTING FORTY-FIRST

"C" Company of the Forty-first New York after the Second Battle of Bull Run, August 30, 1862. When the troops of Generals Milroy and Schurz were hard pressed by overpowering numbers and exhausted by fatigue, this New York regiment, being ordered forward, quickly advanced with a cheer along the War-renton Turnpike and deployed about a mile west of the field of the conflict of July 21, 1861. The fighting men replied with answering shouts, for with the regiment that came up at the double quick galloped a battery of artillery. The charging Confederates were held and this position was assailed time and again. It became the center of the sanguinary combat of the day, and it was here that the "Bull-Dogs" earned their name. Among the first to respond to Lincoln's call, they enlisted in June, '61, and when their first service was over they stepped forward to a man, specifying no term of service but putting their names on the Honor Roll of "For the War."

BRIG.-GEN. RUFUS KING

Brigadier-General King, a division commander in this battle, was a soldier by profession, and a diplomatist and journalist by inheritance—for he was a graduate of West Point, a son of Charles King, editor of the New York *American* in 1827, and a grandson of the elder Rufus, an officer of the Revolution and Minister to the Court of St. James. He had left the army in 1836 to become Assistant Engineer of the New York & Erie Railroad, a post he gave up to become editor of the *Daily Advertiser*, and subsequently of the Milwaukee *Sentinel*. At the outbreak of the war Lincoln had appointed him Minister to Rome, but he asked permission to delay his departure, and was made a Brigadier-General of Volunteers. Later he resigned as Minister, and was assigned to McDowell's corps. At the battle of Manassas, in which the Forty-first New York earned honor, he proved an able leader. In 1867 he was again appointed as Minister of the United States to Italy.

the scene and the two armies rested on their arms until the morning.

The first day's battle is sometimes called the battle of Groveton, but usually it is considered as the first half of the second battle of Bull Run. It was a formidable conflict in itself. The Union loss was at least forty-five hundred men, the Confederate was somewhat larger. Over the gory field lay multitudes of men, the blue and the gray commingled, who would dream of battlefields no more. The living men lay down among the dead in order to snatch a little rest and strength that they might renew the strife in the morning.

It is a strange fact that Lee and Pope each believed that the other would withdraw his army during the night, and each was surprised in the morning to find his opponent still on the ground, ready, waiting, defiant. It was quite certain that on this day, August 30th, there would be a decisive action and that one of the two armies would be victor and the other defeated. The two opposing commanders had called in their outlying battalions and the armies now faced each other in almost full force, the Confederates with over fifty thousand men and the Union forces exceeding their opponents by probably fifteen thousand men. The Confederate left wing was commanded by Jackson, and the right by Longstreet. The extreme left of the Union army was under Fitz John Porter, who, owing to a misunderstanding of orders, had not reached the field the day before. The center was commanded by Heintzelman and the right by Reno.

In the early hours of the morning the hills echoed with the firing of artillery, with which the day was opened. Porter made an infantry attack in the forenoon, but was met by the enemy in vastly superior numbers and was soon pressed back in great confusion. As the hours passed one fearful attack followed another, each side in turn pressing forward and again receding. In the afternoon a large part of

THE ADVANCE THAT BECAME A RETREAT

The Stone Bridge across Bull Run.   When the Federal army silently put Bull Run between itself and Lee on the night of August 30, 1862, Pope's attempt to capture Richmond was turned into a Confederate advance upon Washington.   Lee, on discovering Pope's position at Centreville on the next day, sent "Stonewall" Jackson to turn the Federal right.   Crossing Bull Run at Sudley Ford, Jackson advanced along a country road till he reached the Little River Turnpike, on which the troops bivouacked for the night.   On September 1st he was met near Chantilly by Reno and Kearney, who had been sent by Pope to intercept him.   A fierce encounter followed in a drenching rainstorm.   The brilliant bayonet charge by Birney, in command of the division of General Philip Kearney, who had just fallen, drove back the Confederates, and Birney held the field that night.   The next morning orders came from General Halleck for the broken and demoralized army of Pope to fall back within the defenses of Washington.   Large quantities of Federal stores were left to fall into the hands of Lee, which were of great use in his advance into Maryland.

the Union army made a desperate onslaught on the Confederate left under Jackson. Here for some time the slaughter of men was fearful. It was nearing sunset. Jackson saw that his lines were wavering. He called for reenforcements which did not come and it seemed as if the Federals were about to win a signal victory. But this was not to be. Far away on a little hill at the Confederate right Longstreet placed four batteries in such a position that he could enfilade the Federal columns. Quickly he trained his cannon on the Federal lines that were hammering away at Jackson, and opened fire. Ghastly gaps were soon cut in the Federal ranks and they fell back. But they re-formed and came again and still again, each time only to be mercilessly cut down by Longstreet's artillery. At length, with the coming of darkness, the whole Union front began to waver and show signs of disorder.

General Lee, seeing this, ordered the Confederates in all parts of the field to advance. With wild, triumphant yells they did so. It was now dark and there was little more fighting; but Lee captured several thousand prisoners. Pope retreated across Bull Run with the remnant of his army and by morning was ensconced behind the field-works at Centreville.

There was no mistaking the fact that General Pope had lost the battle and the campaign. He decided to lead his army back to the entrenchments of Washington. After spending a day behind the embankments at Centreville, the retreat was begun. Lee's troops with Jackson in the advance pursued and struck a portion of the retreating army at Chantilly.

It was late in the afternoon of September 1st. The rain, accompanied by vivid lightning and terrific crashes of thunder, was falling in torrents as Stuart's horsemen, sent in advance, were driven back by the Federal infantry. Jackson now pushed two of A. P. Hill's brigades forward to ascertain the condition of the Union army. General Reno was protecting Pope's right flank, and he lost no time in proceeding against Hill. The latter was promptly checked, and both forces took

FAIRFAX COURT HOUSE, VIRGINIA

Pope's retirement from the field of Bull Run gave the famous Confederate cavalry leader, J. E. B. Stuart, a splendid opportunity for the kind of warfare he most delighted in. No sooner had the Federals started than Stuart was following them. Ascertaining that their main body was at Centreville and Fairfax Court House, he planned to make an attack on the pike between the two places. A section of the famous Washington Artillery took position just after dark on August 31st, within range of a road completely filled with a continuous stream of Federal army wagons making their way toward the Court House. A few rounds from the Confederate guns threw "everything into confusion, and such commotion, upsetting, collisions, and smash-ups were rarely ever seen." Stuart bivouacked that night near Chantilly, and after Jackson came up on September 1st, tried to force his way down the pike toward Fairfax Court House. But the Federals were too strong in number at that point. The next day (September 2d) Halleck sent word to Pope to bring his army back to Washington. Stuart then promptly took possession of Fairfax Court House, after a sharp skirmish with some of Sumner's departing troops.

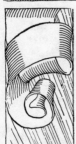

position for battle. One side and then the other fell back in turn as lines were re-formed and urged forward. Night fell and the tempest's fury increased. The ammunition of both armies was so wet that much of it could not be used. Try as they would the Confederates were unable to break the Union line and the two armies finally withdrew. The Confederates suffered a loss of five hundred men in their unsuccessful attempt to demoralize Pope in his retreat, and the Federals more than a thousand, including Generals Stevens and Kearny.

General Kearny might have been saved but for his reckless bravery. He was rounding up the retreat of his men in the darkness of the night when he chanced to come within the Confederate lines. Called on to surrender, he lay flat on his horse's back, sank his spurs into its sides, and attempted to escape. Half a dozen muskets were leveled and fired at the fleeing general. Within thirty yards he rolled from his horse's back dead.

The consternation in Washington and throughout the North when Pope's defeated army reached Arlington Heights can better be imagined than described. General Pope, who bore the brunt of public indignation, begged to be relieved of the command. The President complied with his wishes and the disorganized remnants of the Army of Virginia and the Army of the Potomac were handed to the "Little Napoleon" of Peninsula fame, George B. McClellan.

The South was overjoyed with its victory—twice it had unfurled its banner in triumph on the battlefield at Manassas by the remarkable strategy of its generals and the courage of its warriors on the firing-line. Twice it had stood literally on the road that led to the capital of the Republic, only by some strange destiny of war to fail to enter its precincts on the wave of victory.

PART I
THE RISE OF LEE

ANTIETAM—THE
INVASION OF THE NORTH

THE FIRST STAND
OF "STONEWALL'S" MEN

McCLELLAN'S LAST ADVANCE

This splendid landscape photograph of the pontoon bridge at Berlin, Maryland, was taken in October, 1862. On the 26th McClellan crossed the Potomac here for the last time in command of an army. Around this quiet and picturesque country the Army of the Potomac bivouacked during October, 1862, leaving two corps posted at Harper's Ferry to hold the outlet of the Shenandoah Valley. At Berlin (a little village of about four hundred inhabitants), McClellan had his headquarters during the reorganization of the army, which he considered necessary after Antietam. The many reverses to the Federal arms since the beginning of the war had weakened the popular hold of the Lincoln Administration, and there was constant political pressure for an aggressive move against Lee. McClellan, yielding at last to this demand, began advancing his army into Virginia. Late on the night of November 7th, through a heavy rainstorm, General Buckingham, riding post-

THE CROSSING AFTER ANTIETAM

haste from Washington, reached McClellan's tent at Rectortown, and handed him Stanton's order relieving him from command. Burnside was appointed his successor, and at the moment was with him in the tent. Without a change of countenance, McClellan handed him the despatch, with the words: "Well, Burnside, you are to command the army." Whatever may have been McClellan's fault, the moment chosen for his removal was most inopportune and ungracious. His last advance upon Lee was excellently planned, and he had begun to execute it with great vigor—the van of the army having reached Warrenton on November 7th, opposed only by half of Lee's army at Culpeper, while demonstrations across the gaps of the Blue Ridge compelled the retention of Jackson with the other half in the Shenandoah Valley. Never before had the Federal military prospect been brighter than at that moment.

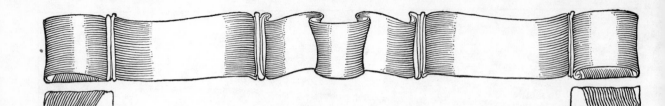

ANTIETAM, OR SHARPSBURG

At Sharpsburg (Antietam) was sprung the keystone of the arch upon which the Confederate cause rested.—James Longstreet, Lieutenant-General C.S.A., in "Battles and Leaders of the Civil War."

A BATTLE remarkable in its actualities but more wonderful in its possibilities was that of Antietam, with the preceding capture of Harper's Ferry and the other interesting events that marked the invasion of Maryland by General Lee. It was one of the bloodiest and the most picturesque conflicts of the Civil War, and while it was not all that the North was demanding and not all that many military critics think it might have been, it enabled President Lincoln to feel that he could with some assurance issue, as he did, his Emancipation Proclamation.

Lee's army, fifty thousand strong, had crossed the Potomac at Leesburg and had concentrated around Frederick, the scene of the Barbara Frietchie legend, only forty miles from Washington. When it became known that Lee, elated by his victory at Second Bull Run, had taken the daring step of advancing into Maryland, and now threatened the capital of the Republic, McClellan, commanding the Army of the Potomac, pushed his forces forward to encounter the invaders. Harper's Ferry, at the junction of the Potomac and the Shenandoah rivers, was a valuable defense against invasion through the Valley of Virginia, but once the Confederates had crossed it, a veritable trap. General Halleck ordered it held and General Lee sent " Stonewall " Jackson to take it, by attacking the fortress on the Virginia side.

Jackson began his march on September 10th with secret instructions from his commander to encompass and capture the

COPYRIGHT 1911, PATRIOT PUB. CO.

LEE LOCKS THE GATES

Sharpsburg, Maryland, September 17, 1862. There were long minutes on that sunny day in the early fall of 1862 when Robert E. Lee, at his headquarters west of Sharpsburg, must have been in almost entire ignorance of how the battle went. Outnumbered he knew his troops were; outfought he knew they never would be. Longstreet, Hood, D. B. Hill, Evans, and D. R. Jones had turned back more than one charge in the morning; but, as the day wore on, Lee perceived that the center must be held. Sharpsburg was the key. He had deceived McClellan as to his numerical strength and he must continue to do so. Lee had practically no reserves at all. At one time General Longstreet reported from the center to General Chilton, Lee's Chief of Staff, that Cooke's North Carolina regiment— still keeping its colors at the front—had not a cartridge left. None but veteran troops could hold a line like this, supported by only two guns of Miller's battery of the Washington Artillery. Of this crisis in the battle General Longstreet wrote afterward: "We were already badly whipped and were holding our ground by sheer force of desperation." Actually in line that day on the Confederate side were only 37,000 men, and opposed to them were numbers that could be footed up to 50,000 more. At what time in the day General Lee must have perceived that the invasion of Maryland must come to an end cannot be told. He had lost 20,000 of his tired, footsore army by straggling on the march, according to the report of Longstreet, who adds: "Nearly one-fourth of the troops who went into the battle were killed or wounded." At dark Lee's rearward movement had begun.

Federal garrison and the vast store of war material at this place, made famous a few years before by old John Brown. To conceal his purpose from the inhabitants he inquired along the route about the roads leading into Pennsylvania. It was from his march through Frederick that the Barbara Frietchie story took its rise. But there is every reason to believe that General Jackson never saw the good old lady, that the story is a myth, and that Mr. Whittier, who has given us the popular poem under the title of her name, was misinformed. However, Colonel H. K. Douglas, who was a member of Jackson's staff, relates, in "Battles and Leaders of the Civil War," an interesting incident where his commander on entering Middletown was greeted by two young girls waving a Union flag. The general bowed to the young women, raised his hat, and remarked to some of his officers, "We evidently have no friends in this town." Colonel Douglas concludes, "This is about the way he would have treated Barbara Frietchie."

On the day after Jackson left Frederick he crossed the Potomac by means of a ford near Williamsport and on the 13th he reached Bolivar Heights. Harper's Ferry lies in a deep basin formed by Maryland Heights on the north bank of the Potomac, Loudon Heights on the south bank, and Bolivar Heights on the west. The Shenandoah River breaks through the pass between Loudon and Bolivar Heights and the village lies between the two at the apex formed by the junction of the two rivers.

As Jackson approached the place by way of Bolivar Heights, Walker occupied Loudon Heights and McLaws invested Maryland Heights. All were unopposed except McLaws, who encountered Colonel Ford with a force to dispute his ascent. Ford, however, after some resistance, spiked his guns and retired to the Ferry, where Colonel Miles had remained with the greater portion of the Federal troops. Had Miles led his entire force to Maryland Heights he could no doubt have held his ground until McClellan came to his relief.

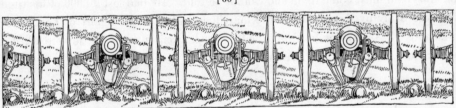

A REGIMENT THAT FOUGHT AT SOUTH MOUNTAIN—THE THIRTY-FIFTH NEW YORK

Here sits Colonel T. G. Morehead, who commanded the 106th Pennsylvania, of the Second Corps. At 7.20 A.M. the order came to advance, and with a cheer the Second Corps—men who for over two years had never lost a gun nor struck a color—pressed forward. But again they were halted. It was almost an hour later when Sedgwick's division, with Sumner at the head, crossed the Antietam. Arriving nearly opposite the Dunker church, it swept out over the cornfields. On it went, by Greene's right, through the West Woods; here it met the awful counter-stroke of Early's reënforced division and, stubbornly resisting, was hurled back with frightful loss.

COLONEL T. G. MOREHEAD
A HERO OF SEDGWICK'S CHARGE

Early in the morning of September 17, 1862, Knap's battery (shown below) got into the thick of the action of Antietam. General Mansfield had posted it opposite the north end of the West Woods, close to the Confederate line. The guns opened fire at seven o'clock. Practically unsupported, the battery was twice charged upon during the morning; but quickly substituting canister for shot and shell, the men held their ground and stemmed the Confederate advance. Near this spot General Mansfield was mortally wounded while deploying his troops. About noon a section of Knap's battery was detached to the assistance of General Greene, in the East Woods.

KNAP'S BATTERY, JUST AFTER THE BLOODY WORK AT ANTIETAM

But General Halleck had ordered him to hold Harper's Ferry to the last, and Miles interpreted this order to mean that he must hold the town itself. He therefore failed to occupy the heights around it in sufficient strength and thus permitted himself to be caught in a trap.

During the day of the 14th the Confederate artillery was dragged up the mountain sides, and in the afternoon a heavy fire was opened on the doomed Federal garrison. On that day McClellan received word from Miles that the latter could hold out for two days longer and the commanding general sent word: "Hold out to the last extremity. If it is possible, re-occupy the Maryland Heights with your entire force. If you can do that I will certainly be able to relieve you. . . . Hold out to the last." McClellan was approaching slowly and felt confident he could relieve the place.

On the morning of the 15th the roar of Confederate artillery again resounded from hill to hill. From Loudon to Maryland Heights the firing had begun and a little later the battle-flags of A. P. Hill rose on Bolivar Heights. Scarcely two hours had the firing continued when Colonel Miles raised the white flag at Harper's Ferry and its garrison of 12,500, with vast military stores, passed into the hands of the Confederates. Colonel Miles was struck by a stray fragment of a Confederate shell which gave him a mortal wound. The force of General Franklin, preparing to move to the garrison's relief, on the morning of the 15th noted that firing at the Ferry had ceased and suspected that the garrison had surrendered, as it had.

The Confederate Colonel Douglas, whose account of the surrender is both absorbing and authoritative, thus describes the surrender in " Battles and Leaders of the Civil War ":

" Under instructions from General Jackson, I rode up the pike and into the enemy's lines to ascertain the purpose of the white flag. Near the top of the hill I met General White and staff and told him my mission. He replied that Colonel Miles had been mortally wounded, that he was in command and

THE FIRST TO FALL

This photograph was taken back of the rail fence on the Hagerstown pike, where "Stonewall" Jackson's men attempted to rally in the face of Hooker's ferocious charge that opened the bloodiest day of the Civil War—September 17, 1862. Hooker, advancing to seize high ground nearly three-quarters of a mile distant, had not gone far before the glint of the rising sun disclosed the bayonet-points of a large Confederate force standing in a cornfield in his immediate front. This was a part of Jackson's Corps which had arrived during the morning of the 16th from the capture of Harper's Ferry and had been posted in this position to surprise Hooker in his advance. The outcome was a terrible surprise to the Confederates. All of Hooker's batteries hurried into action and opened with canister on the cornfield. The Confederates stood bravely up against this fire, and as Hooker's men advanced they made a determined resistance. Back and still farther back were Jackson's men driven across the open field, every stalk of corn in which was cut down by the battle as closely as a knife could have done it. On the ground the slain lay in rows precisely as they had stood in ranks. From the cornfield into a small patch of woods (the West Woods) the Confederates were driven, leaving the sad result of the surprise behind them. As the edge of the woods was approached by Hooker's men the resistance became stronger and more stubborn. Nearly all the units of two of Jackson's divisions were now in action, and cavalry and artillery were aiding them. "The two lines," says General Palfrey, "almost tore each other to pieces." General Starke and Colonel Douglas on the Confederate side were killed. More than half of Lawton's and Hays' brigades were either killed or wounded. On the Federal side General Ricketts lost a third of his division. The energy of both forces was entirely spent and reënforcements were necessary before the battle could be continued. Many of Jackson's men wore trousers and caps of Federal blue, as did most of the troops which had been engaged with Jackson in the affair at Harper's Ferry. A. P. Hill's men, arriving from Harper's Ferry that same afternoon, were dressed in new Federal uniforms—a part of their booty—and at first were mistaken for Federals by the friends who were anxiously awaiting them.

desired to have an interview with General Jackson. . . . I conducted them to General Jackson, whom I found sitting on his horse where I had left him. . . . The contrast in appearances there presented was striking. General White, riding a handsome black horse, was carefully dressed and had on untarnished gloves, boots, and sword. His staff were equally comely in costume. On the other hand, General Jackson was the dingiest, worst-dressed and worst-mounted general that a warrior who cared for good looks and style would wish to surrender to.

"General Jackson . . . rode up to Bolivar and down into Harper's Ferry. The curiosity in the Union army to see him was so great that the soldiers lined the sides of the road. . . . One man had an echo of response all about him when he said aloud: 'Boys, he's not much for looks, but if we'd had him we wouldn't have been caught in this trap.'"

McClellan had failed to reach Harper's Ferry in time to relieve it because he was detained at South Mountain by a considerable portion of Lee's army under D. H. Hill and Longstreet. McClellan had come into possession of Lee's general order, outlining the campaign. Discovering by this order that Lee had sent Jackson to attack Harper's Ferry he made every effort to relieve it.

The affair at Harper's Ferry, as that at South Mountain, was but a prelude to the tremendous battle that was to follow two days later on the banks of the little stream called Antietam Creek, in Maryland. When it was known that Lee had led his army across the Potomac the people were filled with consternation—the people, not only of the immediate vicinity, but of Harrisburg, of Baltimore, of Philadelphia. Their fear was intensified by the memory of the Second Bull Run of a few weeks earlier, and by the fact that at this very time General Bragg was marching northward across Kentucky with a great army, menacing Louisville and Cincinnati.

As one year before, the hopes of the North had centered in George B. McClellan, so it was now with the people of the

THE THRICE–FOUGHT GROUND

The field beyond the leveled fence is covered with both Federal and Confederate dead. Over this open space swept Sedgwick's division of Sumner's Second Corps, after passing through the East and entering the West Woods. This is near where the Confederate General Ewell's division, reënforced by McLaws and Walker, fell upon Sedgwick's left flank and rear. Nearly two thousand Federal soldiers were struck down, the division losing during the day more than forty per cent. of its entire number. One regiment lost sixty per cent.—the highest regimental loss sustained. Later the right of the Confederate line crossed the turnpike at the Dunker church (about half a mile to the left of the picture) and made two assaults upon Greene, but they were repulsed with great slaughter. General D. R. Jones, of Jackson's division, had been wounded. The brave Starke who succeeded him was killed; and Lawton, who followed Starke, had fallen wounded.

RUIN OF MUMMA'S HOUSE, ANTIETAM

A flaming mansion was the guidon for the extreme left of Greene's division when (early in the morning) he had moved forward along the ridge leading to the East Woods. This dwelling belonged to a planter by the name of Mumma. It stood in the very center of the Federal advance, and also at the extreme left of D. H. Hill's line. The house had been fired by the Confederates, who feared that its thick walls might become a vantage-point for the Federal infantry. It burned throughout the battle, the flames subsiding only in the afternoon. Before it, just across the road, a battery of the First Rhode Island Light Artillery had placed its guns. Twice were they charged, but each time they were repulsed. From Mumma's house it was less than half a mile across the open field to the Dunker church. The fence-rails in the upper picture were those of the field enclosing Mumma's land, and the heroic dead pictured lying there were in full sight from the burning mansion.

East. They were ready to forget his failure to capture Richmond in the early summer and to contrast his partial successes on the Peninsula with the drastic defeat of his successor at the Second Bull Run.

When McClellan, therefore, passed through Maryland to the scene of the coming battle, many of the people received him with joy and enthusiasm. At Frederick City, he tells us in his " Own Story," he was " nearly overwhelmed and pulled to pieces," and the people invited him into their houses and gave him every demonstration of confidence.

The first encounter, a double one, took place on September 14th, at two passes of South Mountain, a continuation of the Blue Ridge, north of the Potomac. General Franklin, who had been sent to relieve Harper's Ferry, met a Confederate force at Crampton's Gap and defeated it in a sharp battle of three hours' duration. At the same time the main army under Burnside and Reno encountered a stronger force at Turner's Gap seven miles farther up. The battle here continued many hours, till late in the night, and the Union troops were victorious. General Reno was killed. Lee's loss was nearly twenty-seven hundred, of whom eight hundred were prisoners. The Federals lost twenty-one hundred men and they failed to save Harper's Ferry.

Lee now placed Longstreet and D. H. Hill in a strong position near Keedysville, but learning that McClellan was advancing rapidly, the Confederate leader decided to retire to Sharpsburg, where he could be more easily joined by Jackson.

September 16th was a day of intense anxiety and unrest in the valley of the Antietam. The people who had lived in the farmhouses that dotted the golden autumn landscape in this hitherto quiet community had now abandoned their homes and given place to the armed forces. It was a day of marshaling and maneuvering of the gathering thousands, preparatory to the mighty conflict that was clearly seen to be inevitable. Lee had taken a strong position on the west bank of Antietam

WHERE NUMBERS TOLD

Here, in the old sunken road connecting the Hagerstown and the Keedysville Turnpikes, lies the mute testimony of the stubbornness with which the Confederates stood their ground in the most heroic resistance of the day. North of this sunken road was the original position of the Confederate center under General D. H. Hill when the battle opened at dawn. As the fighting reached flood-tide, Hill sent forward the brigades of Colquitt, Ripley, and McRae to the assistance of Jackson at the left. "The men (says Hill) advanced with alacrity, secured a good position, and were fighting bravely when Captain Thompson, Fifth North Carolina, cried out: 'They're flanking us!' This cry spread like an electric shock along the ranks, bringing up vivid recollections of the flank fire at South Mountain. In a moment they broke and fell to the rear." Rallied again at the sunken road, the forces of Hill now met the combined attack of the divisions of French and Richardson of Sumner's Corps, freshly come on the field. It was resistance to the death; reënforced by the division of Anderson, Hill's men, in the face of the deadly fire poured upon them in the sunken road, bravely assumed the offensive in a determined effort to flank the Federal forces to both left and right. Seizing a vantage-point on higher ground to the left, the Federals drove them back; while on the right Barlow, changing front with his two regiments, poured in a rapid fire, capturing three hundred prisoners and two standards. Then came the direct assault; swept by the enfilading fire from both sides, the remnant of the brave men in the sunken road was driven back, leaving the "bloody lane" behind them. It was not an easy victory for the Federals. The determined fire of the Confederates had brought down a heavy harvest, among which was numbered General Richardson, mortally wounded, who had handled his division in this sanguinary contest with his usual valor and skill.

MAJOR-GENERAL I. B. RICHARDSON

Creek a few miles from where it flows into the Potomac. He made a display of force, exposing his men to the fire of the Federal artillery, his object being to await the coming of Jackson's command from Harper's Ferry. It is true that Jackson himself had arrived, but his men were weary with marching and, moreover, a large portion of his troops under A. P. Hill and McLaws had not yet reached the field.

McClellan spent the day arranging his corps and giving directions for planting batteries. With a few companions he rode along the whole front, frequently drawing the fire of the Confederate batteries and thus revealing their location. The right wing of his army, the corps of Generals Hooker, Mansfield, and Sumner, lay to the north, near the village of Keedysville. General Porter with two divisions of the Fifth Corps occupied the center and Burnside was on the left of the Union lines. Back of McClellan's lines was a ridge on which was a signal station commanding a view of the entire field. Late on the afternoon of the 16th, Hooker crossing the Antietam, advanced against Hood's division on the Confederate left. For several hours there was heavy skirmishing, which closed with the coming of darkness.

The two great armies now lay facing each other in a grand double line three miles in length. At one point (the Union right and the Confederate left) they were so near together that the pickets could hear each other's tread. It required no prophet to foretell what would happen on the morrow.

Beautiful and clear the morning broke over the Maryland hills on the fateful 17th of September, 1862. The sunlight had not yet crowned the hilltops when artillery fire announced the opening of the battle. Hooker's infantry soon entered into the action and encountered the Confederates in an open field, from which the latter were presently pressed back across the Hagerstown pike to a line of woods where they made a determined stand. Hooker then called on General Mansfield to come to his aid, and the latter quickly did so, for he had led

THE HARVEST OF "BLOODY LANE"

Here, at "Bloody Lane" in the sunken road, was delivered the most telling blow of which the Federals could boast in the day's fighting at Antietam, September 17, 1862. In the lower picture we see the officers whose work first began to turn the tide of battle into a decisive advantage which the Army of the Potomac had every reason to expect would be gained by its superior numbers. On the Federal right Jackson, with a bare four thousand men, had taken the fight out of Hooker's eighteen thousand in the morning, giving ground at last to Sumner's fresh troops. On the Federal left, Burnside (at the lower bridge) failed to advance against Longstreet's Corps, two-thirds of which had been detached for service elsewhere. It was at the center that the forces of French and Richardson, skilfully fought by their leaders, broke through the Confederate lines and, sweeping beyond the sunken road, seized the very citadel of the center. Meagher's Irish Brigade had fought its way to a crest from which a plunging fire could be poured upon the Confederates in the sunken road. Meagher's ammunition was exhausted, and Caldwell threw his force into the position and continued the terrible combat. When the Confederates executed their flanking movement to the left, Colonel D. R. Cross, of the Fifth New Hampshire, seized a position which exposed Hill's men to an enfilading fire. (In the picture General Caldwell is seen standing to the left of the tree, and Colonel Cross leans on his sword at the extreme right. Between them stands Lieut.-Colonel George W. Scott, of the Sixty-first New York Infantry, while at the left before the tent stands Captain George W. Bulloch, A.C.S. General Caldwell's hand rests on the shoulder of Captain George H. Caldwell; to his left is seated Lieutenant C. A. Alvord.)

BRIGADIER-GENERAL CALDWELL AND STAFF

his corps across the Antietam after dark the night before. Mansfield, however, a gallant and honored veteran, fell mortally wounded while deploying his troops, and General Alpheus S. Williams, at the head of his first division, succeeded to the command.

There was a wood west of the Sharpsburg and Hagerstown turnpike which, with its outcropping ledges of rock, formed an excellent retreat for the Confederates and from this they pushed their columns into the open fields, chiefly of corn, to meet the Union attacks. For about two hours the battle raged at this point, the lines swaying to and fro, with fearful slaughter on both sides. At length, General Greene, who commanded a division of the fallen Mansfield's corps, gained possession of part of the coveted forest, near a little white church, known as the Dunker's Chapel. This was on high ground and was the key to the Confederate left wing. But Greene's troops were exposed to a galling fire from D. H. Hill's division and he called for reenforcements.

General Sumner then sent Sedgwick's division across the stream and accompanied the troops to the aid of their hard-pressed comrades. And the experience of this body of the gallant Second Corps during the next hour was probably the most thrilling episode of the whole day's battle. Sedgwick's troops advanced straight toward the conflict. They found Hooker wounded and his and Williams' troops quite exhausted. A sharp artillery fire was turned on Sedgwick before he reached the woods west of the Hagerstown pike, but once in the shelter of the thick trees he passed in safety to the western edge. Here the division found itself in an ambush. Heavy Confederate reenforcements—ten brigades, in fact—Walker's men, and McLaws', having arrived from Harper's Ferry—were hastening up, and they not only blocked the front, but worked around to the rear of Sedgwick's isolated brigades. Sedgwick was wounded in the awful slaughter that followed, but he and Sumner finally extricated their men with

THE BLUNDER AT THE BRIDGE

Burnside's Bridge, as it was called after Antietam, bears the name of a noted Federal general—not because of the brilliant maneuver which he vainly tried to execute in his efforts to cross it, but rather because of the gallant resistance offered here by the Confederates. General Toombs, with two Georgia regiments (the Second and the Twentieth) stood off a greatly superior force during the 16th and the greater part of the 17th of September. This bridge (on the road from Sharpsburg to Porterstown and Rohersville) was not forced till late in the afternoon, when Burnside, after a series of delays and ineffectual attempts, managed to throw his troops across Antietam Creek. The battle, however, was then practically decided. Toombs' forces saved the Confederate right wing—to him Lee and Longstreet gave the highest praise.

a loss of two thousand, over three hundred left dead on the ghastly field. Franklin now sent forward some fresh troops and after obstinately fighting, the Federals finally held a corn-field and most of the coveted wood over which the conflict had raged till the ground was saturated with blood.

Before the close of this bloody conflict on the Union right another, almost if not quite as deadly, was in progress near the center. General French, soon joined by General Richardson, both of Sumner's corps, crossed the stream and made a desperate assault against the Southerners of D. H. Hill's division, stationed to the south of where the battle had previously raged—French on a line of heights strongly held by the Confederates, Richardson in the direction of a sunken road, since known as "Bloody Lane." The fighting here was of a most desperate character and continued nearly four hours. French captured a few flags, several hundred prisoners, and gained some ground, but he failed to carry the heights. Richardson was mortally wounded while leading a charge and was succeeded by General Hancock; but his men finally captured Bloody Lane with the three hundred living men who had remained to defend it. The final Federal charge at this point was made by Colonel Barlow, who displayed the utmost bravery and self-possession in the thickest of the fight, where he won a brigadier-generalship. He was wounded, and later carried off the field. The Confederates had fought desperately to hold their position in Bloody Lane, and when it was captured it was filled with dead bodies. It was now about one o'clock and the infantry firing ceased for the day on the Union right, and center.

Let us now look on the other part of the field. Burnside held the Federal left wing against Lee's right, and he remained inactive for some hours after the battle had begun at the other end of the line. In front of Burnside was a triple-arched stone bridge across the Antietam, since known as "Burnside's Bridge." Opposite this bridge, on the slope which extends to a

SHERRICK'S HOUSE

In three distinct localities the battle waxed fierce from dawn to dusk on that terrible day at Antietam, September 17, 1862. First at the Federal right around the Dunker church; then at the sunken road, where the centers of both armies spent themselves in sanguinary struggle; lastly, late in the day, the struggle was renewed and ceased on the Sharpsburg road. When Burnside finally got his troops in motion, Sturgis' division of the Ninth Corps was first to cross the creek; his men advanced through an open ravine under a withering fire till they gained the opposite crest and held it until reënforced by Wilcox. To their right ran the Sharpsburg road, and an advance was begun in the direction of the Sherrick house.

The fighting along the Sharpsburg road might have resulted in a Confederate disaster had it not been for the timely arrival of the troops of General A. P. Hill. His six brigades of Confederate veterans had been the last to leave Harper's Ferry, remaining behind Jackson's main body in order to attend to the details of the surrender. Just as the Federal Ninth Corps was in the height of its advance, a cloud of dust on Harper's Ferry road cheered the Confederates to redoubled effort. Out of the dust the brigades of Hill debouched upon the field. Their fighting blood seemed to have but mounted more strongly during their march of eighteen miles. Without waiting for orders, Hill threw his men into the fight and the progress of the

Ninth Corps was stopped. Lee had counted on the arrival of Hill in time to prevent any successful attempt upon the Confederate right held by Longstreet's Corps, two-thirds of which had been detached in the thick of the fighting of the morning, when Lee's left and center suffered so severely. Burnside's delay at the bridge could not have been more fortunate for Lee if he had fixed its duration himself. Had the Confederate left been attacked at the time appointed, the outcome of Antietam could scarcely have been other than a decisive victory for the Federals. Even at the time when Burnside's tardy advance began, it must have prevailed against the weakened and wearied Confederates had not the fresh troops of A. P. Hill averted the disaster.

GENERAL A. P. HILL, C. S. A.

AFTER THE ADVANCE

In the advance along the Sharpsburg road near the Sherrick house the 79th New York "Highlanders" deployed as skirmishers. From orchards and cornfields and from behind fences and haystacks the Confederate sharpshooters opened upon them, but they swept on, driving in a part of Jones' division and capturing a battery just before A. P. Hill's troops arrived. With these reënforcements the Confederates drove back the brave Highlanders from the suburbs of Sharpsburg, which they had reached. Stubborn Scotch blood would permit only a reluctant retreat. Sharp fighting occurred around the Sherrick house with results seen in the lower picture. Night closed the battle, both sides exhausted.

high ridge, were Confederate breastworks and rifle-pits, which commanded the bridge with a direct or enfilading fire. While the Federal right was fighting on the morning of the 17th, McClellan sent an order to Burnside to advance on the bridge, to take possession of it and cross the stream by means of it. It must have been about ten o'clock when Burnside received the order as McClellan was more than two miles away.

Burnside's chief officer at this moment was General Jacob D. Cox (afterward Governor of Ohio), who had succeeded General Reno, killed at South Mountain. On Cox fell the task of capturing the stone bridge. The defense of the bridge was in the hands of General Robert Toombs, a former United States senator and a member of Jefferson Davis' Cabinet. Perhaps the most notable single event in the life of General Toombs was his holding of the Burnside Bridge at Antietam for three hours against the assaults of the Federal troops. The Confederates had been weakened at this point by the sending of Walker to the support of Jackson, where, as we have noticed, he took part in the deadly assault upon Sedgwick's division. Toombs, therefore, with his one brigade had a heavy task before him in defending the bridge with his small force, notwithstanding his advantage of position.

McClellan sent several urgent orders to advance at all hazards. Burnside forwarded these to Cox, and in the fear that the latter would be unable to carry the bridge by a direct front attack, he sent Rodman with a division to cross the creek by a ford some distance below. This was accomplished after much difficulty. Meanwhile, in rapid succession, one assault after another was made upon the bridge and, about one o'clock, it was carried, at the cost of five hundred men. The Confederates fell back. A lull in the fighting along the whole line of battle now ensued.

Burnside, however, received another order from McClellan to push on up the heights and to the village of Sharpsburg. The great importance of this move, if successful, was

THE FLOOD–TIDE OF THE FEDERAL ADVANCE

This Lutheran church on Main Street, to the east of Sharpsburg, marked the end of the Federal assault upon Lee's position at Antietam, as the little church of the non-resistant Dunkers to the north of the town had marked its beginning in the early morning. About three o'clock in the afternoon Burnside's skirmishers advanced to the first cross-street beyond this church, threatening the town itself. Out on the hills beyond the town, Main Street becomes the Shepherdstown road, and along this were arriving and hurrying through the town the anxiously awaited forces of A. P. Hill. From that moment the Federals got no nearer Sharpsburg. Hill drove them back steadily beyond the church, recapturing the battery which they had wrested from the troops of Jones and which had done damage to the little church as well as to the Confederates. Hill's men, taking Rodman's division in flank, poured in a fire in which Rodman met his death. Panic among his troops was averted only by Scammon, who (leading Cox's division) checked Hill for a breathing space; but Burnside's forces were steadily pushed back until at nightfall they lay discomfited, holding the bridge on the banks of Antietam creek, which he had wrested from Toombs' two Georgia regiments.

that it would cut Lee out from his line of retreat by way of Shepherdstown.

After replenishing the ammunition and adding some fresh troops, Cox advanced at three o'clock with the utmost gallantry toward Sharpsburg. The Confederates disputed the ground with great bravery. But Cox swept all before him and was at the edge of the village when he was suddenly confronted by lines in blue uniforms who instantly opened fire. The Federals were astonished to see the blue-clad battalions before them. They must be Union soldiers; but how did they get there? The matter was soon explained. They were A. P. Hill's division of Lee's army which had just arrived from Harper's Ferry, and they had dressed themselves in the uniforms that they had taken from the Federal stores.

Hill had come just in time to save Lee's headquarters from capture. He checked Cox's advance, threw a portion of the troops into great confusion, and steadily pressed them back toward the Antietam. In this, the end of the battle, General Rodman fell mortally wounded. Cox retired in good order and Sharpsburg remained in the hands of the Confederates.

Thus, with the approach of nightfall, closed the memorable battle of Antietam. For fourteen long hours more than one hundred thousand men, with five hundred pieces of artillery, had engaged in titanic combat. As the pall of battle smoke rose and cleared away, the scene presented was one to make the stoutest heart shudder. There lay upon the ground, scattered for three miles over the valleys and the hills or in the improvised hospitals, more than twenty thousand men. Horace Greeley was probably right in pronouncing this the bloodiest day in American history.

Although tactically it was a drawn battle, Antietam was decisively in favor of the North inasmuch as it ended the first Confederate attempt at a Northern invasion. General Lee realized that his ulterior plans had been thwarted by this engagement and after a consultation with his corps commanders

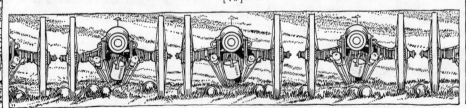

THE MEDIATOR

President Lincoln's Visit to the Camps at Antietam, October 8, 1862.   Yearning for the speedy termination of the war, Lincoln came to view the Army of the Potomac, as he had done at Harrison's Landing.   Puzzled to understand how Lee could have circumvented a superior force on the Peninsula, he was now anxious to learn why a crushing blow had not been struck.   Lincoln (after Gettysburg) expressed the same thought: "Our army held the war in the hollow of their hand and they would not close it!"   On Lincoln's right stands Allan Pinkerton, the famous detective and organizer of the Secret Service of the army.   At the President's left is General John A. McClernand, soon to be entrusted by Lincoln with reorganizing military operations in the West.

he determined to withdraw from Maryland. On the night of the 18th the retreat began and early the next morning the Confederate army had all safely recrossed the Potomac.

The great mistake of the Maryland campaign from the standpoint of the Confederate forces, thought General Longstreet, was the division of Lee's army, and he believed that if Lee had kept his forces together he would not have been forced to abandon the campaign. At Antietam, he had less than forty thousand men, who were in poor condition for battle while McClellan had about eighty-seven thousand, most of whom were fresh and strong, though not more than sixty thousand were in action.

The moral effect of the battle of Antietam was incalculably great. It aroused the confidence of the Northern people. It emboldened President Lincoln to issue five days after its close the proclamation freeing the slaves in the seceded states. He had written the proclamation long before, but it had lain inactive in his desk at Washington. All through the struggles of the summer of 1862 he had looked forward to the time when he could announce his decision to the people. But he could not do it then. With the doubtful success of Federal arms, to make such a bold step would have been a mockery and would have defeated the very end he sought.

The South had now struck its first desperate blow at the gateways to the North. By daring, almost unparalleled in warfare, it had swung its courageous army into a strategical position where with the stroke of fortune it might have hammered down the defenses of the National capital on the south and then sweep on a march of invasion into the North. The Northern soldiers had parried the blow. They had saved themselves from disaster and had held back the tide of the Confederacy as it beat against the Mason and Dixon line, forcing it back into the State of Virginia where the two mighty fighting bodies were soon to meet again in a desperate struggle for the right-of-way at Fredericksburg.

PART I
THE RISE OF LEE

FREDERICKSBURG
DISASTER FOR A NEW UNION LEADER

THE MILL ACROSS THE RIVER

FREDERICKSBURG

A PHOTOGRAPH TAKEN JUST AFTER THE BATTLE OF DECEMBER, 1862

Two magnificent armies faced one another here in the middle of December, 1862. Along the ground we see spread before us on the east side of the Rappahannock—the famous Stafford Heights—the men in blue were massed in a long line of camps. In the town were scattered forces of Confederate troops, and along the river front each house was a temporary citadel; even cannon frowned from the windows. The winding river, now unbridged and at high water, separated the Army of Northern Virginia under Lee from the Army of the Potomac under Burnside. Fredericksburg, deserted by women, children, the aged, and the infirm, lay helpless before the Federal guns. But along the hill against the horizon stretched Lee's army, under able generals, in an impregnable position. Between it and the town lay open ground with a few scattered houses. Stretching across the river we can see the ruins of the bridges. For a month Burnside had waited for pontoons to enable him to cross in force. On a foggy morning after their arrival, the 11th of December, a landing was effected. The fierce fire of 147 guns from Stafford Heights played havoc among the houses. The sharpshooters that had bothered the pontoniers were driven back, and soon all the Confederate forces had gathered along the ridge a mile to the west of the town. By the 12th the Federal army had crossed and deployed for battle.

THE DEATH-TRAP ON TELEGRAPH ROAD

Here Sumner's right grand division of the Army of the Potomac exemplified an implicit obedience of orders more magnificent even than that of the "Six Hundred" at Balaklava. Advancing along the Telegraph Road, seen at the right of the picture, the divisions of French and Hancock, already depleted by cruel artillery fire, charged up Marye's Heights, the eminence at the center of the picture. There a blinding flash of flame first disclosed the ambuscade in the sunken road. Ranged in ranks, first four and then six men deep, the Confederates kept up a continuous volleying against which no troops could stand. First the divisions of French and Hancock went down before it—then that of Howard. To the left the supporting divisions of Sturgis and Getty shared the efforts of their comrades with like result. Griffin's and Humphreys' divisions followed later—all to no avail. Six desperate charges were made upon Cobb's and Kershaw's troops. When darkness put an end to the slaughter, seven thousand Federal killed and wounded lay at the foot of Marye's Heights.

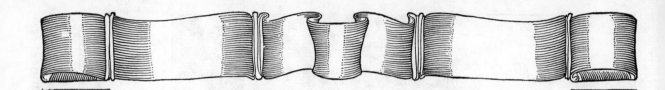

FREDERICKSBURG—DISASTER FOR A NEW UNION LEADER

The Army of the Potomac had fought gallantly; it had not lost a single cannon, all its attacks being made by masses of infantry; it had experienced neither disorder nor rout. But the defeat was complete, and its effects were felt throughout the entire country as keenly as in the ranks of the army. The little confidence that Burnside had been able to inspire in his soldiers had vanished, and the respect which everybody entertained for the noble character of the unfortunate general could not supply its place.—*Comte de Paris, in "History of the Civil War in America."*

THE silent city of military graves at Fredericksburg is a memorial of one of the bloodiest battles of the Civil War. The battle of Antietam had been regarded a victory by the Federals and a source of hope to the North, after a wearisome period of inaction and defeats. General George B. McClellan, in command of the Army of the Potomac, failed to follow up this advantage and strike fast and hard while the Southern army was shattered and weak. President Lincoln's impatience was brought to a climax; McClellan was relieved and succeeded by General Ambrose E. Burnside, who was looked upon with favor by the President, and who had twice declined this proffered honor. It was on November 5, 1862, nearly two months after Antietam, when this order was issued. The Army of the Potomac was in splendid form and had made plans for a vigorous campaign. On the 9th Burnside assumed command, and on the following day McClellan took leave of his beloved troops.

Burnside at once changed the whole plan of campaign, and decided to move on Fredericksburg, which lay between the Union and Confederate armies. He organized his army into

THE SECOND LEADER AGAINST RICHMOND

Major-General Ambrose Everett Burnside was a West Point graduate, inventor of a breech-loading rifle, commander of a brigade in the first battle of Bull Run, captor of Roanoke Island and Newberne (North Carolina), and commander of the Federal left at Antietam. He was appointed to the command of the Army of the Potomac and succeeded General George B. McClellan on November 8, 1862. He was a brave soldier, but was an impatient leader and inclined to be somewhat reckless. He pressed rapidly his advance against Lee and massed his entire army along Stafford Heights, on the east bank of the Rappahannock, opposite Fredericksburg. According to General B. B. Franklin (who commanded the left grand division of the army), the notion that a serious battle was necessary to Federal control of the town "was not entertained by any one." General Sumner (who led the advance of Burnside's army) held this opinion but he had not received orders to cross the river. Crossing was delayed nearly a month and this delay resulted in the Federal disaster on December 13th. This put an abrupt end to active operations by Burnside against Lee. This picture was taken at Warrenton, November 24th, on the eve of the departure of the army for its march to Fredericksburg.

three grand divisions, under Generals Sumner, Hooker, and Franklin, commanding the right, center, and left, and moved his troops from Warrenton to Falmouth. A delay of some two weeks was due to the failure of arrival of the pontoons. In a council of war held on the night of December 10th the officers under Burnside expressed themselves almost unanimously as opposed to the plan of battle, but Burnside disregarded their views and determined to carry out his original plans immediately. After some delay and desultory fighting for two days, the crossing of the army was effected by the morning of December 13th. By this time General Robert E. Lee, commanding the Confederates, had his army concentrated and entrenched on the hills surrounding the town. In their efforts to place their bridges the Federals were seriously hindered by the firing of the Confederate sharpshooters— "hornets that were stinging the Army of the Potomac into a frenzy." The Confederate fire continued until silenced by a heavy bombardment of the city from the Federal guns, when the crossing of the army into Fredericksburg was completed without further interference.

The forces of Lee were in battle array about the town. Their line stretched for five miles along the range of hills which spread in crescent shape around the lowland where the city lay, surrounding it on all sides save the east, where the river flowed. The strongest Confederate position was on the slopes of the lowest hill of the range, Marye's Heights, which rose in the rear of the town. Along the foot of this hill there was a stone wall, about four feet in height, bounding the eastern side of the Telegraph road, which at this point runs north and south, being depressed a few feet below the surface of the stone wall, thus forming a breastwork for the Confederate troops. Behind it a strong force was concealed, while higher up, in several ranks, the main army was massed, stretching along the line of hills. The right wing, consisting of thirty thousand troops on an elevation near Hamilton's Cross-

THE BUSY BASE OF THE ARMY OF THE POTOMAC

Aquia Creek Landing, Virginia, February, 1863. In the movements of Burnside and Hooker along the Rappahannock in the winter of 1862–3 this point became the base of supplies for the Army of the Potomac. Transports and supply-ships from Alexandria were bringing down troops, food, clothing, arms, ammunition, and artillery, and unloading them at the pontoon piers, such as shown in this picture, whence they were forwarded along the line of the Richmond, Fredericksburg & Potomac Railroad to general headquarters at Falmouth Station. The position at Aquia Creek had been occupied alternately by the Federal and Confederate forces from the beginning of the war. Federal troops landed here in August, 1862, before the second battle of Bull Run. After Lee's brilliant victory at Chancellorsville, which drove Hooker in defeat north of the Rappahannock, the great Confederate leader pressed boldly forward. The Federal base of supplies remained at Aquia Creek until Hooker's army marched toward the upper Potomac in pursuit.

ing of the Fredericksburg and Potomac Railroad, was commanded by "Stonewall" Jackson. The left, on Marye's Heights and Marye's Hill, was commanded by the redoubtable Longstreet. The Southern forces numbered about seventy-eight thousand.

Into the little city below and the adjoining valleys, the Federal troops had been marching for two days. Franklin's Left Grand Division of forty thousand was strengthened by two divisions from Hooker's Center Grand Division, and was ordered to make the first attack on the Confederate right under Jackson. Sumner's Right Grand Division, also reenforced from Hooker's forces, was formed for assault against the Confederate's strongest point at Marye's Hill.

All this magnificent and portentous battle formation had been effected under cover of a dense fog, and when it lifted on that fateful Saturday there was revealed a scene of truly military grandeur. Concealed by the somber curtain of nature the Southern hosts had fixed their batteries and entrenched themselves most advantageously upon the hills, and the Union legions, massed in menacing strength below, now lay within easy cannon-shot of their foe. The Union army totaled one hundred and thirteen thousand men. After skirmishing and gathering of strength, it was at length ready for the final spring and the death-grapple.

When the sun's rays broke through the fog during the forenoon of December 13th, Franklin's Grand Division was revealed in full strength in front of the Confederate right, marching and countermarching in preparation for the coming conflict. Officers in new, bright uniforms, thousands of bayonets gleaming in the sunshine, champing steeds, rattling gun-carriages whisking artillery into proper range of the foe, infantry, cavalry, batteries, with officers and men, formed a scene of magnificent grandeur which excited the admiration even of the Confederates. This maneuver has been called the grandest military scene of the war.

THE DETAINED GUNS

Fredericksburg, February, 1863. In the foreground, looking from what is approximately the same position as the opening picture, are three guns of Tyler's Connecticut battery. It was from all along this ridge that the town had suffered its bombardment in December of the previous year. Again the armies were separated by the Rappahannock River. There was a new commander at the head of the Army of the Potomac—General Hooker. The plundered and deserted town now held by the Confederates was to be made the objective of another attack. The heights beyond were once more to be assaulted; bridges were to be rebuilt. But all to no purpose. This ground of much contention was deserted some time before Lee advanced to his invasion of Pennsylvania. Very slowly the inhabitants of Fredericksburg had returned to their ruined homes. The town was a vast Federal cemetery, the dead being buried in gardens and backyards, for during its occupancy almost every dwelling had been turned into a temporary hospital. After the close of the war these bodies were gathered and a National Cemetery was established on Willis' Hill, on Marye's Heights, the point successfully defended by Lee's veterans.

Heavy pontoon-boats, each on its separate wagon, were sometimes as necessary as food or ammunition. At every important crossing of the many rivers that had to be passed in the Peninsula Campaign the bridges had been destroyed. There were few places where these streams were fordable. Pontoons, therefore, made a most important adjunct to the Army of the Potomac.

PONTOON-BOATS IN TRANSIT

Yet with all this brave show, we have seen that Burnside's subordinate officers were unanimous in their belief in the rashness of the undertaking. Enthusiasm was sadly lacking. The English military writer, Colonel Henderson, has explained why this was so:

And yet that vast array, so formidable of aspect, lacked that moral force without which physical power, even in its most terrible form, is but an idle show. Not only were the strength of the Confederate position, the want of energy of preliminary movements, the insecurity of their own situation, but too apparent to the intelligence of the regimental officers and men, but they mistrusted their commander. Northern writers have recorded that the Army of the Potomac never went down to battle with less alacrity than on this day at Fredericksburg.

The first advance began at 8:30 in the morning, while the fog was still dense, upon Jackson's right. Reynolds ordered Meade with a division, supported by two other divisions under Doubleday and Gibbon, to attack Jackson at his weakest point, the extreme right of the Confederate lines, and endeavor to seize one of the opposing heights. The advance was made in three lines of battle, which were guarded in front and on each flank by artillery which swept the field in front as the army advanced. The Confederates were placed to have an enfilading sweep from both flanks along the entire front line of march. When Reynolds' divisions had approached within range, Jackson's small arms on the left poured in a deadly fire, mowing down the brave men in the Union lines in swaths, leaving broad gaps where men had stood.

This fire was repeated again and again, as the Federals pressed on, only to be repulsed. Once only was the Confederate line broken, when Meade carried the crest, capturing flags and prisoners. The ground lost by the Confederates was soon recovered, and the Federals were forced to retire. Some of the charges made by the Federals during this engagement were heroic in the extreme, only equaled by the opposition met

THE FLAMING HEIGHTS

This photograph from the Fredericksburg river-bank recalls a terrible scene.   On those memorable days of December 11 and 12, 1862, from these very trenches shown in the foreground, the ragged gray riflemen saw on that hillside across the river the blue of the uniforms of the massed Federal troops.   The lines of tents made great white spaces, but the ground could hardly be seen for the host of men who were waiting, alas! to die by thousands on this coveted shore.   From these hills, too, burst an incessant flaming and roaring cannon fire.   Siege-guns and field artillery poured shot and shell into the town of Fredericksburg.   Every house became a target, though deserted except for a few hardy and venturesome riflemen.   There was scarcely a dwelling that escaped.   Ruined and battered and bloody, Fredericksburg three times was a Federal hospital, and its backyards became little cemeteries.

A TARGET AT FREDERICKSBURG FOR THE FEDERAL GUNS

from the foe. In one advance, knapsacks were unslung and bayonets fixed; a brigade marched across a plowed field, and passed through broken lines of other brigades, which were retiring to the rear in confusion from the leaden storm.

The fire became incessant and destructive; many fell, killed or wounded; the front line slackened its pace, and without orders commenced firing. A halt seemed imminent, and a halt in the face of the terrific fire to which the men were exposed meant death; but, urged on by regimental commanders in person, the charge was renewed, when with a shout they leaped the ditches, charged across the railroad, and upon the foe, killing many with the bayonet and capturing several hundred prisoners. But this was only a temporary gain. In every instance the Federals were shattered and driven back. Men were lying dead in heaps, the wounded and dying were groaning in agony. Soldiers were fleeing; officers were galloping to and fro urging their lines forward, and begging their superior officers for assistance and reenforcement.

A dispatch to Burnside from Franklin, dated 2:45, was as follows: " My left has been very badly handled; what hope is there of getting reenforcements across the river? " Another dispatch, dated 3:45, read: " Our troops have gained no ground in the last half hour."

In their retreat the fire was almost as destructive as during the assault. Most of the wounded were brought from the field after this engagement, but the dead were left where they fell. It was during this engagement that General George D. Bayard was mortally wounded by a shot which had severed the sword belt of Captain Gibson, leaving him uninjured. The knapsack of a soldier who was in a stooping posture was struck by a ball, and a deck of cards was sent flying twenty feet in the air. Those witnessing the ludicrous scene called to him, " Oh, deal me a hand! " thus indicating the spirit of levity among soldiers even amid such surroundings. Another soldier sitting on the ground suddenly leaped high above the

THE BRIDGES THAT A BAND OF MUSIC THREATENED

At Franklin Crossing, on the Rappahannock, occurred an incident that proves how little things may change the whole trend of the best-laid plans. The left Union wing under the command of General Franklin, composed of the First Army Corps under General Reynolds, and the Sixth under General W. S. Smith, was crossing to engage in the battle of Fredericksburg. For two days they poured across these yielding planks between the swaying boats to the farther shore. Now, in the crossing of bridges, moving bodies of men must break step or even well-built structures might be threatened. The colonel of one of the regiments in General Devens' division that led the van ordered his field music to strike up just as the head of the column swept on to the flimsy planking; before the regiment was half-way across, unconsciously the men had fallen into step and the whole fabric was swaying to the cadenced feet. Vibrating like a great fiddle-string, the bridge would have sunk and parted, but a keen eye had seen the danger. "Stop that music!" was the order, and a staff officer spurred his horse through the men, shouting at top voice. The lone charge was made through the marching column: some jumped into the pontoons to avoid the hoofs; a few went overboard; but the head of the column was reached at last, and the music stopped. A greater blunder than this, however took place on the plains beyond. Owing to a misunderstanding of orders, 37,000 troops were never brought into action; 17,000 men on their front bore the brunt of a long day's fighting.

heads of his comrades as a shell struck the spot, scooping a wheelbarrowful of earth, but the man was untouched.

Entirely independent of the action in which the Left Grand Division under Franklin was engaged against the right wing of the Confederate line, Sumner's Right Grand Division was engaged in a terrific assault upon the works on Marye's Heights, the stronghold of the Confederate forces. Their position was almost impregnable, consisting of earthworks, wood, and stone barricades running along the sunken road near the foot of Marye's Hill. The Federals were not aware of the sunken road, nor of the force of twenty-five hundred under General Cobb concealed behind the stone wall, this wall not being new work as a part of the entrenchments, but of earlier construction. When the advance up the road was made they were harassed by shot and shell and rifle-balls at every step, but the men came dashing into line undismayed by the terrific fire which poured down upon them.

The Irish Brigade, the second of Hancock's division, under General Meagher, made a wonderful charge. When they returned from the assault but two hundred and fifty out of twelve hundred men reported under arms from the field, and all these were needed to care for their wounded comrades. The One Hundred and Sixteenth Pennsylvania regiment was new on the field of battle, but did fearless and heroic service. The approach was completely commanded by the Confederate guns. Repeatedly the advance was repulsed by well-directed fire from the batteries.

Once again Sumner's gallant men charged across a railroad cut, running down one side and up the other, and still again attempted to escape in the same manner, but each time they were forced to retire precipitately by a murderous fire from the Confederate batteries. Not only was the Confederate fire disastrous upon the approach and the successive repulses by the foe, but it also inflicted great damage upon the masses of the Federal army in front of Marye's Hill.

MEN WHO CHARGED ON MARYE'S HEIGHTS

Officers of the famous "Irish Brigade," which lost more than 41 per cent. of its strength in the first assault at Marye's Heights. The "Irish Brigade" (consisting of the Twenty-eighth Massachusetts, the Sixty-third, Sixty-ninth, and Eighty-eighth New York, and the One Hundred and Sixteenth Pennsylvania) was commanded by General Thomas F. Meagher and advanced in Hancock's division to the first assault on December 13, 1862. At Antietam this brigade had spent its ammunition at the sunken road and then retired in splendid order. Again, in the charge at Marye's, the lines of the Irish soldiers were "beautifully and rapidly formed," and they moved steadily up the ridge until within a few yards of another and more deadly sunken road, the unexpected fire from which mowed them down. Of the 1,315 men which Meagher led into battle, 545 fell in that charge. Hancock's entire command sustained that day a loss of 40.2 per cent., the second highest percentage of any division in any one engagement in the war. After the charge on Marye's Heights it numbered only 2,800 men. This group was photographed at Harrison's Landing, on the James River, in July, 1862.

The Confederates' effective and successful work on Marye's Hill in this battle was not alone due to the natural strength of their position, but also to the skill and generalship of the leaders, and to the gallantry, courage, and well-directed aim of their cannoneers and infantry.

Six times the heroic Union troops dashed against the invulnerable position, each time to be repulsed with terrific loss. General Couch, who had command of the Second Corps, viewing the scene of battle from the steeple of the court-house with General Howard, says: "The whole plain was covered with men, prostrate and dropping, the live men running here and there, and in front closing upon each other, and the wounded coming back. I had never before seen fighting like that, nothing approaching it in terrible uproar and destruction."

General Howard reports that Couch exclaimed: "Oh, great God! see how our men, our poor fellows, are falling!" At half-past one Couch signaled Burnside: "I am losing. Send two rifle batteries."

The point and method of attack made by Sumner was anticipated by the Confederates, careful preparation having been made to meet it. The fire from the Confederate batteries harassed the Union lines, and as they advanced steadily, heroically, without hurrah or battle-cry, the ranks were cut to pieces by canister and shell and musket-balls. Heavy artillery fire was poured into the Union ranks from front, right, and left with frightful results. Quickly filling up the decimated ranks they approached the stone wall masking the death-trap where General Cobb lay with a strong force awaiting the approach. Torrents of lead poured into the bodies of the defenseless men, slaying, crushing, destroying the proud army of a few hours before. As though in pity, a cloud of smoke momentarily shut out the wretched scene but brought no balm to the helpless victims of this awful carnage. The ground was so thickly strewn with dead bodies as seriously to impede the movements of a renewed attack. These repeated assaults in such good

THE SUMMIT OF SLAUGHTER

Marye's House marked the center of the Confederate position on the Heights, before which the Federals fell three deep in one of the bravest and bloodiest assaults of the war. The eastern boundary of the Marye estate was a retaining wall, along which ran a sunken road; on the other side of this was a stone wall, shoulder high, forming a perfect infantry parapet. Here two brigades of Confederates were posted and on the crest above them were the supporting batteries, while the slope between was honeycombed with the rifle-pits of the sharpshooters, one of which is seen in the picture. Six times did the Federals, raked by the deadly fire of the Washington Artillery, advance to within a hundred yards of the sunken road, only to be driven back by the rapid volleys of the Confederate infantry concealed there. Less than three of every five men in Hancock's division came back from their charge on these death-dealing heights. The complete repulse of the day and the terrific slaughter were the barren results of an heroic effort to obey orders.

order caused some apprehension on the part of General Lee, who said to Longstreet after the third attack, "General, they are massing very heavily and will break your line, I am afraid." But the great general's fears proved groundless.

General Cobb was borne from the field mortally wounded, and Kershaw took his place in the desperate struggle. The storm of shot and shell which met the assaults was terrific. Men fell almost in battalions; the dead and wounded lay in heaps. Late in the day the dead bodies, which had become frozen from the extreme cold, were stood up in front of the soldiers as a protection against the awful fire to shield the living, and at night were set up as dummy sentinels.

The steadiness of the Union troops, and the silent, determined heroism of the rank and file in these repeated, but hopeless, assaults upon the Confederate works, were marvelous, and amazed even their officers. The real greatness in a battle is the fearless courage, the brave and heroic conduct, of the men under withering fire. It was the enlisted men who were the glory of the army. It was they, the rank and file, who stood in the front, closed the gaps, and were mowed down in swaths like grass by cannon and musket-balls.

After the sixth disastrous attempt to carry the works of the Confederate left it was night; the Federal army was repulsed and had retired; hope was abandoned, and it was seen that the day was lost to the Union side. Then the shattered Army of the Potomac sought to gather the stragglers and care for the wounded. Fredericksburg, the beautiful Virginia town, was a pitiable scene in contrast to its appearance a few days before. Ancestral homes were turned into barracks and hospitals. The charming drives and stately groves, the wonted pleasure grounds of Colonial dames and Southern cavaliers, were not filled with grand carriages and gay parties, but with war horses, soldiers, and military accouterments. Aside from desultory firing by squads and skirmishers at intervals there was no renewal of the conflict.

THE FATEFUL CROSSING

From this, the Lacy House, which Sumner had made his headquarters, he directed the advance of his right grand division of the Army of the Potomac on December 11, 1862. Little did he dream that his men of the Second Corps were to bear the brunt of the fighting and the most crushing blow of the defeat on the 13th. Soon after three o'clock on the morning of the 11th the columns moved out with alacrity to the river bank and before daybreak, hidden at first by the fog, the pontoniers began building the bridges. Confederate sharpshooters drove off the working party from the bridge below the Lacy House and also from the middle bridge farther down. As the mist cleared, volunteers ferried themselves over in the boats and drove off the riflemen. At last, at daybreak of the 12th, the town of Fredericksburg was occupied, but the whole of another foggy day was consumed in getting the army concentrated on the western shore. Nineteen batteries (one hundred and four guns) accompanied Sumner's troops, but all save seven of these were ordered back or left in the streets of Fredericksburg. Late on the morning of the 13th the confused and belated orders began to arrive from Burnside's headquarters across the river; one was for Sumner to assault the Confederate batteries on Marye's Heights. At nightfall Sumner's men retired into Fredericksburg, leaving 5,444 dead or dying on the field. "Oh, those men, those men over there! I cannot get them out of my mind!" wailed Burnside in an agony of failure. Yet he was planning almost in the same breath to lead in person his old command, the Ninth Corps, in another futile charge in the morning. On the night of the 14th, better judgment prevailed and the order came to retire across the Rappahannock.

Here, on the heights behind Fredericksburg, Lee's veterans who had fought at Antietam opposed the Army of the Potomac under its new commander. Had Lee been given his choice he could not have selected a more advantageous position. Burnside's futile attempts to wrest these heights from the Confederates cost him 12,653 men in killed, wounded, and missing. On the heights behind Fredericksburg, Lee's soldiers, working night and day, had thrown up a double line of strong entrenchments and constructed a road to facilitate the transfer of troops behind the defenses. Everything that the engineering talent of the Confederacy could suggest had been done. By the time Burnside moved his 113,000 troops against the 78,000 of Lee, Jackson, and Longstreet on December 13, 1862, Marye's Heights had been made impregnable. Four months later, in the Chancellorsville campaign (May 3, 1863), Sedgwick's men fought over this same ground and carried the position. But then the main body of Lee's army was hotly engaged with Hooker and the Heights were not strongly defended. This photograph of Willis's Hill (just south of Marye's) was taken after Sedgwick occupied the position in 1863. Willis's Hill was, with great appropriateness, made a National Cemetery at Fredericksburg after the war.

WILLIS'S HILL,

NEAR MARYE'S HEIGHTS

THE PLANS THAT FAILED

From his headquarters at the Phillips house, Burnside directed the disastrous maneuvers of his army during the battle of December 13th. On December 9th Burnside called his generals together and persisted in his plan for a direct assault upon Lee, who was strongly entrenched in a position of his own choosing. The slaughter at Marye's Heights on the 13th proved him in the wrong. Nevertheless, Burnside on the field that night gave orders to renew the attack the next morning. Returning to the Phillips house about 1 A.M., he found among the others Colonel Rush C. Hawkins, who had come at the request of Generals Willcox, Humphreys, Meade, and Getty, who had all faced that terrible fire on Telegraph Road. A conference ensued in the presence of Sumner, Hooker, and Franklin, and Burnside was at last dissuaded.

THE UNLUCKY HEADQUARTERS

The ruins of the Phillips house stand as an aftermath of Burnside's unfortunate career at the head of the Army of the Potomac. The wisest decision that he made in that house was in the early morning of December 14th—not to renew the attack. In the old mansion he had formed the fatal plan of direct assault. Here also he issued his order for the famous "mud march" by which, in the dead of winter, he sought to retrieve failure by putting his army in motion to flank Lee, January 21, 1863. All his efforts had come to naught, and not one of his generals longer agreed with him. His resignation from the command followed on January 26th. In February the Phillips house was set on fire; and in the picture on the preceding page the photographer has caught the Federals (now commanded by Hooker) trying to extinguish the flames.

The bloody carnage was over, the plan of Burnside had ended in failure, and thousands of patriotic and brave men, blindly obedient to their country's command, were the toll exacted from the Union army. Burnside, wild with anguish at what he had done, walking the floor of his tent, exclaimed, "Oh, those men—those men over there," pointing to the battlefield, "I am thinking of them all the time." In his report of the battle to Washington, Burnside gave reasons for the issue, and in a manly way took the responsibility upon himself, and most highly commended his officers and men. He said, "For the failure in the attack I am responsible, as the extreme gallantry, courage, and endurance shown by them [officers and men] were never excelled."

President Lincoln's verdict in regard to this battle is adverse to the almost unanimous opinion of the historians. In his reply, December 22d, to General Burnside's report of the battle, he says, "Although you were not successful, the attempt was not an error, nor the failure other than an accident." Burnside, at his own request, was relieved of the command of the Army of the Potomac, however, on January 25, 1863, and was succeeded by General Hooker. The Union loss in killed, wounded, and missing was 12,653, and the Confederates lost 5,377.

After the battle the wounded lay on the field in their agony exposed to the freezing cold for forty-eight hours before arrangements were effected to care for them. Many were burned to death by the long, dead grass becoming ignited by cannon fire. The scene witnessed by the army of those screaming, agonizing, dying comrades was dreadful and heartrending. Burnside's plan had been to renew the battle, but the overwhelming opinion of the other officers prevailed. The order was withdrawn and the defeated Union army slipped away under the cover of darkness on December 15th, and encamped in safety across the river. The battle of Fredericksburg had passed into history.

———

CHANCELLORSVILLE AND JACKSON'S FLANKING MARCH

———

READY TO COVER THE RAPPAHANNOCK—THE 150TH PENNSYLVANIA,
THREE WEEKS BEFORE THE BATTLE OF CHANCELLORSVILLE

WAR'S HEAVIEST LABOR

Here a construction corps is rebuilding the railroad bridge across Bull Run. The men are armed with crowbars and axes, and in the constant wielding of such peaceful implements throughout the war many who never fired a musket became expert in the occupations of peace. This photograph was taken in March, 1863, while Hooker was reëstablishing railway communications to make possible his contemplated advance toward Gordonsville, Virginia, with the expectation of driving Lee back upon Richmond. During the previous year, in the disastrous campaign of Pope, most of the bridges along the Orange & Alexandria Railroad had been destroyed and much of the line torn up. In order to flank Lee's position at Fredericksburg, it was imperative for the Army of the Potomac to abandon its base at Aquia Creek and draw supplies overland from Alexandria. In the spring Hooker was pushing the railroad repairs.

RAPID REPAIRS

This picture of the almost completed bridge across Bull Run shows how thoroughly the work was done—and how quickly, for the photograph was taken in March, 1863, only a short time after that on the opposite page. The hopes of Hooker and his army ran high; rested and heavily reinforced, it again outnumbered Lee's Army of Northern Virginia. It seemed certain that such a superior force must at last wrest a decisive victory from the Confederates. Hooker's plan of campaign was excellent. Demonstrating strongly against Lee's right, he intended to cross the fords of the Rappahannock and Rapidan with his main body and, flanking Lee by the left, draw him from his fastness at Fredericksburg to battle on the open plain. Cavalry was to be sent two weeks in advance of the infantry to sweep around in Lee's rear toward Gordonsville and cut his communications, to compel a retreat upon Richmond. But it was not Lee who retreated after Chancellorsville!

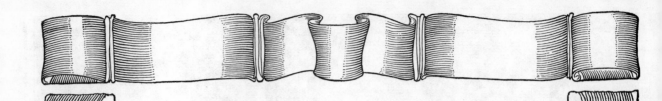

CHANCELLORSVILLE AND JACKSON'S FLANKING MARCH

The interval of two months between the battles of Chancellorsville and Gettysburg was for the South—notwithstanding the irreparable loss it sustained in the death of Jackson—the brightest period of the Civil War. But its brightness was that of a false and treacherous light. The over-confidence born of the victory of Chancellorsville carried the Army of Northern Virginia against the impregnable front of the Federal lines at Gettysburg; and it was the victory of Gettysburg that sustained the Army of the Potomac in its desperate wrestling in the Wilderness, and in gaining the point of vantage from which it finally started on the arduous, decisive, and fateful race to Appomattox.—*Major John Bigelow, Jr., U.S.A., in "The Campaign of Chancellorsville."*

THE Rappahannock River flows out of the hills at the foot of the Blue Ridge Mountains in a southeasterly course. Falmouth is on the north bank, about a mile from Fredericksburg, which lies on the opposite shore. Along the banks of this peaceful river were fought some of the most important battles of the Civil War. This region was the scene of the conflict of Fredericksburg, December 12–13, 1862, and the later battle of May 1–5, 1863. Chancellorsville is a little over two miles south of the river and about ten miles west of Fredericksburg.

After the Fredericksburg campaign the Union forces encamped at Falmouth for the winter, while Lee remained with the Southern army on the site of his successful contest at Fredericksburg. Thus the two armies lay facing each other within hailing distance, across the historic river, waiting for the coming of spring. Major-General Joseph Hooker, popularly known as "Fighting Joe" Hooker, who had succeeded Burnside in command of the Army of the Potomac, soon had

A MAN OF WHOM MUCH WAS EXPECTED

General Joseph Hooker.   A daring and experienced veteran of the Mexican War, Hooker had risen in the Civil War from brigade commander to be the commander of a grand division of the Army of the Potomac, and had never been found wanting.   His advancement
to the head of the Army of the Potomac, on January 26, 1863, was a tragic episode in his own career and in that of the Federal arms.
Gloom hung heavy over the North after Fredericksburg.   Upon Hooker fell the difficult task of redeeming the unfulfilled political
pledges for a speedy lifting of that gloom.   It was his fortune only to deepen it.

the troops on a splendid campaign footing by a positive and vigorous method of reorganization, and aroused them to enthusiastic loyalty.

It was the month of April, and field and woodland had begun to put on the bright colors of spring. There was activity about the Federal army headquarters that indicated a renewal of hostilities. The hospitals had been well cleared, the forces had been recruited, ammunition and arms replenished and put in order, horses groomed and well fed, uniforms renewed, and the Army of the Potomac was in excellent condition to advance against its foe. President Lincoln had visited the camp, and reviewed the army, thrilling the men with his inspiring presence and personality. It was well known that he had a very deep concern in the welfare of the soldiers. After the review he asked, "What will become of all these men when the war is over?" His parting admonition to Hooker was this wise advice, "In your next battle, put in all your men." By a strange fatality that is just what Hooker failed to do, and a great misfortune overtook his army.

Hooker abandoned Burnside's method of organization. Under "Fighting Joe," instead of three grand divisions, there were seven army corps, each under a major-general, and a cavalry corps. At this time the Union forces aggregated between one hundred and twenty-five and one hundred and thirty thousand men; Lee's forces were estimated at about sixty thousand. Hooker's corps commanders were: Reynolds, in command of the First; Couch, the Second; Sickles, the Third; Meade, the Fifth; Sedgwick, the Sixth; Howard, the Eleventh; Slocum, the Twelfth, and Stoneman, who was in command of the cavalry corps.

Hooker conceived, a plan of campaign which was ingenious and masterful, and had he carried it out there would have been a different story to tell about Chancellorsville. The plan was to deploy a portion of the army to serve as a decoy to Lee, while the remainder of the host at the same time

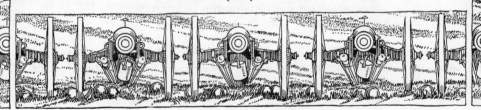

NEW LEADERS AND NEW PLANS

General Joseph Hooker and his Staff. These were the men whose work it was, during the winter after Fredericksburg, to restore the *esprit du corps* of the Army of the Potomac. The tireless energy and magnetic personality of Hooker soon won officers from their disaffection and put an end to desertions—which had been going on at the rate of two hundred per day before he took command. By spring everything seemed propitious for an aggressive campaign, the plans for which were brilliantly drawn and at first vigorously carried out, giving truth to Lincoln's expressed belief that Hooker was "a trained and skilful soldier." In that remarkable letter of admonition to Hooker upon assuming command, Lincoln added: "But beware of rashness, beware of rashness; with energy and with sleepless vigilance go forward and give us victories." By some strange fate it was not rashness but quite the contrary which compassed the failure of "Fighting Joe" Hooker at Chancellorsville. His first forward advance was executed with his usual bold initiative. Before Lee could fully divine his purpose, Hooker with thirty-six thousand men was across his left flank in a favorable position, with the main body of his army at hand ready to give battle. Then came Hooker's inexplicable order to fall back upon Chancellorsville. That very night, consulting in the abandoned Federal position, Lee and Jackson formed the plan which drove Hooker back across the Rappahannock in ignominious defeat.

occupied the vicinity of Chancellorsville, a country mansion, in the center of the wilderness that stretched along the Rappahannock.

The movement of the army began on the 27th of April when Sedgwick was sent east of Fredericksburg with a large force to attract the attention of the Confederates. Another force was left in camp to give the appearance that the main army was still there, while in fact it was secretly being moved to Chancellorsville. The strategy was carried out successfully. On April 30th the army, except a force under Sedgwick composing the First, Third, and Sixth Corps, was concentrated on Lee's left flank, the entire field and its approaches being commanded by the Fifth, Eleventh, and Twelfth Corps, part of the Second Corps, and Stoneman's cavalry of the Army of the Potomac. Victory seemed assured. Hooker, in an order issued on that day, said, "Now the enemy must flee shamefully or come out of his defenses to accept battle on our own ground, to his certain destruction." The contemplated field of battle was high ground about half way between this plateau and the Chancellor house. The Federal army was not yet in position on this open and favorably located field. At eleven o'clock in the morning Hooker started the movement of the army to the point where he intended it to be in line of battle at two o'clock on the afternoon of May 1st.

Lee was a great general and a master in strategy. He had learned of Hooker's plan and, paying but little attention to Sedgwick, had collected his forces and turned to face Hooker. By a rapid night march he met the Union army before it had reached its destination. He was pushed back, however, by Sykes, of Meade's corps, who occupied the position assigned to him. Meade was on the left, and Slocum on the right, with adequate support in the rear. All was in readiness and most favorable for the "certain destruction" of the Confederates predicted by "Fighting Joe" when, to the amazement and consternation of all his officers, Hooker

LEADERS OF THE FRUITLESS RAID

Major-General George Stoneman and Staff; photographed in April, 1863, a month before it fell to the lot of these gallant cavalry officers to lead ten thousand sabers on a daring but futile expedition. Sweeping around in the rear of the Confederate army, it was their intention to cut Lee's railroad communication with Richmond. According to Hooker's plan, this advance movement was to begin April 13th, two weeks before that of his main army, but heavy rains delayed the expedition until the 27th and Hooker's whole force set out simultaneously with the cavalry. Thus Stoneman's work was wasted, for the Army of the Potomac was defeated and in full retreat before the cavalry could strike. On the 5th of May Stoneman recalled his detachments and, leaving his headquarters at Louisa Court House, rejoined the army at Falmouth on the 8th. The most daring raid of the expedition was performed by Colonel Kilpatrick, with his Second New York Cavalry. Dashing across the country, he passed within two and a half miles of Richmond, creating great consternation. Turning down the peninsula, he ended his long ride at Gloucester Point, which was garrisoned by the Federals. With great boldness the regiment rode forth from this refuge. Eluding the Confederates and repulsing a strong force, it rebuilt a bridge and returned safely to Falmouth on June 3d, bringing two hundred prisoners, forty wagons, and a thousand contraband slaves. Hooker, dissatisfied with what the cavalry had accomplished, removed Stoneman from his command.

ordered the whole army to retire to the position it had occupied the day before, leaving the advantage to his opponents.

Lee quickly moved his army into the position thus relinquished, and began feeling the Federal lines with skirmishers and some cannonading during the evening of May 1st. By the next morning the two armies were in line of battle.

The danger in which the Confederate army now found itself was extreme. One large Federal army was on its front, while another was at its rear, below Fredericksburg. But Lee threw the hopes of success into one great and decisive blow at Hooker's host. Dividing an army in the face of the foe is extremely dangerous and contrary to all accepted theories of military strategy; but there comes a time when such a course proves the salvation of the legions in peril. Such was the case at Chancellorsville on May 2, 1863.

At 7 A.M. the cannonading began its death-song and was soon followed by infantry demonstrations, but without serious results. The action was continued. Early in the afternoon, Hooker by a ruse was beguiled into the belief that Lee's army was in full retreat. What Hooker had seen and believed to be a retreat was the marching of Jackson's forces, about twenty-six thousand strong, from the battlefield. What he did not see, however, was that, after a few miles, Jackson turned abruptly and made for the right flank of the Federal host, the Eleventh Corps, under Howard. It was after half-past five when Jackson broke from the woods into which he had marched in a paralyzing charge upon the unprepared troops of Howard.

The approach of this Confederate force was first intimated to the Federals by the bending of shrubbery, the stampede of rabbits and squirrels, and the flocks of birds in wild flight, as before a storm. Then appeared a few skirmishers, then a musket volley, and then the storm broke in all its fury —the war scream, the rattling musketry, the incessant roar of cannon. The Confederates fought heroically. The knowledge

THE CORPS THAT STOOD ALONE

Major-General John Sedgwick and Staff. Sedgwick's Sixth Corps alone and unaided executed the most successful maneuver during the Chancellorsville battles of May 1–4, 1863. For two days Sedgwick had been keeping up a strong demonstration against Lee's extreme right below Fredericksburg. On the night of May 2d, after Jackson had routed the entire Eleventh Corps, came the order from Hooker for Sedgwick to move forward toward Chancellorsville, "attack and destroy any forces met with on the march," then fall upon Lee's rear. By midnight the Sixth Corps was in motion and at dawn advanced against Marye's Heights. Only after a fierce uphill fight was that bloody field won from Early's 9,000 Confederates. At night, forced back by Lee, he established communication with Hooker, but could get no definite orders. Next morning word came not to attack unless Hooker did likewise. But Hooker's inactivity encouraged Lee to send heavy forces to crush the Sixth Corps. All the afternoon, cut off from help, the corps fought off assault after assault till nightfall of May 4th. Then, upon the receipt of orders, Sedgwick retired north of the Rappahannock.

SICKLES REVIEWS HIS EIGHTEEN THOUSAND TROOPS, UNAWARE OF JACKSON'S FLANKING MARCH

The photograph, presented one-half above and one-half below, is a reflection of history in the very making. It was at midnight on May 1, 1863, that Lee and Jackson sat on two cracker-boxes before their fire in the abandoned Union camp, and conceived the audacious idea of flanking the Federals. It was 5.30 the next morning that Jackson formed his devoted veterans in column, then bade his last farewell to his chief, and rode into the tangled forest. And it was the same morning that a Union photographer made this picture of Major-General Daniel E. Sickles reviewing his Third Corps of the Army of the Potomac, 18,000 horse, foot, and artillery—all unsuspecting that a couple of miles distant 31,000 in gray were pushing across their front and around to the unprotected rear of the Union encampment. The confidence of the Federals was only natural. Who would have suspected that Lee, with less than 45,000 men, all told, would deliberately have detached more than two-thirds of them in the face of Hooker's encamped 70,000? But Lee was a military genius, and genius knows when to dare—especially with a leader in the field like "Stonewall" Jackson, no less secret than swift. And so it befell that when the Confederate column was spied passing over a bare hill about a mile and a half from the left of Sickles's line, General Hooker supposed that such a movement could mean only a retreat. He ordered a pursuit. This drew a division away from a point where soon it was sorely needed. For Jackson's Corps, having passed around the Federal right, formed in battle-line, burst through the woods in the rear of the unsuspecting Federals, and drove them in utter rout. It was a piece of strategy as daring as it was masterly.

"STONEWALL" JACKSON—TWO WEEKS BEFORE HIS MORTAL WOUND

The austere, determined features of the victor of Chancellorsville, just as they appeared two weeks before the tragic shot that cost the Confederacy its greatest Lieutenant-General—and, in the opinion of sound historians, its chief hope for independence. Only once had a war photograph of Jackson been taken up to April, 1863, when, just before the movement toward Chancellorsville, he was persuaded to enter a photographer's tent at Hamilton's Crossing, some three miles below Fredericksburg, and to sit for his last portrait. At a glance one can feel the self-expression and power in this stern worshiper of the God of Battles; one can understand the eulogy written by the British military historian, Henderson: "The fame of 'Stonewall' Jackson is no longer the exclusive property of Virginia and the South: it has become the birthright of every man privileged to call himself an American,"

that "Old Jack" was on the field was inspiration enough for them. The charge was so precipitous, so unexpected and terrific that it was impossible for the Federals to hold their lines and stand against the impact of that awful onslaught which carried everything before it. The regiments in Jackson's path, resisting his advance, were cut to pieces and swept along as by a tidal wave, rolled up like a scroll, multitudes of men, horses, mules, and cattle being piled in an inextricable mass. Characteristic of Jackson's brilliant and unexpected movements, it was like an electric flash, knocking the Eleventh Corps into impotence, as Jackson expected it would. This crowning and final stroke of Jackson's military genius was not impromptu, but the result of his own carefully worked-out plan, which had been approved by Lee.

General Hooker was spending the late afternoon hours in his headquarters at the Chancellor house. To the eastward there was considerable firing, where his men were carrying out the plan of striking Lee in flank. Jackson was retreating, of that he was sure, and Sickles, with Pleasanton's cavalry and other reenforcements, was in pursuit. Everything seemed to be going well. About half-past six the sounds of battle grew suddenly louder and seemed to come from another direction. A staff-officer went to the front of the house and turned his field-glass toward the west.

"My God, here they come!"

At the startled cry Hooker sprang upon his horse and dashed down the road. He encountered portions of the Eleventh Corps pouring out of the forest—a badly mixed crowd of men, wagons, and ambulances. They brought the news that the right wing was overwhelmed. Hurriedly Hooker sought his old command, Berry's division of the Third Corps, stationed in support of the Eleventh. "Forward, with the bayonet!" he commanded.

An officer who witnessed the scene says the division advanced with a firm and steady step, cleaving the multitude

WILDERNESS CHURCH—THE SCENE OF JACKSON'S SECOND RUSH

The shots that riddled the roof of this humble meeting-house were fired on an evening of triumph and panic. Beyond the church, as the sun sank low on May 2d, stretched the main Union line, Howard's Eleventh Corps. The troops had stacked their arms and lay at ease. Supper was cooking. Suddenly bugle-calls came from the west. Then a roar of human voices swept the forest. A double battle-line in gray burst from the woods, ran over the gunners, and shattered the divisions into fragments. Gallant Federal officers did their best to re-form their lines. With the little church at about the center, a stand was made by five thousand men of Schurz's division, with some of Devens'—but without respite Jackson gave the call to advance. After twenty minutes of furious fighting, the Confederate battle-flag flew in the clearing. It was then that the fugitives from the Eleventh Corps came in sight.

of disbanded Federals as the bow of a vessel cleaves the waves of the sea. It struck the advance of the Confederates obliquely and checked it, with the aid of the Twelfth Corps artillery.

A dramatic, though tragic, feature of the rout was the charge of the Eighth Pennsylvania cavalry, under Major Keenan, in the face of almost certain death, to save the artillery of the Third Corps from capture. The guns rested upon low ground and within reach of the Confederates. The Federals had an equal opportunity to seize the artillery, but required a few minutes to prepare themselves for action. The Confederate advance must be checked for these few moments, and for this purpose Keenan gallantly led his five hundred cavalrymen into the woods, while his comrades brought the guns to bear upon the columns in gray. He gained the necessary time, but lost his life at the head of his regiment, together with Captain Arrowsmith and Adjutant Haddock, who fell by his side.

The light of day had faded from the gruesome scene. The mighty turmoil was silenced as darkness gathered, but the day's carnage was not ended. No camp-fires were lighted in the woods or on the plain. The two hostile forces were concealed in the darkness, watching through the shadows, waiting for—they knew not what. Finally at midnight the order "Forward" was repeated in subdued tones along the lines of Sickles' corps. Out over the open and into the deep, dark thicket the men in blue pursued their stealthy advance upon the Confederate position. Then the tragedies of the night were like that of the day, and the moon shed her peaceful rays down upon those shadowy figures as they struggled forward through the woods, in the ravines, over the hillocks. The Federals, at heavy loss, gained the position, and the engagement assumed the importance of a victory.

It was on this day that death robbed the South of one of her most beloved warriors. After darkness had

Within an hour after Jackson's sudden and deadly charge, his men captured Dowdall's Tavern. Here Howard, commander of the Eleventh Corps, now fleeing before the Confederate rush, was holding his headquarters when the blow fell. The trenches in the picture below were the goal in a race between Jackson's men and the men of Williams's Federal division. This had been sent to support Sickles and tried too late to recover the position that it had left, unaware of the Confederate flanking movement. Jackson captured two hundred men of the One Hundred and Twenty-eighth Pennsylvania as they tried to get to their places. Williams after falling back finally checked the Confederates, aided by Barry of the Third Corps and fresh artillery. As night fell, Jackson with his staff ventured on his last reconnaissance. The picture on the

DOWDALL'S TAVERN

right shows the tangled wood through which he passed and the fury of the fire that lopped off the stunted trees. Through a fatal mischance, some Confederates stationed along the road to the north of this spot fired upon what they thought to be a Federal scouting party—and there mortally wounded their own general. Jackson had turned back along the road itself, and his men had orders to fire upon any advance from the Federal position. The next day, with a cry of "Remember Jackson!" the line in gray again swept forward, and by nine in the morning had carried the rude breastworks in the left-hand picture. Hooker withdrew his entire army. Yet the Confederate victory lacked the completeness that would have been expected with Jackson in the saddle; and the Confederacy had lost one of its greatest captains.

WHERE THE FEDERALS MADE A STAND
SOUTH OF THE "PLANK ROAD"

TREES SHATTERED BY THE FIRING NEAR
THE SPOT WHERE JACKSON FELL

overspread the land, Jackson, accompanied by members of his staff, undertook a reconnaissance of the Federal lines. He was planning a night attack. He came upon a line of Union infantry lying on its arms and was forced to turn back along the plank road, on both sides of which he had stationed his own men with orders to fire upon any body of men approaching from the direction of the Federal battle-lines. The little cavalcade of Confederate officers galloped along the highway, directly toward the ambuscade, and apparently forgetful of the strict orders left with the skirmishers. A sudden flash of flame lighted the scene for an instant, and within that space of time the Confederacy was deprived of one of its greatest captains—Jackson was severely wounded, and by his own men and through his own orders. When the news spread through Jackson's corps and through the Confederate army the grief of the Southern soldiers was heartbreaking to witness. The sorrow spread even into the ranks of the Federal army, which, while opposed to the wounded general on many hard-fought battle-grounds, had learned to respect and admire " Stonewall " Jackson.

The loss of Jackson to the South was incalculable. Lee had pronounced him the right arm of the whole army. Next to Lee, Jackson was considered the ablest general in the Confederate army. His shrewdness of judgment, his skill in strategy, his lightning-like strokes, marked him as a unique and brilliant leader. Devoutly religious, gentle and noble in character, the nation that was not to be disunited lost a great citizen, as the Confederate army lost a great captain, when a few days later General Jackson died.

That night orders passed from the Federal headquarters to Sedgwick, below Fredericksburg, eleven miles away. Between him and Hooker stood the Confederate army, flushed with its victories of the day. Immediately in his front was Fredericksburg, with a strong guard of Southern warriors. Beyond loomed Marye's Heights, the battle-ground on which

THE DEMOLISHED HEADQUARTERS

From this mansion, Hooker's headquarters during the battle of Chancellorsville, he rode away after the injury he received there on May 3d, never to return. The general, dazed after Jackson's swoop upon the right, was besides in deep anxiety as to Sedgwick. The latter's forty thousand men had not yet come up. Hooker was unwilling to suffer further loss without the certainty of his coöperation. So he decided to withdraw his army. The movement was the signal for increased artillery fire from the Confederate batteries, marking the doom of the old Chancellor house. Its end was accompanied by some heart-rending scenes. Major Bigelow thus describes them: "Missiles pierced the walls or struck in the brickwork; shells exploded in the upper rooms, setting the building on fire; the chimneys were demolished and their fragments rained down upon the wounded about the building. All this time the women and children (including some slaves) of the Chancellor family, nineteen persons in all, were in the cellar. The wounded were removed from in and around the building, men of both armies nobly assisting one another in the work."

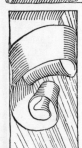

Burnside had in the preceding winter left so many of his brave men in the vain endeavor to drive the Confederate defenders from the crest.

The courageous Sedgwick, notwithstanding the formidable obstacles that lay on the road to Chancellorsville, responded immediately to Hooker's order. He was already on the south side of the river, but he was farther away than Hooker supposed. Shortly after midnight he began a march that was fraught with peril and death. Strong resistance was offered the advancing blue columns as they came to the threshold of Fredericksburg, but they swept on and over the defenders, and at dawn were at the base of the heights. On the crest waved the standards of the Confederate Washington Artillery. At the foot of the slope was the stone wall before which the Federals had fought and died but a few months before, in the battle of Fredericksburg. Reenforcements were arriving in the Confederate trenches constantly. The crest and slopes bristled with cannon and muskets. The pathways around the heights were barricaded. The route to the front seemed blocked; still, the cry for help from Hooker was resounding in the ears of Sedgwick

Gathering his troops, he attacked directly upon the stone wall and on up the hillside, in the face of a terrific storm of artillery and musketry. The first assault failed; a flank movement met with no better success; and the morning was nearly gone when the Confederates finally gave way at the point of the bayonet before the irresistible onset of men in blue. The way to Chancellorsville was open; but the cost to the Federals was appalling. Hundreds of the soldiers in blue lay wrapped in death upon the bloody slopes of Marye's Heights.

It was the middle of the afternoon, and not at daybreak, as Hooker had directed, when Sedgwick appeared in the rear of Lee's legions. A strong force of Confederates under Early prevented his further advance toward a juncture with Hooker's army at Chancellorsville. Since five o'clock in the

THE STONE WALL AT FREDERICKSBURG

Behind the deadly stone wall of Marye's Heights after Sedgwick's men had swept across it in the gallant charge of May 3, 1863. This was one of the strongest natural positions stormed during the war. In front of this wall the previous year, nearly 6,000 of Burnside's men had fallen, and it was not carried. Again in the Chancellorsville campaign Sedgwick's Sixth Corps was ordered to assault it. It was defended the second time with the same death-dealing stubbornness but with less than a fourth of the former numbers—9,000 Confederates against 20,000 Federals. At eleven o'clock in the morning the line of battle, under Colonel Hiram Burnham, moved out over the awful field of the year before, supported to right and left by flanking columns. Up to within twenty-five yards of the wall they pressed, when again the flame of musketry fire belched forth, laying low in six minutes 36.5 per cent. of the Fifth Wisconsin and the Sixth Maine. The assailants wavered and rallied, and then with one impulse both columns and line of battle hurled themselves upon the wall in a fierce hand-to-hand combat. A soldier of the Seventh Massachusetts happened to peer through a crack in a board fence and saw that it covered the flank of the double line of Confederates in the road. Up and over the fence poured the Federals and drove the Confederates from the heights.

morning the battle had been raging at the latter place, and Jackson's men, now commanded by Stuart, though being mowed down in great numbers, vigorously pressed the attack of the day while crying out to one another "Remember Jackson," as they thought of their wounded leader.

While this engagement was at its height General Hooker, leaning against a pillar of the Chancellor house, was felled to the ground, and for a moment it was thought he was killed. The pillar had been shattered by a cannon-ball. Hooker soon revived under the doctor's care and with great force of will he mounted his horse and showed himself to his anxious troops. He then withdrew his army to a stronger position, well guarded with artillery. The Confederates did not attempt to assail it. The third day's struggle at Chancellorsville was finished by noon, except in Lee's rear, where Sedgwick fought all day, without success, to reach the main body of Hooker's army. The Federals suffered very serious losses during this day's contest. Even then it was believed that the advantage rested with the larger Army of the Potomac and that the Federals had an opportunity to win. Thirty-seven thousand Union troops, the First, and three-quarters of the Fifth Corps, had been entirely out of the fight on that day. Five thousand men of the Eleventh Corps, who were eager to retrieve their misfortune, were also inactive.

When night came, and the shades of darkness hid the sights of suffering on the battlefield, the Federal army was resting in a huge curve, the left wing on the Rappahannock and the right on the Rapidan. In this way the fords across the rivers which led to safety were in control of the Army of the Potomac. Lee moved his corps close to the bivouacs of the army in blue. But, behind the Confederate battle-line, there was a new factor in the struggle in the person of Sedgwick, with the remnants of his gallant corps, which had numbered nearly twenty-two thousand when they started for the front, but now were depleted by their terrific charge upon Marye's Heights

THE WORK OF ONE SHELL

Part of the Havoc Wrought on Marye's Heights by the Assault of Sedgwick on May 3, 1863.   No sooner had they seized the stone wall than the victorious Federals swarmed up and over the ridge above, driving the Confederates from the rifle-pits, capturing the guns of the famous Washington Artillery which had so long guarded the Heights, and inflicting slaughter upon the assaulting columns.   If Sedgwick had had cavalry he could have crushed the divided forces of Early and cleared the way for a rapid advance to attack Lee's rear.   In the picture we see Confederate caisson wagons and horses destroyed by a lucky shot from the Second Massachusetts' siege-gun battery planted across the river at Falmouth to support Sedgwick's assault.   Surveying the scene stands General Herman Haupt, Chief of the Bureau of Military Railways, the man leaning against the stump.   By him is W. W. Wright, Superintendent of the Military Railroad.   The photograph was taken on May 3d, after the battle.   The Federals held Marye's Heights until driven off by fresh forces which Lee had detached from his main army at Chancellorsville and sent against Sedgwick on the afternoon of the 4th.

OVER THE RUINED TOWN

Here stand the Federal cannoneers at their posts on the last morning of the Chancellorsville struggle, ready to open fire with their 32-pounders against the fateful Marye's Heights across the river—where Sedgwick and his gallant Sixth Corps were to pluck the only shred of victory that remained to the beaten Army of the Potomac at the close of Hooker's futile and costly campaign. On the night of May 2d came the order to advance. The men of the Sixth Corps, already drawn up in battle, slept on their arms till dawn, ready to push forward and play their part in the conflict, the distant heavy booming of which had shaken the air as they had stood all day impatiently waiting. The troops of the Sixth Corps marched out across the plain from the river at four o'clock in the morning; and as they reached the eastern part of Fredericksburg the Confederate batteries opened upon them from above, while the skirmishers rose in swarms before them and poured volley after volley into their ranks, the conflict being hottest around a large mansion

FEDERAL BATTERY BEFORE FREDERICKSBURG, MAY 3, 1863

in the town, where both sides dodged behind the garden-fence of the outhouses and fought furiously. For a brief interval the Federals were held in check, but the rifled guns on Stafford Heights were already hurling their huge shells across the river and the wide valley, to burst in the Confederate works on the ridge before which Sedgwick's men waited for the order to charge. Field batteries were unlimbered and these added their iron hail to the hammering that was being inflicted on Marye's Heights, where so many brave Federals had lost their lives the previous December. At half-past ten Sedgwick, seeing that the Heights could be taken only by direct assault, ordered General Newton to command the charge, and the two commanders anxiously watched for the outcome of another hurling of flesh and blood up the slope against the sunken road which held such bitter memories. The columns went forward as coolly as did Pickett's men at Gettysburg, closing up ranks as men fell, till they swept over the hilltop, and Marye's Heights was won.

and the subsequent hard and desperate struggle with Early in the afternoon.

Lee was between two fires—Hooker in front and Sedgwick in the rear, both of whose forces were too strong to be attacked simultaneously. Again the daring leader of the Confederate legions did the unexpected, and divided his army in the presence of the foe, though he was without the aid of his great lieutenant, "Stonewall" Jackson.

During the night Lee made his preparations, and when dawn appeared in the eastern skies the movement began. Sedgwick, weak and battered by his contact with Early on the preceding afternoon, resisted bravely, but to no avail, and the Confederates closed in upon him on three sides, leaving the way to Banks's Ford on the Rappahannock open to escape. Slowly the Federals retreated and, as night descended, rested upon the river bank. After dark the return to the northern side was begun by Sedgwick's men, and the Chancellorsville campaign was practically ended.

The long, deep trenches full of Federal and Confederate dead told the awful story of Chancellorsville. If we gaze into these trenches, which by human impulse we are led to do, after the roar and din of the carnage is still, the scene greeting the eye will never be forgotten. Side by side, the heroes in torn and bloody uniforms, their only shrouds, were gently laid.

The Union loss in killed and wounded was a little over seventeen thousand, and it cost the South thirteen thousand men to gain this victory on the banks of the Rappahannock. The loss to both armies in officers was very heavy.

The two armies were weary and more than decimated. It appeared that both were glad at the prospect of a cessation of hostilities. On the night of May 5th, in a severe storm, Hooker conveyed his corps safely across the river and settled the men again in their cantonments of the preceding winter at Falmouth. The Confederates returned to their old encampment at Fredericksburg.

BATON ROUGE—AN ARSENAL RECAPTURED

HOMES DESTROYED TO CLEAR THE WAY FOR
FORTS—BATON ROUGE, 1862

ON THE MISSISSIPPI

As the Federal forces gradually recovered the Mississippi for the Union, many troops were necessary to hold its banks. Whole regiments were detached from the main army for this purpose. The Thirteenth Connecticut was organized in November, 1861, and belonged to Grover's division of the Nineteenth Army Corps. Here a portion of the regiment is seen drawn up on the banks of the Mississippi, in Louisiana. From their neat appearance and white gloves they have evidently been on headquarters duty, and possibly have been in recent touch with the quartermaster's stores; their uniforms are in fine condition and their caps brand new. After its service in the vicinity of the Mississippi, where the regiment had taken part in the operations against Port Hudson and the capture of Donaldsonville and the constant fighting and skirmishing in western Louisiana, the Thirteenth Connecticut went on the ill-fated Red River expedition and bore itself bravely at Monett's Bluff and Cane River Crossing. The men from Connecticut assisted the Michigan and Wisconsin woodsmen in building the famous dam at Alexandria that released the imprisoned gunboats. During July and August the seasoned veterans enjoyed a well-earned furlough after their arduous campaign, and upon its expiration they returned to duty and were attached to Sheridan's Army of the Shenandoah, for service in the East.

PATROLLING THE RIVER

To split the Confederacy apart was the Federal aim in the fall of 1862. It was necessary to the possession and command of the great waterway of the Mississippi that a constant patrol should be established after it was opened, and for this purpose, aside from the heavily armored gunboats, there was maintained a fleet of light-draught stern- and side-wheel vessels. This vessel (pictured by the Southern photographer Lytle) is No. 8 of the lightly armored "tin-clads." It was by means of these vessels of light draught that the shallow tributaries could be used as highways for the transportation of troops and supplies. The fleet or flotilla was at first really a division of the army. The crews were a miscellaneous lot of artillery-men and drafts made up from regi-ments in the service along the river. The early organization caused great confusion. In numerous cases naval officers in command of vessels were given military rank. Captain Foote found that he ranked only as a colonel, and that every brigadier could inter-fere with him. In November, 1861, he received the appointment of flag-officer that gave him the same rank as a major-general, and put him above the orders of any except the comman-der of the department; still he com-manded soldiers, and it was not until late in the year of 1861 that any trained naval men of the rank and file were placed on the river gunboats.

THE CAMP THAT BECAME A BATTLE-FIELD

The Federal Camp at Baton Rouge, Photographed Before the Battle of August 5, 1862. When the operations in the vicinity of Vicksburg had come to an end the Second Brigade (under the command of General Thomas Williams) of the Department of the Gulf once more went into camp at Baton Rouge, pitching tents within the limits of the city. On the 5th the Confederates under General J. C. Breckinridge attacked in two divisions in the early morning, their movements being hidden by a very dense fog. At first the Confederates were most successful and they seized a camp that lay in front of the Union battle-line. But the Federals soon advanced; the Confederates made three charges upon them but were finally driven back in much disorder. General Williams was killed. Baton Rouge was evacuated shortly after. The town was not burned on account of its many public institutions.

WHERE THE HOSPITALS FURNISHED REËNFORCEMENTS

The Federal Camp Banks, at Baton Rouge, near the Penitentiary, taken in late July, 1862. This is another view of what was soon to become a battle-field. We are looking down at the camp of the Seventh Vermont and the Twenty-first Indiana; on the extreme right is the camp of Nims' battery. This point was attacked fiercely, as it was supposed to be held by regiments much depleted by sickness, but at the first alarm the men in the hospitals picked up their rifles and fell into line. After General Williams' death the command devolved upon Colonel Cahill, of the Ninth Connecticut, an Irish regiment. By evening the Confederates had abandoned the ground that they had won in the fight.

THE BREAD–LINE AT BATON ROUGE

This picture was taken just at the close of the war in 1865. It is a remarkable and interesting picture. The Verandah House, the building shown on the left, is where General W. T. Sherman stopped in 1859, when he was Superintendent of the Louisiana Seminary of Learning and Military Academy. The group of colored people lining the sidewalk are waiting for their issue of rations. The skill of Lytle, the photographer, is shown by the fact that the man walking is hardly blurred and the mule's ears in the foreground might have been taken by an instantaneous shutter. The view below shows the home of the Union soldiers who remained in Baton Rouge from its occupation on May 12, 1862. Brigadier-General Thomas Williams had been assigned from Butler's force at New Orleans to assist Farragut to clear the Mississippi. Williams' headquarters was Baton Rouge, but during most of May, June, and July he was in the vicinity of Vicksburg operating in conjunction with Farragut's fleet. When he arrived at Baton Rouge at the end of July the barracks was almost a hospital, for half the men were on the sick-list.

THE COURT HOUSE AT BATON ROUGE

The Parade of a Part of a Regiment of Federal Troops at Baton Rouge. It would take a long search to find a finer body of men than these trained and seasoned veterans here drawn up in line. The campaign on the lower Mississippi was a survival of the fittest in more ways than one. Sickness was rife, and only those in the best condition and the hardiest kept in trim for active service. In many cases regiments could muster only 120 men. Camp fevers and the threat of the yellow scourge were always present. The returns of the regiments employed in the vicinity of New Orleans show a startling mortality. The Thirteenth Connecticut lost by disease 160 men. The Twenty-first Indiana, whose casualty list in the battle of Baton Rouge was 126, lost twice that number from sickness. A larger proportion of sick to killed and wounded prevailed in the Fourteenth Maine and the Seventh Vermont—the former losing 332 and the latter 407.

DRESS–PARADE OF FEDERAL TROOPS AT BATON ROUGE

BY ORDER OF THE COMMANDING OFFICER

Buildings in Line of Fire Condemned and Destroyed at Baton Rouge by Order of Colonel Halbert E. Paine. This view was photographed by Mr. Lytle after the drawn battle of the 5th of August, 1862, when the Federals had retreated from their outer camps and had concentrated on the Arsenal grounds between the cemetery and the river bank, at the northwestern end of the town. In order that the houses should not afford protection to any attacking party, those in the immediate vicinity (on the southeastern flank of the fortified Arsenal) were set on fire and razed to the ground. In this picture the heavy stockade that surrounded the garrison is plainly visible, as is also the roof of one of the barracks. Nevertheless, although the Federal troops were never attacked in their stronghold, General Butler determined to concentrate his forces in New Orleans, and Baton Rouge was abandoned.

THE ASSAULT
ON CORINTH

PUSHING THROUGH TENNESSEE, 1862

UNION BRIDGE OVER THE ELK RIVER AT PULASKI

THE RUSE OF THE WHISTLES

The Tishomingo Hotel was an old hostelry forming practically the railway station at Corinth, Miss., and here was played a little comedy by way of prelude to the tragic spectacle that was to happen on this very scene. After the battle of Shiloh, General Beauregard retreated to Corinth, where soon the Confederate army numbered about eighty thousand men. Halleck, who had assumed command in person, after a little delay started in pursuit at the head of the largest army ever assembled west of the Alleghanies, numbering more than 135,000 effective men. But the great forces did not come to decisive blows; Halleck, as usual, did not act with energy. For more than a month he went on gathering still more reenforcements, planning and organizing, all the time closing in slowly on Corinth. It was expected that a conclusive battle would soon take place, but Beauregard did not risk the test of arms. Keeping his intentions absolutely secret, he decided to evacuate. This plan was carried out with great cleverness; his army with its stores and munitions

THE GUARDED TRACK, CORINTH, MISSISSIPPI, 1862

boarded the assembled railway trains on the night of May 29, 1862, and the roads to the southward were filled with wagons and marching troops. But along the Confederate front the watch-fires burned brightly; and Halleck's army, waiting within earshot, heard sounds of commotion—the tooting of locomotive whistles and, with every fresh clear blast, loud cheers. It was rumored through the Federal camp that strong Confederate reenforcements were arriving. Into the gray of the morning this continued. The troops awoke with the nervous expectancy of battle, but before them lay a deserted town. The whistling and the cheering had covered Beauregard's retreat. The "movement of artillery" that had been reported had been some old wagons driven round in a circle. General Pope was sent in pursuit of the wily Confederate leader, but failed to force him to a stand. The evacuation had opened the Tennessee River, and finally resulted in giving the Federals the control of the Mississippi from Cairo to Memphis.

WHERE TRAGEDY FOLLOWED COMEDY AT CORINTH

Across the road, at the extreme right, against Battery Robinett, frowning above the camp, the Confederates charged on October 4th with terrible results, some of which are shown in the picture following. Only a short distance down the track from the old hotel and railway station shown in the preceding picture, the photographer had aimed his camera to take this view.

Months had passed since over this very ground had swept two charges memorable in the annals of the Civil War. On the left of the picture is Battery Williams. Over this foreground the Confederates bravely advanced in the attempt to take two positions. By firmly holding his ground, General Rosecrans leaped at once into national fame.

THE DAY AFTER THE MAGNIFICENT ASSAULT THAT FAILED

As the camera snapped, October 5, 1862, every object in this picture was a tragedy. Directly in the foreground lies a Confederate soldier who had swept along in the grand and terrible charge against the ramparts of Battery Robinett, to fall within fifty yards of the goal. Even nearer the battery lies the battle-charger of the colonel of the Texas Brigade. And to the left has been reverently laid the body of Colonel Rogers himself—the brave leader who leaped from his dying horse, seized the colors, and on foot dashed up the parapet straight into the last charge of grape-shot. "Then," writes one of the Federal defenders (General John Crane, the adjutant of the Seventeenth Wisconsin), "we learned who it was—Colonel William P. Rogers, of the Second Texas. General Rosecrans asked us to uncover his face; he said, 'He was one of the bravest men that ever led a charge. Bury him with military honors and mark his grave so that his friends may claim him.'" Colonel Rogers is said to have been the fifth standard-bearer to fall in that last desperate charge of the Texas Brigade.

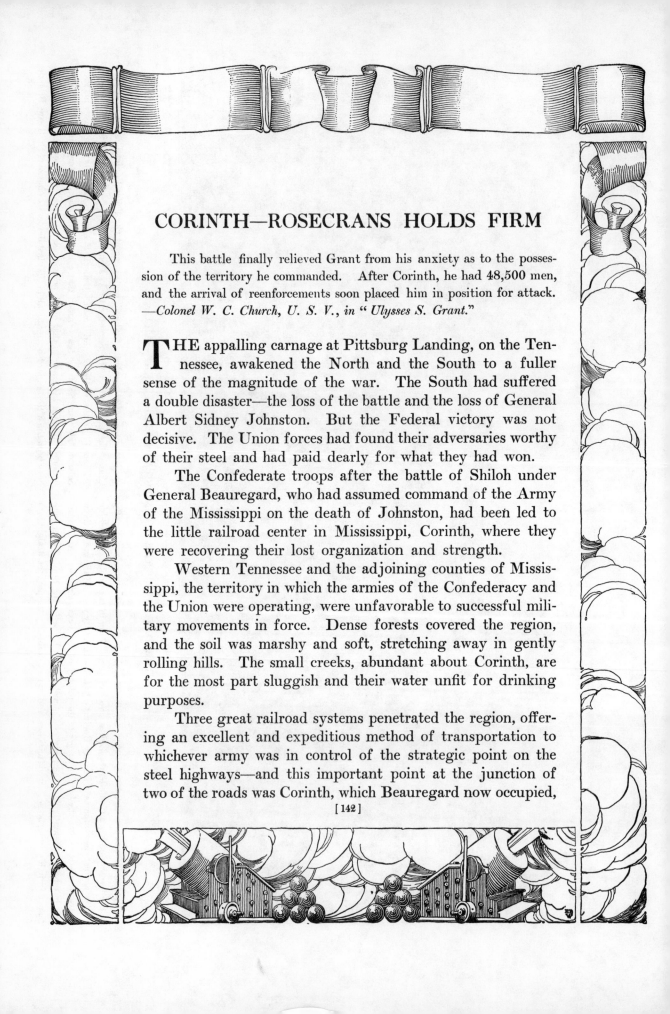

CORINTH—ROSECRANS HOLDS FIRM

This battle finally relieved Grant from his anxiety as to the possession of the territory he commanded. After Corinth, he had 48,500 men, and the arrival of reenforcements soon placed him in position for attack. —*Colonel W. C. Church, U. S. V., in " Ulysses S. Grant."*

THE appalling carnage at Pittsburg Landing, on the Tennessee, awakened the North and the South to a fuller sense of the magnitude of the war. The South had suffered a double disaster—the loss of the battle and the loss of General Albert Sidney Johnston. But the Federal victory was not decisive. The Union forces had found their adversaries worthy of their steel and had paid dearly for what they had won.

The Confederate troops after the battle of Shiloh under General Beauregard, who had assumed command of the Army of the Mississippi on the death of Johnston, had been led to the little railroad center in Mississippi, Corinth, where they were recovering their lost organization and strength.

Western Tennessee and the adjoining counties of Mississippi, the territory in which the armies of the Confederacy and the Union were operating, were unfavorable to successful military movements in force. Dense forests covered the region, and the soil was marshy and soft, stretching away in gently rolling hills. The small creeks, abundant about Corinth, are for the most part sluggish and their water unfit for drinking purposes.

Three great railroad systems penetrated the region, offering an excellent and expeditious method of transportation to whichever army was in control of the strategic point on the steel highways—and this important point at the junction of two of the roads was Corinth, which Beauregard now occupied,

GENERAL EARL VAN DORN, C.S.A.

THE CONFEDERATE COMMANDER AT CORINTH

General Earl Van Dorn was born in Mississippi in 1821; he was graduated from West Point in 1842, and was killed in a personal quarrel in 1863. Early in the war General Van Dorn had distinguished himself by capturing the steamer "Star of the West" at Indianola, Texas. He was of a tempestuous nature and had natural fighting qualities. During the month of August he commanded all the Confederate troops in Mississippi except those under General Price, and it was his idea to form a combined movement with the latter's forces and expel the invading Federals from the northern portion of his native State and from eastern Tennessee. The concentration was made and the Confederate army, about 22,000 men, was brought into the disastrous battle of Corinth. Brave were the charges made on the entrenched positions, but without avail.

THE CONFEDERATE SECOND IN COMMAND

General Sterling Price was a civilian who by natural inclination turned to soldiering. He had been made a brigadier-general during the Mexican War, but early allied himself with the cause of the Confederacy. At Pea Ridge, only seven months before the battle of Corinth, he had been wounded. Of the behavior of his men, though they were defeated and turned back on the 4th, he wrote that it was with pride that sisters and daughters of the South could say of the officers and men, "My brother, father, fought at Corinth." And nobly they fought indeed. General Van Dorn, in referring to the end of that bloody battle, wrote these pathetic words: "Exhausted from loss of sleep, wearied from hard marching and fighting, companies and regiments without officers, our troops—let no one censure them—gave way. The day was lost."

GENERAL STERLING PRICE, C.S.A.

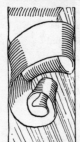

and upon which the Federal authorities cast longing glances as soon as the present campaign had begun.

However, it became clear to Beauregard that although his opponent did not immediately pursue, it would be impossible to hold Corinth. Soon after Shiloh the Union army was re-enforced to more than double the strength it had been before. Four days after the battle, General H. W. Halleck arrived at the Landing and took command in person; ten days later General John Pope, who had captured Island No. 10, on April 7th, joined his army to that at the Landing, and this, with other reenforcements, raised the number to a hundred thousand.

Beauregard had been joined by Van Dorn and Sterling Price from beyond the Mississippi, but, although the rolls showed now a force of over one hundred and twelve thousand he could not muster much more than fifty thousand men at any time and he prepared to give up Corinth whenever the great Northern force should move against it. About the 1st of May the movement of the Federal hosts, reorganized and now consisting of the Army of the Tennessee under General Thomas, the Army of the Ohio under Buell, and the Army of the Mississippi under Pope, began. Grant was second in command of the whole force, under Halleck. Slowly and cautiously, entrenching at every night halt, Halleck moved upon Corinth, guarding always against attack. He arrived before the town on May 25th. He met with but slight resistance. But Beauregard, although he had thrown up entrenchments and was maintaining a bold front, stealthily prepared to evacuate the town and save his army. Troops, provided with three days' cooked rations, manned the trenches confronting the Federal line, waiting for the order to advance. The Confederate soldiers had no inkling of the intentions of their leader. As the days passed and the command to attack was not given, the men behind the breastworks became restless.

Meanwhile, the patients in the hospitals within the town were being hurried away, and with great trainloads of stores

BEFORE THE SOD HID THEM

The Gathered Confederate Dead Before Battery Robinett—taken the morning after their desperate attempt to carry the works by assault.   No man can look at this awful picture and wish to go to war.   These men, a few hours before, were full of life and hope and courage.   Without the two last qualities they would not be lying as they are pictured here.   In the very foreground, on the left, lies their leader, Colonel Rogers, and almost resting on his shoulder is the body of the gallant Colonel Ross.   We are looking from the bottom of the parapet of Battery Robinett.   Let an eye-witness tell of what the men saw who looked toward the houses on that bright October day, and then glanced along their musket-barrels and pulled the triggers: "Suddenly we saw a magnificent brigade emerge in our front; they came forward in perfect order, a grand but terrible sight.   At their head rode the commander, a man of fine physique, in the prime of life—quiet and cool as though on a drill.   The artillery opened, the infantry followed; notwithstanding the slaughter they were closer and closer.   Their commander [Colonel Rogers] seemed to bear a charmed life. He jumped his horse across the ditch in front of the guns, and then on foot came on.   When he fell, the battle in our front was over."

were sent south over the Mobile and Ohio Railroad. On the night of the 29th, the preparations for the evacuation of the town by the Confederates were completed. Most of the troops were withdrawn from the trenches to the railroad, and there instructed concerning the part they were to play in the strategy to deceive the Federals.

Late that night a train rolled into the station, and the Federal pickets heard a lusty cheer arise from the Confederate ranks. Other trains followed, and the sounds of exuberation increased. Word quickly spread through the Federal camps that heavy reenforcements had come to the Confederates. The Northerners spent the early morning hours preparing to resist the attack they expected would be made with the coming of dawn.

At break of day the Federals, waiting in battle-line, could see no signs of life in the pits confronting them. The pickets crept forward to investigate. A thunderous explosion shook the town. It was the destruction of the last of the Confederate stores. The Southerners had evacuated the village, and Corinth, with all its strategic advantage, with its command of the great railroads connecting the Mississippi valley with the Atlantic coast and with the Gulf of Mexico, fell into the hands of the North. Both of the great armies were quickly broken up. Halleck, in possession of Corinth, looked to Chattanooga as the next objective, and Buell led the Army of the Ohio back to middle Tennessee as a preliminary move in that direction.

In the midsummer, Halleck was made general-in-chief of all the Northern armies and went to Washington. He left Grant in control of the West. Meantime, Beauregard was relieved of the command of the Confederate Army of the Mississippi and it was handed over to General Bragg. Leaving a portion of his army in Mississippi with Van Dorn and Price, Bragg began, late in August, his famous expedition into Kentucky, pursued by Buell with the Army of the Ohio. A part of the Federal Army of the Mississippi remained at Corinth,

THE BATTERY THAT CONTROLLED THE RIGHT OF WAY

Battery Williams, that can just be seen at the left of the picture, controlled the cutting through which the Memphis & Charleston Road ran on its way between Corinth and the Mississippi. It faced the right flank of Fort Robinett, distant about half a mile. During the action of October 4th, when the gallant Texans bravely assailed Battery Robinett, Battery Williams with all its guns was playing steadily upon the Confederate left flank, and so closely did they follow that brave and brilliant charge that two shells from the battery landed inside the Federal earthworks and burst there. Most of the houses seen in the mid-distance are barracks erected by the Fifty-seventh and Fifty-second Illinois Infantry. It was directly from this ground, in front of the railway station, that the Confederate advance took place. A short distance to the left of the freight-house stood a small cottage. General Rosecrans, as he rode along the Federal line, noticed that the porch and windows were filled with Confederates, who were firing at long range at the batteries. Immediately he ordered two field-pieces to open upon the dwelling with grape and canister. Hardly a man escaped alive. The town suffered severely from the fire of both Confederate and Federal artillery, but most of the inhabitants had retreated to their cellars and no casualties were reported. Note the bales of precious cotton gathered from some storehouse, worth almost their weight in gold before the war was over.

where there were immense military stores, under the command of General William S. Rosecrans. After inflicting a defeat on Sterling Price, September 19th, in a severe combat at Iuka, Mississippi, Rosecrans was settled snugly at Corinth with two divisions and cavalry of his army, and two divisions of the Federal Army of West Tennessee, in all about twenty-three thousand men. Van Dorn then joined his Army of West Tennessee with Price's Corps, or Army of the West, and decided to make a desperate attempt to capture Corinth. It was a daring venture, for Corinth was well fortified and Rosecrans' army was slightly larger than his own.

The battle of Corinth, October 3–4, 1862, does not compare in magnitude with the greatest battles of the war; but for ferocity of fighting, it was not surpassed by any. Rosecrans did not believe that Van Dorn would attack him, and when the latter appeared in force in the neighborhood on October 3rd he supposed that it was only a feint and that the real object of the Confederate attack was to be Jackson, about sixty miles north, in Tennessee, where Grant's headquarters were, or Bolivar, Tennessee, about forty miles northwest, where Hurlbut's division of Grant's Army of West Tennessee was at that time located.

However, Rosecrans was prepared for any emergency. He sent Colonel Oliver with three regiments to take an advanced position on a hill, near the Chewalla road, to watch the movements of the Confederates. A desultory cannonade was begun and soon Rosecrans sent General McArthur to the front with his brigade. In a short time a sharp battle was raging. Then came a sudden determined Confederate charge by which the Union forces were driven from the hill and two of their heavy guns captured. The Union commander was now convinced that the attack was no feint, but that the purpose of the Southern general was to make a grand assault on Corinth with a view of defeating its defenders and capturing the great stores within its fortifications.

WINTER QUARTERS AT CORINTH

A Photograph Taken During the Federal Occupation, Winter of 1862. These little cottages—bungalows we should call them—resemble much the summer residences erected by the holiday-makers on the sea-coast at some wintering resort. Many were built by soldier-carpenters who found time to turn their hands to carpentering, and even to architectural decoration. All trades were represented in the army, and during a lull in the fighting the men plied their avocations. Besides the artisans that were of use to the commanding generals—such as mechanics, locomotive engineers, machinists, and farriers—there were tailors and shoemakers, watchmakers and barbers, and all the little trades by which men with time on their hands could turn an honest penny. Some regiments became renowned for the neatness of their quarters. It was a matter of prideful boastings. In this picture a soldier has fashioned a well-cut overcoat out of a gaudy blanket. These are officers' quarters. The man smoking the long cigar as he sits on the veranda railing is a captain. A bearded lieutenant stands on the steps of the second house, and another young officer has apparently adopted for the time a tow-headed child of a Corinth family.

The hours of the afternoon were given to disposing the various divisions of the army to the best advantage for the defense of the town; but it was no easy task because of the annoying Confederate fire from the surrounding hills. Before either side opened a general engagement it was night, and both armies slept on their arms, confident that a fierce battle was in store for the coming day.

The early hours of the night were spent by Rosecrans in rearranging his battle-lines, and before he went to sleep about 3 A.M., his forces had drawn closer to the town. The Federal left, under McKean, rested near Corona College; next in line was Stanley, in support of Battery Robinett, a small fortification mounting three guns; in the center of the battle-line, was Davies, and Hamilton was assigned to the right wing. Thus stood the weary warriors in blue, who had struggled desperately in the terrific heat of the preceding day and were now exhausted. The line was crescent shaped, and covered the northern and western approaches to Corinth, extended a mile in length and rested on the edge of the town. The Confederate divisions, commanded by Lovell, Maury, and Hébert stood arrayed in another great crescent, conforming to the curve of Rosecrans' battle-line. About four o'clock on the morning of the 4th the sleeping village was awakened by the shells that shrieked over the housetops and fell bursting in the streets.

During the night a Confederate battery had been planted a few hundred yards from the Union lines, opposite Stanley's position, and now opened with several Parrott guns. Little damage was done, except that the teamsters, sutlers, and other non-combatants were kept in a ferment of excitement. No reply was made till near daylight, when a Union battery opened on the Confederate guns, and the latter were silenced and disabled in a few minutes. Indian summer had descended over the land, bringing its enervating heat from which the soldiers of both armies suffered. The sun peeped over the eastern hills, and its rays were soon beating down upon the bivouacs.

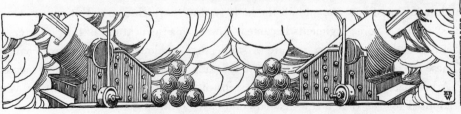

PHOTOGRAPHERS OF THE WESTERN ARMIES

The Civil War was the first great war to be photographed. The art had just arisen. The daguerreotype had been superseded by the tintype, and the wet-plate method (still in vogue in the best portrait galleries) was then in the height of its excellence. It is a fortunate thing in recording the history of the time that the camera was in existence. In Corinth there was a firm of photographers occupying a little wooden shack in the outskirts of the town. They did a thriving business during the occupancy by the Confederates and by the Federals. George Armstead was a wonderful photographer—rivaling Brady at his best. In the picture he is standing back to the left, near where some of his negatives are printing in the sun; in front of the shop a drummer-boy stands with folded arms near the civilians who loll against the post. What would we not give for a nearer glimpse of the samples of Armstead's work on the right of the doorway! The little frame of portrait tintypes on the other side would also give us to-day a thrill of interest. They are the only relics, perhaps, of men who lie in far-off graves—duplicates of the only mementoes that their people, who are now old, possess. In turning the pages of this volume many will exclaim, "Look, there he is!"

During the day the temperature rose to ninety-four degrees in the shade.

Soon after daybreak the skirmishers of both sides began with scattering shots, which presently came thicker and faster; the batteries came into play, and shells were falling and bursting all around. So it continued until half-past nine. Then came a sudden and amazing change in the whole aspect of the battle. A vast column of gleaming bayonets was seen to flash from the woods east of the Memphis and Charleston Railroad; long lines of determined, gray-clad troops of Price's divisions quickly formed and began to march swiftly and steadily along the Purdy road, toward Davies and Hamilton, behind whom lay the town of Corinth. Presently the great column took the shape of a wedge as it moved impetuously forward.

General Rosecrans was prepared for the charge. He had skilfully planned to entice the Confederates to attack at a point where his carefully placed batteries and infantry could sweep the road with direct, cross, and enfilading fires. There was an outburst from the Federal guns. Gaps were torn in the moving gray column, but they were instantly filled and the lines moved on with great steadiness. A gently sloping hill led up to the Federal position. As Price's troops began the ascent, volley after volley of grape, canister, and shell were poured into their ranks, but still they marched on with a valor not surpassed by Leonidas and his Spartans at Thermopylæ.

Colonel Sweeny, who commanded a brigade of Davies' division on that memorable 4th of October, gives a vivid picture of this remarkable charge:

An ominous silence took place for a few moments, when a sharp rattling of musketry was heard, accompanied by heavy volleys, and the enemy's columns burst from the woods in front and to the right, driving the sharpshooters before them and following close upon their heels. Colonel Burke's regiment fought like heroes and disputed every inch of ground as they fell back on my position. I cautioned my men, who were lying on the ground, to reserve their fire until the enemy got within

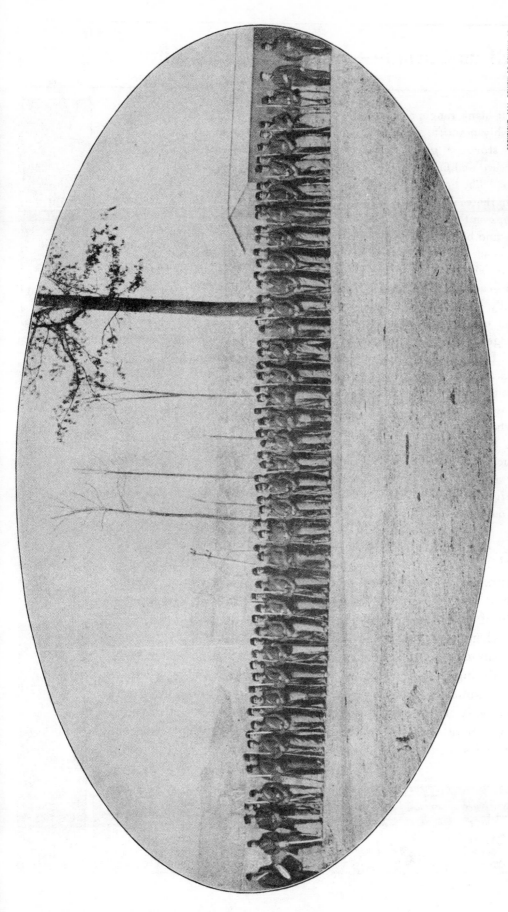

OHIO TROOPS ON THE BATTLE-FIELD OF CORINTH

The Eighty-first Ohio, pictured here drawn up at "parade rest," enlisted in August, 1861; when its term expired in 1864, it reënlisted and served to the end of the war. The youth of these men is very evident; yet when this picture was taken they were already tried and proved veterans. Attached to Sweeney's division of the Sixteenth Army Corps, they fought through most of the actions in Tennessee and Mississippi, but were not present at the time of the Confederate attack on the fortifications we see behind them—Battery Williams to the left, and Battery Robinett to the right. The Eightieth Ohio was present at this action and was attached to the second brigade of the second division of the Army of the Mississippi under Rosecrans. Its commander, Major Lanning, was killed. Well can Ohio be proud of her record in the war; nearly twenty-one thousand men remained in the field and served after their three-years' enlistment had expired, and most of these reën-listments embraced a very large proportion of the original volunteers of '61.

point-blank range, and then fire low and keep perfectly cool. It was a terribly beautiful sight to see the columns advance, in despite of a perfect storm of grape and canister, shell, and rifle-ball; still on they marched and fired, though their ranks were perceptibly thinned at every step. The brigade stood firm as a rock, and the men loaded and fired with the coolness and precision of veterans, when all of a sudden the troops on the right of the redan (a brigade of Hamilton's division) gave way and broke. The First Missouri Artillery, in the redan, and the two pieces on the left of the Fifty-second Illinois limbered up and galloped off in wild confusion through our reserves, killing several of our men and scattering the rest. My line remained still unbroken, pouring deadly volleys into the enemy's ranks, who, taking advantage of the panic on the right, moved their columns obliquely in that direction and charged up to the redan. . . .

I now ordered the line to charge on the enemy, who had by this time gained the crest of the hill in our front. With a shout that was heard through our whole lines the men of the First Brigade rushed upon them. Those who had given way a short time before, being evidently ashamed of the momentary panic that had seized them, seemed determined to wipe out the stain upon their courage by their reckless daring. The foe, reluctant to abandon the advantage they had gained, fought stubbornly for a while, but was finally compelled to give way, retreating in great confusion through the swamps and abatis to the woods, hotly pursued by our men.

In spite of the desperate resistance, the center of the Federal line was penetrated, and Price's troops drove the regiments back into the town, scattering the Union soldiers among the houses. The storming Confederates advanced to the north side of the square and posted themselves around a house close to where General Halleck had maintained his headquarters the summer before. Two field-pieces opened upon them, and the daring Southerners were whirled back, leaving seven of their number dead in the dooryard, after one round of grape and canister. Union troops stationed in the town hurried up and General Sullivan immediately supported the shattered center. His men retook Battery Powell while General Hamilton

A CAMP MEETING WITH A PURPOSE

There was something of extreme interest taking place when this photograph was taken at Corinth. With arms stacked, the soldiers are gathered about an improvised stand sheltered with canvas, listening to a speech upon a burning question of the hour—the employment of colored troops in the field. A question upon which there were many different and most decided opinions prevailing in the North, and but one nearly universal opinion holding south of Mason and Dixon's line. General Thomas, at the moment this photograph was taken, was addressing the assembled troops on this subject. Some prominent Southeners, among them General Patrick Cleburne, favored the enrollment of Negroes in the Confederate army.

collected his scattered division and charged upon the Confederate left, driving it across an open field over which the recaptured Union artillery hurled a pitiless fire. It was now one o'clock in the afternoon and the battle on the Federal right was over.

The Confederate commanders had planned a general assault, Price and Van Dorn acting in concert, but on different points of Rosecrans' line. Van Dorn delayed in reaching his position, and Price's majestic and thrilling charge had been in progress half an hour or more when the standards of the Army of West Tennessee emerged from the woods, in front of Stanley's division and batteries Robinett and Williams. The Federal troops were eagerly watching affairs on their right, when their attention was called to the gray wave plunging over fallen trees and through growths of underbrush in front of Battery Robinett. A sheet of flame burst from the fort, and the advance line of Confederates was enveloped in smoke, many of its numbers falling dead and wounded. A second storming column appeared, and again the Federal guns smote the daring Confederates. Again and again the courageous Southerners charged until they finally won the ditch surrounding the battery, and after a desperate hand-to-hand fight gained the interior of the fort, the defenders falling back to another position. At the head of the attacking regiments stood Colonel W. P. Rogers of the Second Texas regiment of Maury's division.

The Southerners had almost gained this important point in the Federal line, when a burst of flame appeared in Battery Williams, and two shells hurtled across the intervening space and fell into the Confederate ranks. Simultaneously, Fuller's Ohio brigade of Stanley's division and the Eleventh Missouri appeared in the rear of the fort where they had been concealed, and delivered six successive volleys into the gray ranks at the front of the battery. When the smoke cleared the front of the fort was clear of living Confederates. They could not stand the terrific storm of lead and iron. Many of them fell to rise

[156]

PROVOST MARSHAL'S HEADQUARTERS AT CORINTH

During the occupation of a town where soldiers were in predominance, there was one man who was responsible for the conduct of the troops, and also for the practical government and policing of the streets, and the control of the inhabitants' actions. Such was the provost marshal. He was head constable, police-court judge, health department, and general almoner. Negroes from the outlying districts had flocked, as usual, into Corinth in nondescript wagons drawn by oxen and mules, and sometimes both, as we see here pictured.

FOOD FOR POWDER

Give a glance at these seventeen men, who, for some reason that we cannot tell, have chosen to stand before the camera and be "taken." Note one thing first—there is not one smiling face nor one look of the holiday soldier about this little group. Able, grim, stern-hearted veterans—their faces show it. Among them all there is not a single merry-maker. These men have faced death often, they have seen their comrades die. They have looked across the sights of their muskets at the ragged men in gray, and peered through the enveloping smoke to see if their shots have told. These are not the machine-made soldiers of the European armies. They are the development of the time and hour. The influence of emigration is plainly shown. Here is a Scotchman—

FEDERAL TROOPS AT CORINTH

An old soldier of the Queen, perhaps, who knew the Mutiny and the Crimea. Here are Swedes and Germans, Irish and French; but, predominating, is the American type—the Yankee, and the man of many blends from the mid-West and the North woods. There are two or three regulars standing in the center—artillerymen with bell buttons. On the extreme right are two men of the saber, with short jackets. Beyond them is the battle-field of October. It is now winter, but these men saw that field shrouded in battle smoke. They saw Price and Van Dorn's brave troops come yelling and charging across the railway track and the road beyond up to the very guns of Battery Robinett, which we see rising like a mound or hillock beyond the line of the railway shed.

no more. The others began to waver. Then came a panic.
They broke and fled in great disorder. Volley after volley
was fired at the fleeing men. They were now pursued by the
victors, across ravines, over hills, and among the fallen trees.
Many threw away their guns and surrendered, others escaped,
and still others gave their lives for the cause in which they
believed. Fifty-six bodies of brave Confederates were found in
a space of a few rods about Battery Robinett and were buried
in one pit. Among them was Colonel Rogers, who had fallen
while planting his battle-flag on the parapet. The wild shouts
of the victorious Federals rang through the streets of Corinth,
above the moaning of the wounded and dying. By two o'clock
Rosecrans was convinced that the Confederate generals did
not intend to make another attack and were retreating in force,
but his troops were too weary to follow after on that day.

Later in the afternoon McPherson arrived with four regiments sent by Grant, and these were ordered to begin the
pursuit at daylight the next morning. Meanwhile, Hurlbut
with his division was hastening from Bolivar to the Confederate rear. On the night of the 4th he bivouacked on the west
bank of the Hatchie River near Davis' Bridge, right in the
path of Van Dorn. The following morning General Ord
arrived and took command of the Federal forces.

Owing to a number of mishaps and delays Rosecrans
never overtook the Confederate army, but when Van Dorn's
advance guard attempted to seize the Hatchie bridge on the
morning of the 5th, it was most spiritedly attacked and driven
off by Ord, who was severely wounded. Although the Confederates greatly outnumbered their opponents, Van Dorn,
fearful of Rosecrans in his rear, moved down the east bank of
the Hatchie, crossed six miles below, and made his way to
Holly Springs. On these three October days the Federals
lost over twenty-five hundred and the Confederates forty-eight
hundred. Of these over two thousand had been captured by
Rosecrans and Ord.

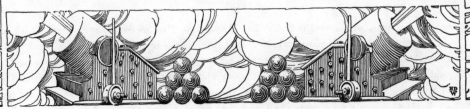

PART II
OPENING THE MISSISSIPPI

———

THE MIDWINTER COMBAT
AT STONE'S RIVER

———

THE MURFREESBORO COURTHOUSE UNDER GUARD—1863

THE SINEWS OF WAR

This busy scene along the Nashville wharf on December 18, 1862, gives a clear idea of the magnitude of the preparations at the Federal army base thirteen days before the battle opened around Murfreesboro, at which point Bragg was threatening Nashville. Rosecrans could not move forward to attack him without supplies, and the river steamers which played so important a part in all the military operations in the West were hurrying up the Cumberland heavily loaded with the munitions and sustenance that made possible the coming battles. The first boat completely visible in the picture at the right is the " Mercury," a famous Ohio River packet at the time. Next to her lies the " Lizzie Martin," and then the " Palestine," another Ohio racer. She has a hole stove in her prow just above the water-line, and the ship's carpenter in his yawl is busily repairing it. Confederate batteries constantly menaced the Federal transports as they plied up and down the rivers. The renowned Tom Napier sometimes scared and captured a vessel with his dummy wooden guns.

SUPPLY STEAMERS AT NASHVILLE, DECEMBER, 1862

Beyond the "Palestine" lie the "Reveillie," the "Irene," the "Belle Peoria" (a famous Mississippi boat from St. Louis), and last the "Rob Roy"—all discharging their tons of freight, paid for by the Government at war-time prices. On the snow-covered wharf are piled barrels of whiskey (the standard brand familiarly known as "Cincinnati rot-gut," distilled for the Government's own use), while the roustabouts are rolling ashore barrels of sugar and hogsheads of molasses to be mixed with the coffee which weary soldiers are to brew for themselves in the field. There are thousands of barrels of flour still to be unloaded. In symmetrical piles lie myriad boxes each stencilled "Pilot bread from U. S. Government Bakery, Evansville, Ind." Many an old Confederate knew the taste of this hard-tack and had to depend upon capturing a supply of it to stay his hunger. Confederate prisoners in their confinement watched many such scenes as this, wondering what newcomers would be added to their numbers during the ensuing campaign.

CONFEDERATES WHO FOUGHT THE GUNS AT STONE'S RIVER

The Washington Artillery, mustered in at New Orleans, was one of the crack military organizations of the Confederacy. In this rare picture a Confederate photographer has caught a jolly group of them, confident and care-free, whiling away the hours in camp. The photograph was taken the year before the battle of Stone's River. Ere that conflict the youngsters had received their baptism of fire at Shiloh and had acquitted themselves like men. Their gallant force was attached to Anderson's First Brigade and then to General Samuel Jones's Corps, of Bragg's army. At the battle of Stone's River they fought in Breckinridge's division of Hardee's Corps. It was they who made the daring rush to plant their batteries on the hill, and suffered so severely from the galling fire of

MEN OF THE FAMOUS WASHINGTON ARTILLERY

Mendenhall's Federal gun across the river. On that hard-fought battlefield they were differently occupied than in the picture. Their deeds in the swift moments of the conflict were not acted out to the accompaniment of a merry tune; each man played his part amid the roar of cannon and the clash of arms, and many paid the piper with his life for that awful music. Even in the confident poses and smiling faces of the picture are apparent all the dash and spirit which they displayed later at Stone's River. This brave Confederate organization distinguished itself on all the fields where it fought. Not till Chancellorsville did it ever lose a gun; in that engagement five pieces were captured from it, when Sedgwick's 20,000 wrested Marye's Heights from the 9,000 Lee had left there.

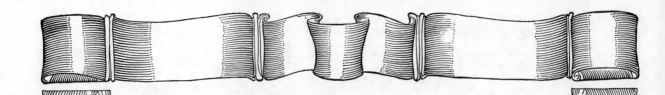

STONE'S RIVER, OR MURFREESBORO

As it is, the battle of Stone's River seems less clearly a Federal victory than the battle of Shiloh. The latter decided the fall of Corinth; the former did not decide the fall of Chattanooga. Offensively it was a drawn battle, as looked at from either side. As a defensive battle, however, it was clearly a Union victory.—*John Fiske in "The Mississippi Valley in the Civil War."*

THE battle of Corinth developed a man—William S. Rosecrans—whose singular skill in planning the battle, and whose dauntless courage in riding between the firing-lines at the opportune moment, drew the country's attention almost as fully as Grant had done at Fort Donelson. And at this particular moment the West needed, or thought it needed, a man. The autumn months of 1862 had been spent by Generals Bragg and Buell in an exciting race across Kentucky, each at the head of a great army. Buell had saved Louisville from the legions of Bragg, and he had driven the Confederate Army of the Mississippi from the State; but he had not prevented his opponent from carrying away a vast amount of plunder, nor had he won decisive results at the battle of Perryville, which took place October 8, 1862, four days after the battle of Corinth. Thereupon the Federal authorities decided to relieve Buell of the Army of the Ohio and to give it to General Rosecrans.

On October 30, 1862, Rosecrans assumed command at Nashville of this force, which was now designated as the Army of the Cumberland. Bragg had concentrated his army at Murfreesboro, in central Tennessee, about thirty miles southeast of Nashville and a mile east of a little tributary of the Cumberland River called Stone's River. Here occurred, two months later, the bloodiest single day's battle in the West,

[166]

THE GUARDED DEPOT—STEVENSON IN 1862

This little Alabama town first became the subject of a war photograph during General Buell's campaign. It sprang into strategic importance as a base of supplies, and in order to hold it Buell sent forward Colonel A. S. Barker, who began the construction of extensive defenses, pressing into service some five hundred Negroes. Barker succeeded in completing two large redoubts and seven lockhouses; so defensible was the position made that during Hood's invasion of Tennessee it was not attacked by the Confederates.

THE STRENGTHENED FORTS

This picture of Fort Barker, at Stevenson, shows the care with which the Federals defended this advance base. In this fort, which was about 150 feet square, there were barbette platforms for seven guns and an extensive magazine, and bomb-proof. Fort Mitchell, south of the station on the other side of the railroad, was equally strong. The two forts guarded the approach from the north.

which has taken the double name of the town and the river. Beside the winding little stream ran the turnpike to Nashville and the Nashville and Chattanooga Railroad.

Bragg had the advantage in cavalry. In addition to Wheeler's command there were the troops of Forrest and Morgan, who acted independently of the Army of the Mississippi, now known as the Army of Tennessee. These men, with several hundred horsemen, raided through the country, regardless of mud, snow, or ice, and at one time threatened Nashville, the Federal supply-depot. They tore up railroads, burned bridges, and left a trail of destruction in their wake. One night, early in December, Morgan pounced upon the town of Hartsville, overpowered the guard of several hundred Federal troops, captured and carried them to Murfreesboro.

Christmas day, in 1862, was passed by Bragg's army in whatever festivities the little town of Murfreesboro could afford. The fratricidal strife that was draining both the North and the South was forgotten for the moment. A general belief had circulated in the Confederate camps that the Federal commander, harassed on every side by the raiders, would have enough to do to keep his army intact, and would not make a general advance on Bragg. But soon there was a different story to tell. On the day after Christmas, the news reached the little town that the Federal army had emerged from Nashville, that it was headed directly for Murfreesboro, and that a great battle was imminent.

The battle-ground toward which the Federal army was marching was broken and heavily wooded, with an occasional open field, and gentle rises on which artillery and infantry could be posted. But cavalry was practically useless in this rough country. Stone's River, which ran through the battle-ground, was tortuous in its channel and shallow; its banks were fringed with clumps of cedar brakes. Numerous turnpikes converged at the little town of Murfreesboro from the surrounding towns; the principal highway being the Nashville

LEADERS OF A GALLANT STAND AT STONE'S RIVER

General William P. Carlin and Staff. Early in the war Carlin made a name for himself as colonel of the Thirty-eighth Illinois Infantry, which was stationed at Pilot Knob, Mossouri, and was kept constantly alert by the raids of Price and Jeff Thompson. Carlin rose rapidly to be the commander of a brigade, and joined the forces in Tennessee in 1862. He distinguished himself at Perryville and in the advance to Murfreesboro. At Stone's River his brigade, almost surrounded, repulsed an overwhelming force of Confederates. This picture was taken a year after that battle, while the brigade was in winter quarters at Ringgold, Georgia. The band-stand was built by the General's old regiment.

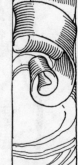

turnpike, which, after crossing the river, took the general direction of its course for some distance.

General Bragg did not lose a moment in marshaling his army into well-drawn battle-lines. His army was in two corps with a cavalry division under General Wheeler, Forrest and Morgan being on detached service. The left wing, under General Hardee, and the center, under Polk, were sent across Stone's River, the right wing, a division under John C. Breckinridge, remaining on the eastern side of the stream to guard the town. The line was three miles in length, and on December 30th the Federal host that had come from Nashville stood opposite, in a parallel line. It was also in three sections. The left wing, opposite Breckinridge, was commanded by Thomas L. Crittenden, whose brother was a commander in the Confederacy. They were sons of the famous United States senator from Kentucky, John J. Crittenden. The Federal center, opposite Polk, was commanded by George H. Thomas, and the right wing, opposing the Confederate left, was led by Alexander McD. McCook, one of the well-known "Fighting McCook" brothers. The effective Federal force was about forty-three thousand men; the Confederate army numbered about thirty-eight thousand. That night they bivouacked within musket range of each other and the camp-fires of each were clearly seen by the other as they shone through the cedar groves that interposed. Thus lay the two great armies, ready to spring upon each other in deadly combat with the coming of the morning.

Rosecrans had permitted McCook to thin out his lines over too much space, while on that very part of the field Bragg had concentrated his forces for the heaviest attack. The plans of battle made by the two opposing commanders were strikingly similar. Rosecrans' plan was to throw his left wing, under Crittenden, across the river upon the Confederate right under Breckinridge, to crush it in one impetuous dash, and to swing around through Murfreesboro to the Franklin road and

MEN WHO LEARNED WAR WITH SHERMAN

The Twenty-first Michigan Infantry. In the Murfreesboro campaign, the regiment, detached from its old command, fought in the division of Brigadier-General "Phil" Sheridan, a leader who became scarcely less renowned in the West than Sherman and gave a good account of himself and his men at Stone's River. Most of the faces in the picture are those of boys, yet severe military service has already given them the unmistakable carriage of the soldier. The terrible field of Chickamauga lay before them, but a few months in the future; and after that, rejoining their beloved "Old Tecumseh," they were to march with him to the sea and witness some of the closing scenes in the struggle.

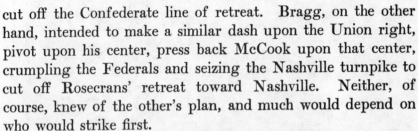

cut off the Confederate line of retreat. Bragg, on the other hand, intended to make a similar dash upon the Union right, pivot upon his center, press back McCook upon that center, crumpling the Federals and seizing the Nashville turnpike to cut off Rosecrans' retreat toward Nashville. Neither, of course, knew of the other's plan, and much would depend on who would strike first.

At the early light of the last day of the year the Confederate left wing moved upon the Union right in a magnificent battle-line, three-quarters of a mile in length and two columns deep. At the same time the Confederate artillery opened with their cannon. McCook was astonished at so fierce and sudden a charge. The gallant Patrick Cleburne, one of the ablest commanders in the Southern armies, led his division, which had been brought from the Confederate right, in the charge. The Federal lines were ill prepared for this sudden onslaught, and before McCook could arrange them several batteries were overpowered and eleven of the heavy guns were in the hands of the Confederates.

Slowly the Union troops fell back, firing as they went; but they had no power to check the impetuous, overwhelming charge of the onrushing foe. McCook's two right divisions, under Johnson and Jeff. C. Davis, were driven back, but his third division, which was commanded by a young officer who had attracted unusual attention at the battle of Perryville— Philip H. Sheridan—held its ground. At the first Confederate advance, Sill's brigade of Sheridan's division drove the troops in front of it back into their entrenchments, and in the charge the brave Sill lost his life.

While the battle raged with tremendous fury on the Union right, Rosecrans was three miles away, throwing his left across the river. Hearing the terrific roar of battle at the other end of the line, Rosecrans hastened to begin his attack on Breckinridge hoping to draw a portion of the Confederate force away from McCook. But as the hours of the forenoon

COPYRIGHT, 1911, REVIEW OF REVIEWS CO.

FIGHTERS IN THE WEST

This picture of Company B of the Twenty-first Michigan shows impressively the type of men that the rough campaigning west of the Alleghanies had molded into veterans. These were Sherman's men, and under the watchful eye and in the inspiring presence of that general thousands of stalwart lads from the sparsely settled States were becoming the very bone and sinew of the Federal fighting force. The men of Sherman, like their leader, were forging steadily to the front. They had become proficient in the fighting which knows no fear, in many hard-won combats in the early part of the war. Greater and more magnificent conflicts awaited those who did not find a hero's grave.

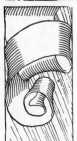

passed he was dismayed as he noted that the sound of battle was coming nearer, and he rightly divined that his right wing was receding before the dashing soldiers of the South. He ordered McCook to dispute every inch of the ground; but McCook's command was soon torn to pieces and disorganized, except the division of Sheridan.

The latter stood firm against the overwhelming numbers, a stand that attracted the attention of the country and brought him military fame. He checked the onrushing Confederates at the point of the bayonet; he formed a new line under fire. In his first position Sheridan held his ground for two hours. The Confederate attack had also fallen heavily on Negley, who was stationed on Sheridan's left, and on Palmer, both of Thomas' center. Rousseau commanding the reserves, and Van Cleve of Crittenden's forces were ordered to the support of the Union center and right. Here, for two hours longer the battle raged with unabated fury, and the slaughter of brave men on both sides was appalling. Three times the whole Confederate left and center were thrown against the Union divisions, but failed to break the lines. At length when their cartridge boxes were empty Sheridan's men could do nothing but retire for more ammunition, and they did this in good order to a rolling plain near the Nashville road. But Rousseau of Thomas' center was there to check the Confederate advance.

It was now past noon, and still the battle roar resounded unceasingly through the woods and hills about Murfreesboro. Though both hosts had struggled and suffered since early morning, they still held to their guns, pouring withering volleys into each other's ranks. The Federal right and center had been forced back at right angles to the position they had held when day dawned; and the Confederate left was swung around at right angles to its position of the morning. The Federal left rested on Stone's River, while Bragg's right was on the same stream and close to the line in blue. Meantime, Rosecrans had massed his artillery on a little hill over-

AN UNCEASING WORK OF WAR

In the picture the contraband laborers often pressed into service by Federals are repairing the "stringer" track near Murfreesboro after the battle of Stone's River. The long lines of single-track road, often involving a change from broad-gauge to narrow-gauge, were entirely inadequate for the movement of troops in that great area. In these isolated regions the railroads often became the supreme objective of both sides. When disinclined to offer battle, each struck in wild raids against the other's line of communication. Sections of track were tipped over embankments; rails were torn up, heated red-hot in bonfires, and twisted so that they could never be used again. The wrecking of a railroad might postpone a maneuver for months, or might terminate a campaign suddenly in defeat. Each side in retreat burned its bridges and destroyed the railroad behind it. Again advancing, each had to pause for the weary work of repair.

looking the field of action. He had also re-formed the broken lines of the right and center and called in twelve thousand fresh troops. Then, after a brief lull, the battle opened again and the ranks of both sides were torn with grape and canister and bursting shells.

In answer to Bragg's call for reenforcements came Breckinridge with all but one brigade of his division, a host of about seven thousand fresh troops. The new Confederate attack began slowly, but increased its speed at every step. Suddenly, a thundering volley burst from the line in blue, and the front ranks of the attacking column disappeared. Again, a volley tore through the ranks in gray, and the assault was abandoned.

The battle had raged for nearly eleven hours, when night enveloped the scene, and the firing abated slowly and died away. It had been a bloody day—this first day's fight at Stone's River—and except at Antietam it had not thus far been surpassed in the war. The advantage was clearly with the Confederates. They had pressed back the Federals for two miles, had routed their right wing and captured many prisoners and twenty-eight heavy guns. But Rosecrans determined to hold his ground and try again.

The next day was New Year's and but for a stray fusillade, here and there, both armies remained inactive, except that each quietly prepared to renew the contest on the morrow. The renewal of the battle on January 2nd was fully expected on both sides, but there was little fighting till four in the afternoon. Rosecrans had sent General Van Cleve's division on January 1st across the river to seize an elevation from which he could shell the town of Murfreesboro. Bragg now sent Breckinridge to dislodge the division, and he did so with splendid effect. But Breckinridge's men came into such a position as to be exposed to the raking fire of fifty-two pieces of Federal artillery on the west side of the river. Returning the deadly and constant fire as best they could, they stood the storm of shot and shell for half an hour when they retreated to a place

ALONG THE HAZARDOUS ADVANCE FROM MURFREESBORO

Portion of the Bridgeport Bridge from Long Island to the East Bank of the Tennessee. The island, 1,232 feet at this point, divides the stream opposite Bridgeport, Alabama. The Union troops crossed at four points (at all of which the river was very wide), the division of Reynolds to the north of Bridgeport by means of captured boats, while that of Brannan crossed on rafts. The main crossing of McCook's Corps was at Caperton's Ferry, where the one complete pontoon-bridge had been laid. The army was all across by September 10th, but even greater difficulties now confronted it. The greatest of these obstacles were the steeps of Raccoon Mountain—the towering heights of Lookout Mountain rising before them, almost impassable to wagons and destitute of water. Beyond these, Missionary Ridge and a succession of lesser ranges must be crossed before Bragg's railroad connections with Atlanta could be struck at Dalton. Yet the trains which had already been brought across the Cumberland Mountains into Tennessee must ever be carried forward, loaded with twenty-five days' supplies and ammunition enough for the two great battles that were to follow.

of safety, leaving seventeen hundred of their number dead or wounded on the field. That night the two armies again lay within musket shot of each other. The next day brought no further conflict and during that night General Bragg moved away to winter quarters at Shelbyville, on the Elk River.

Murfreesboro, or Stone's River, was one of the great battles of the war. The losses were about thirteen thousand to the Federals and over ten thousand to the Confederates. Both sides claimed victory—the South because of Bragg's signal success on the first day; the North because of Breckinridge's fearful repulse at the final onset and of Bragg's retreating in the night and refusing to fight again. A portion of the Confederate army occupied Shelbyville, Tennessee, and the larger part entrenched at Tullahoma, eighteen miles to the southeast.

Six months after the battle of Stone's River, the Federal army suddenly awoke from its somnolent condition—a winter and spring spent in raids and unimportant skirmishes—and became very busy preparing for a long and hasty march. Rosecrans' plan of campaign was brilliant and proved most effective. He realized that Tullahoma was the barrier to Chattanooga, and determined to drive the Confederates from it.

On June 23, 1863, the advance began. The cavalry, under General Stanley, had received orders to advance upon Shelbyville on the 24th, and during that night to build immense and numerous camp-fires before the Confederate stronghold at Shelbyville, to create the impression that Rosecrans' entire army was massing at that point. But the wily leader of the Federals had other plans, and when Stanley, supported by General Granger, had built his fires, the larger force was closing in upon Tullahoma.

The stratagem dawned upon Bragg too late to check Rosecrans' plans. Stanley and Granger made a brilliant capture of Shelbyville, and Bragg retired to Tullahoma; but finding here that every disposition had been made to fall upon his rear, he continued his southward retreat toward Chattanooga.

THE SIEGES OF VICKSBURG
AND PORT HUDSON

CONFEDERATE FORTS THAT HELD THE STEEP RIVER-BANKS
AT PORT HUDSON, 1863

FEDERAL GUNS AND A CONFEDERATE CAMERA

The Second, Fourth, and Sixth Massachusetts Light Artillery at Baton Rouge, in May, 1862, photographed by Lytle, of the Confederate Secret Service. When Farragut's fleet, after the capture of New Orleans, moved up the Mississippi on May 2d, General Williams, with fourteen hundred men, including two sections of Everett's (Sixth) battery, accompanied it. The ambitious plan was the opening of the Mississippi and the establishment of communication with the Federal forces to the north. Occupying Baton Rouge, the expedition pushed on to Vicksburg. Here Farragut's guns could not be sufficiently elevated to silence the batteries on the bluff,

THE FIRST BATTERIES SENT AGAINST VICKSBURG

in the face of which Williams could not land.   After three weeks on the crowded transports, the men were returned to Baton Rouge and went into camp.   On the 20th of June, General Williams again set out for Vicksburg with four regiments and Nims's (Second) and Everett's (Sixth) Massachusetts batteries.   At Ellis's Bluff, and again at Grand Gulf, the troops drove off the Confederate field-batteries that opened on the gunboats.   But at Vicksburg no effective land attack could be made and the troops, whose numbers had been reduced by overwork, malaria, and scurvy from thirty-two hundred to but eight hundred fit for duty, returned to Baton Rouge.

FORWARDING THE RAW RECRUITS—CAIRO

In the fall of 1862 all the available river-steamers were busy transporting newly organized regiments from Cairo to Memphis to take part in the independent expedition against Vicksburg, which had been proposed by Major-General John A. McClernand and in command of which he had been placed by secret orders from Lincoln and Stanton. Not even Grant was informed of this division of authority. McClernand, who was influential in the West, raised in Indiana, Illinois, and Iowa some thirty regiments of volunteers, two-thirds of which had been forwarded to Cairo and Memphis by November 10th, and at the latter place were being drilled into shape by Sherman. Both Sherman and Grant supposed that they were the promised reënforcements for the expedition which they had planned together. On December 12th Sherman was ready to move, and on the 19th transports arrived at Memphis and the embarkation of the troops began. Next day they moved down the river, convoyed by Porter's fleet. On the 26th Sherman landed thirteen miles up the Yazoo River and advanced to Chickasaw Bluffs, where on the 29th he assaulted the defenses of Vicksburg to the north. The news of the failure of Grant's land expedition at Oxford had reached McClernand instead of Sherman, and as the latter general emerged from the swamps with his defeated divisions, McClernand, on New Year's Day, met him at the mouth of the Yazoo and superseded him in command.

FEDERAL TRANSPORTS ON THE MISSISSIPPI
ONE SMOKESTACK DAMAGED BY CONFEDERATE FIRE FROM THE RIVER BANK

WHERE GRANT'S CAMPAIGN WAS HALTED

The Courthouse at Oxford, Mississippi. The second attempt to capture Vicksburg originated with Grant. Since he had sprung into fame at Fort Donelson early in 1862, he had done little to strengthen his reputation; but to all urgings of his removal Lincoln replied: "I can't spare this man; he fights." He proposed to push southward through Mississippi to seize Jackson, the capital. If this could be accomplished, Vicksburg (fifty miles to the west) would become untenable. At Washington his plan was overruled to the extent of dividing his forces. Sherman, with a separate expedition, was to move from Memphis down the Mississippi directly against Vicksburg. It was Grant's hope that by marching on he could unite with Sherman in an assault upon this key to the Mississippi. Pushing forward from Grand Junction, sixty miles, Grant reached Oxford December 5. 1862, but his supplies were still drawn from Columbus, Kentucky, over a single-track road to Holly Springs, and thence by wagon over roads which were rapidly becoming impassable. Delay ensued in which Van Dorn destroyed Federal stores at Holly Springs worth $1,500,000. This put an end to Grant's advance. In the picture we see an Illinois regiment guarding some of the 1200 Confederate prisoners taken during the advance and here confined in the Courthouse.

VICKSBURG PROVES IMPREGNABLE

Chickasaw Bayou. Here rested Sherman's extreme left, December 28, 1862, after a day's advance over bottom-lands of extreme difficulty. From this point, after sharp skirmishing which discomforted the advancing Federals, at nightfall the Confederates retired to their works on the bluff beyond, confident of being able to repel the assault that was to come. That confidence was not misplaced. Sherman had miscalculated in two particulars—chiefly in supposing that Grant was close at hand to support him. Furthermore, he did not know that his movements had been daily reported and that Johnston and Pemberton were fully aware of his strength. On the very day that Sherman landed on the Yazoo, Pemberton arrived in Vicksburg with reënforcements, bringing the garrison up to twelve thousand, while Sherman supposed that he was to contend with but half that number. Fully prepared for uncompromising defense, the Confederates were bound to win.

WHERE SHERMAN FAILED

Chickasaw Bluffs. Stretching northeast from Vicksburg, Walnut Hill forms a perfect natural fortress overlooking the bottom-lands toward the Yazoo, rising to a height of two hundred feet, as seen in the picture. In the whole twelve miles between Haynes' Bluff (where Sherman landed) and Vicksburg, there were but five points where troops could pass from the Yazoo through the network of bayous and swamps to attack this bluff, and all these points were commanded by Confederate batteries. Sherman had considerable difficulty in properly posting his troops during the determined skirmishing kept up by the Confederates on the 28th. On the 29th, at noon, he gave the signal for the assault. The two brigades of De Courcy and Blair, together with the Fourth Iowa—six thousand men in all—bore the brunt of the fighting and charged gallantly up to the Confederate works. There, unsupported, they were cut to pieces by the cross-fire that was poured upon them. Sherman, who had lost nearly two thousand, decided that the position was impregnable. A thousand men could have held it against ten times their number.

THE LEADER AT HAYNES' BLUFF

U. S. S. *Choctaw*, resting peacefully at Vicksburg after the surrender. She had led the other gunboats in the attack upon Haynes' Bluff on the Yazoo, simultaneous with Sherman's second demonstration against the defenses northeast of Vicksburg. Grant distracted Pemberton long enough to enable the Federals to concentrate to the south of the city for its final investment. Since the end of January, Grant (again in supreme command) had been working hard with tentative operations, first for the completion of the canal begun by General Williams the previous year, then for the cutting of the levee at Yazoo Pass to flood the bottom-lands and enable gunboats to engage in amphibious warfare.

"WHISTLING DICK"—THE PET OF THE CONFEDERATE GUNNERS

This 18-pounder rifle, made at the Tredegar Iron Works at Richmond, was mounted in the Vicksburg water-batteries overlooking the Mississippi. Porter's fleet was exposed to its fire when it passed down the river on the night of April 16, 1863. From the peculiar sound of its missiles speeding through the air it earned the nickname "Whistling Dick." It was a monster of its time; its fire sunk the Federal gunboat *Cincinnati* on May 28th. Finally it was disabled and silenced by the Federal batteries from across the river.

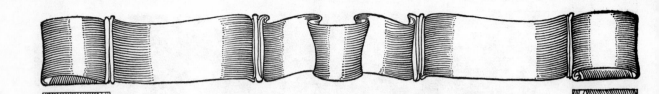

VICKSBURG AND PORT HUDSON

On the banks of this, the greatest river in the world, the most decisive and far-reaching battle of the war was fought. Here at Vicksburg over one hundred thousand gallant soldiers and a powerful fleet of gunboats and ironclads in terrible earnestness for forty days and nights fought to decide whether the new Confederate States should be cut in twain; whether the great river should flow free to the Gulf, or should have its commerce hindered. We all know the result—the Union army under General Grant, and the Union navy under Admiral Porter were victorious. The Confederate army, under General Pemberton, numbering thirty thousand men, was captured and General Grant's army set free for operating in other fields. It was a staggering blow from which the Confederacy never rallied.—*Lieutenant-General Stephen D. Lee, C.S.A., at the dedication of the Massachusetts Volunteers' statue at the Vicksburg National Military Park, Vicksburg, Mississippi, November 14, 1903.*

THE Mississippi River, in its lower course, winds like a mighty serpent from side to side along a vast alluvial bottom, which in places is more than forty miles in width. On the eastern bank, these great coils here and there sweep up to the bluffs of the highlands of Tennessee and Mississippi. On these cliffs are situated Memphis, Port Hudson, Grand Gulf, and Vicksburg. The most important of these from a military point of view was Vicksburg, often called the " Gibraltar of the West." Situated two hundred feet above the current, on a great bend of the river, its cannon could command the waterway for miles in either direction, while the obstacles in the way of a land approach were almost equally insurmountable.

The Union arms had captured New Orleans, in the spring of 1862, and Memphis in June of that year; but the Confederates still held Vicksburg and Port Hudson and the two hundred and fifty miles of river that lies between them. The military

WHERE VICKSBURG'S FATE WAS SEALED

The Battle-field of Champion's Hill. Here on May 16, 1863, Grant crowned his daring maneuver against Vicksburg from the south with complete success. Once across the river below Grand Gulf, after an easy victory at Port Gibson, he was joined by Sherman. The army struck out across the strange country south of the Big Black River and soon had driven Pemberton's southern outposts across that stream. Grant was now on solid ground; he had successfully turned the flank of the Confederates and he grasped the opportunity to strike a telling blow. Pressing forward to Raymond and Jackson, he captured both, and swept westward to meet the astounded Pemberton, still vacillating between attempting a junction with Johnston or attacking Grant in the rear. But Grant, moving with wonderful precision, prevented either movement. On May 16th a battle ensued which was most decisive around Champion's Hill. Pemberton was routed and put to flight, and on the next day the Federals seized the crossings of the Big Black River. Spiking their guns at Haynes' Bluff, the Confederates retired into Vicksburg, never to come out again except as prisoners. In eighteen days from the time he crossed the Mississippi, Grant had gained the advantage for which the Federals had striven for more than a year at Vicksburg.

object of the Federal armies in the West was to gain control of the entire course of the great Mississippi that it might " roll unvexed to the sea," to use Lincoln's terse expression, and that the rich States of the Southwest, from which the Confederacy drew large supplies and thousands of men for her armies, might be cut off from the rest of the South. If Vicksburg were captured, Port Hudson must fall. The problem, therefore, was how to get control of Vicksburg.

On the promotion of Halleck to the command of all the armies of the North, with headquarters at Washington, Grant was left in superior command in the West and the great task before him was the capture of the " Gibraltar of the West." Vicksburg might have been occupied by the Northern armies at any time during the first half of the year 1862, but in June of that year General Bragg sent Van Dorn with a force of fifteen thousand to occupy and fortify the heights. Van Dorn was a man of prodigious energy. In a short time he had hundreds of men at work planting batteries, digging rifle-pits above the water front and in the rear of the town, mounting heavy guns and building bomb-proof magazines in tiers along the hillsides. All through the summer, the work progressed under the direction of Engineer S. H. Lockett, and by the coming of winter the city was a veritable Gibraltar.

From the uncompleted batteries on the Vicksburg bluffs, the citizens and the garrison soldiers viewed the advance division of Farragut's fleet, under Commander Lee, in the river, on May 18, 1863. Fifteen hundred infantry were on board, under command of General Thomas Williams, and with them was a battery of artillery. Williams reconnoitered the works, and finding them too strong for his small force he returned to occupy Baton Rouge. The authorities at Washington now sent Farragut peremptory orders to clear the Mississippi and accordingly about the middle of June, a flotilla of steamers and seventeen mortar schooners, under Commander D. D. Porter, departed from New Orleans and steamed up the river.

THE BRIDGE THE CONFEDERATES BURNED AT BIG BLACK RIVER

THE FIRST FEDERAL CROSSING—SHERMAN'S PONTOONS

The pursuit of Pemberton's army brought McClernand's Corps to the defenses of the Big Black River Bridge early on May 17, 1863. McPherson was close behind. McClernand's division carried the defenses and Bowen and Vaughn's men fled with precipitate haste over the dreary swamp to the river and crossed over and burned the railroad and other bridges just in time to prevent McClernand from following. The necessary delay was aggravating to Grant's forces. The rest of the day and night was consumed in building bridges. Sherman had the only pontoon-train with the army and his bridge was the first ready at Bridgeport, early in the evening.

Simultaneously Farragut headed a fleet of three war vessels and seven gunboats, carrying one hundred and six guns, toward Vicksburg from Baton Rouge. Many transports accompanied the ships from Baton Rouge, on which there were three thousand of Williams' troops.

The last days of June witnessed the arrival of the combined naval forces of Farragut and Porter below the Confederate stronghold. Williams immediately disembarked his men on the Louisiana shore, opposite Vicksburg, and they were burdened with implements required in digging trenches and building levees.

The mighty Mississippi, at this point and in those days, swept in a majestic bend and formed a peninsula of the western, or Louisiana shore. Vicksburg was situated on the eastern, or Mississippi shore, below the top of the bend. Its batteries of cannon commanded the river approach for miles in either direction. Federal engineers quickly recognized the strategic position of the citadel on the bluff; and also as quickly saw a method by which the passage up and down the river could be made comparatively safe for their vessels, and at the same time place Vicksburg "high and dry" by cutting a channel for the Mississippi through the neck of land that now held it in its sinuous course.

While Farragut stormed the Confederate batteries at Vicksburg, Williams began the tremendous task of diverting the mighty current across the peninsula. Farragut's bombardment by his entire fleet failed to silence Vicksburg's cannon-guards, although the defenders likewise failed to stop the progress of the fleet. The Federal naval commander then determined to dash past the fortifications, trusting to the speed of his vessels and the stoutness of their armor to survive the tremendous cannonade that would fall upon his flotilla. Early in the morning of June 28th the thrilling race against death began, and after two hours of terrific bombardment aided by the mortar boats stationed on both banks, Farragut's fleet with

Vicksburg, taken under fire.

THE GATE TO THE MISSISSIPPI

The handwriting is that of Surgeon Bixby, of the Union hospital ship "Red Rover." In his album he pasted this unique photograph from the western shore of the river where the Federal guns and mortars threw a thousand shells into Vicksburg during the siege. The prominent building is the courthouse, the chief landmark during the investment. Here at Vicksburg the Confederates were making their last brave stand for the possession of the Mississippi River, that great artery of traffic. If it were wre ted from them the main source of their supplies would be cut off. Pemberton, a brave and capable officer and a Pennsylvanian by birth, worked unremittingly for the cause he had espoused. Warned by the early attacks of General Williams and Admiral Farragut, he had left no stone unturned to render Vicksburg strongly defended. It had proved impregnable to attack on the north and east, and the powerful batteries planted on the river-front could not be silenced by the fleet nor by the guns of the Federals on the opposite shore. But Grant's masterful maneuver of cutting loose from his base and advancing from the south had at last out-generaled both Pemberton and Johnston. Nevertheless, Pemberton stoutly held his defenses. His high river-battery is photographed below, as it frowned upon the Federals opposite.

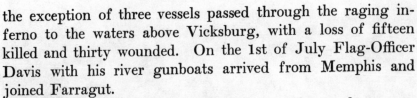

the exception of three vessels passed through the raging inferno to the waters above Vicksburg, with a loss of fifteen killed and thirty wounded. On the 1st of July Flag-Officer Davis with his river gunboats arrived from Memphis and joined Farragut.

Williams and his men, including one thousand negroes, labored like Titans to complete their canal, but a sudden rise of the river swept away the barriers with a terrific roar, and the days of herculean labor went for naught. Again Williams' attempt to subdue the stronghold was abandoned, and he returned with his men when Farragut did, on July 24th, to Baton Rouge to meet death there on August 5th when General Breckinridge made a desperate but unsuccessful attempt to drive the Union forces from the Louisiana capital.

Farragut urged upon General Halleck the importance of occupying the city on the bluff with a portion of his army; but that general gave no heed; and while even then it was too late to secure the prize without a contest, it would have been easy in comparison to that which it required a year later.

In the mean time, the river steamers took an important part in the preliminary operations against the city. Davis remained at Memphis with his fleet for about three weeks after the occupation of that city on the 6th of June, meanwhile sending four gunboats and a transport up the White River, with the Forty-sixth Indiana regiment, under Colonel Fitch. The object of the expedition, undertaken at Halleck's command, was to destroy Confederate batteries and to open communication with General Curtis, who was approaching from the west. It failed in the latter purpose but did some effective work with the Southern batteries along the way.

The one extraordinary incident of the expedition was the disabling of the *Mound City,* one of the ironclad gunboats, and the great loss of life that it occasioned. When near St. Charles the troops under Fitch were landed, and the *Mound City* moving up the river, was fired on by concealed batteries

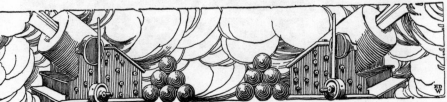

THE WELL–DEFENDED CITADEL

Behind these fortifications Pemberton, driven from the Big Black River, gathered his twenty-one thousand troops to make the last stand for the saving of the Mississippi to the Confederacy.   In the upper picture we see Fort Castle, one of the strongest defenses of the Confederacy.   It had full sweep of the river; here "Whistling Dick" (one of the most powerful guns in possession of the South) did deadly work.   In the lower picture we see the fortifications to the east of the town, before which Grant's army was now entrenching.   When Vicksburg had first been threatened in 1862, the Confederate fortifications had been laid out and work begun on them in haste with but five hundred spades, many of the soldiers delving with their bayonets.   The sites were so well chosen and the work so well done that they had withstood attacks for a year.   They were to hold out still longer.   By May 18th the Federals had completely invested Vicksburg, and Grant and Sherman rode out to Haynes' Bluff to view the open river to the north, down which abundant supplies were now coming for the army.   Sherman, who had not believed that the plan could succeed, frankly acknowledged his mistake.   But the Mississippi was not yet theirs.   Sherman, assaulting the fortifications of Vicksburg, the next day, was repulsed.   A second attack, on the 22d, failed and on the 25th Grant settled down to starve Pemberton out.

under the direction of Lieutenant Dunnington. A 32-pound shot struck the vessel, crashed through the side and passed through the steam-drum. The steam filled the vessel in an instant. Many of the men were so quickly enveloped in the scalding vapor that they had no chance to escape. Others leaped overboard, some being drowned and some rescued through the efforts of the *Conestoga* which was lying near. While straining every nerve to save their lives, the men had to endure a shower of bullets from Confederate sharpshooters on the river banks. Of the one hundred and seventy-five officers and men of the *Mound City* only twenty-five escaped death or injury in that fearful catastrophe. Meanwhile, Colonel Fitch with his land forces rushed upon the Confederate batteries and captured them. The unfortunate vessel was at length repaired and returned to service.

For some time it had been known in Federal military and naval circles that a powerful ironclad similar to the famous *Monitor* of Eastern waters was being rushed to completion up the Yazoo. The new vessel was the *Arkansas*. She and a sister ship were building at Memphis when the capture of that city was anticipated by the destruction of one of them. The work on the *Arkansas* was far enough advanced for her to be taken to Yazoo City for the finishing touches. The Union fleet was not unduly terrified by tales of the monster, but nevertheless Farragut and Davis determined to find out what they could about her. Three vessels were chosen for the reconnaissance— the ironclad *Carondelet,* the wooden *Tyler,* and the Ellet ram *Queen of the West.* Bravely they steamed up the Yazoo on the morning of July 15th, but before they had gone more than six miles they encountered the *Arkansas,* under the command of Captain Isaac N. Brown, coming down the river.

The *Carondelet,* though supported at a distance by the *Tyler,* fled before her stronger antagonist, being raked from stem to stern, struck several times with solid shot, and saved from destruction only by running into shallow water where

[196]

THE WORK OF THE BESIEGERS

Battery Sherman, on the Jackson Road, before Vicksburg. Settling down to a siege did not mean idleness for Grant's army. Fortifications had to be opposed to the formidable one of the Confederates and a constant bombardment kept up to silence their guns, one by one. It was to be a drawn-out duel in which Pemberton, hoping for the long-delayed relief from Johnston, held out bravely against starvation and even mutiny. For twelve miles the Federal lines stretched around Vicksburg, investing it to the river bank, north and south. More than eighty-nine battery positions were constructed by the Federals. Battery Sherman was exceptionally well built—not merely revetted with rails or cotton-bales and floored with rough timber, as lack of proper material often made necessary. Gradually the lines were drawn closer and closer as the Federals moved up their guns to silence the works that they had failed to take in May. At the time of the surrender Grant had more than 220 guns in position, mostly of heavy caliber. By the 1st of July besieged and besiegers faced each other at a distance of half-pistol shot. Starving and ravaged by disease, the Confederates had repelled repeated attacks which depleted their forces, while Grant, reenforced to three times their number, was showered with supplies and ammunition that he might bring about the long-delayed victory which the North had been eagerly awaiting since Chancellorsville.

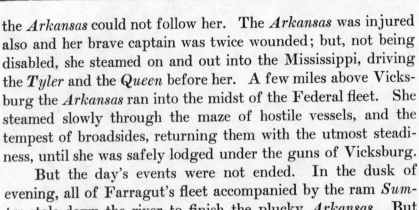

the *Arkansas* could not follow her. The *Arkansas* was injured also and her brave captain was twice wounded; but, not being disabled, she steamed on and out into the Mississippi, driving the *Tyler* and the *Queen* before her. A few miles above Vicksburg the *Arkansas* ran into the midst of the Federal fleet. She steamed slowly through the maze of hostile vessels, and the tempest of broadsides, returning them with the utmost steadiness, until she was safely lodged under the guns of Vicksburg.

But the day's events were not ended. In the dusk of evening, all of Farragut's fleet accompanied by the ram *Sumter* stole down the river to finish the plucky *Arkansas*. But she changed her position as soon as it was dark and the Union vessels had difficulty in finding her. They came down the river amid the roar of cannon, but only one 11-inch shot struck her as the fleet went by, and down the river, and the broadsides from the *Arkansas* killed five and wounded sixteen of the Union crews. None of Farragut's fleet was ever seen above Vicksburg again. It returned to New Orleans, July 24th.

The *Arkansas* had another fight for her life on July 22d. Commander William D. Porter with the *Essex*, aided by the *Queen of the West,* made the attack. The crew of the *Arkansas* had been reduced by half, but the remainder fought savagely and saved their vessel from destruction.

The month of July had not been favorable to the Federal hopes. Farragut had returned to New Orleans. General Williams had gone with him as far as Baton Rouge. Davis now went with his fleet back to Helena. Halleck was succeeded by Grant. Vicksburg entered upon a period of quiet.

But this condition was temporary. The city's experience of blood and fire had only begun. During the summer and autumn of 1862, the one thought uppermost in the mind of General Grant was how to gain possession of the stronghold. He was already becoming known for his bull-dog tenacity. In the autumn, two important changes took place, but one day apart. On October 14th, General John C. Pemberton

A GOOD POLITICIAN WHO BECAME A GREAT SOLDIER

MAJOR–GENERAL JOHN ALEXANDER LOGAN AND STAFF IN VICKSBURG, JULY, 1863

John A. Logan, a War Democrat who left Congress to fight as a private in a Michigan regiment at Bull Run, was one of the mainstays of the Federal cause in the West. A successful lawyer and brilliant orator, he proved to be one of the most successful civilian generals of the war. In Grant's Vicksburg campaign, Logan's soldierly qualities came particularly into prominence. His division of McPherson's Corps distinguished itself in the battle of Raymond, Mississippi, and again at that of Champion's Hill, which sounded the knell of Vicksburg. It was Logan's division that marched in on the Jackson road to take possession of the fallen city, July 4, 1863. For his services in the campaign Logan was made a major-general.

succeeded Van Dorn in command of the defenses of Vicksburg, and on the next day David D. Porter succeeded Davis as commander of the Federal fleet on the upper Mississippi.

So arduous was the task of taking Vicksburg that the wits of General Grant, and those of his chief adviser, General W. T. Sherman, were put to the test in the last degree to accomplish the end. Grant knew that the capture of this fortified city was of great importance to the Federal cause, and that it would ever be looked upon as one of the chief acts in the drama of the Civil War.

The first plan attempted was to divide the army, Sherman taking part of it from Memphis and down the Mississippi on transports, while Grant should move southward along the line of the Mississippi Central Railroad to cooperate with Sherman, his movements to be governed by the efforts of the scattered Confederate forces in Mississippi to block him. But the whole plan was destined to failure, through the energies of General Van Dorn and others of the Confederate army near Grant's line of communication.

The authorities at Washington preferred the river move upon Vicksburg, as the navy could keep the line of communication open. The stronghold now stood within a strong line of defense extending from Haynes' Bluff on the Yazoo to Grand Gulf on the Mississippi, thirty miles below Vicksburg. To prepare for Sherman's attack across the swamps of the Yazoo, Admiral Porter made several expeditions up that tortuous stream to silence batteries and remove torpedoes. In one of these he lost one of the Eads ironclads, the *Cairo*, blown up by a torpedo, and in another the brave Commander Gwin, one of the heroes of Shiloh, was mortally wounded.

Sherman, with an army of thirty-two thousand men, left Memphis on December 20th, and landed a few days later some miles north of Vicksburg on the banks of the Yazoo. On the 29th he made a daring attack in three columns on the Confederate lines of defense at Chickasaw Bayou and suffered a

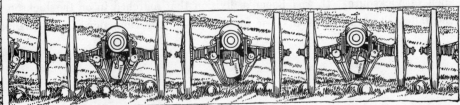

INVESTING BY INCHES

Logan's Division undermining the most formidable redoubt in the defenses of Vicksburg. The position was immediately in front of this honeycombed slope on the Jackson road. Upon these troops fell most of the labor of sapping and mining, which finally resulted in the wrecking of the fort so gallantly defended by the veterans of the Third Louisiana. As the Federal lines crept up, the men working night and day were forced to live in burrows. They became proficient in such gopher work as the picture shows. Up to the "White House" (Shirley's) the troops could be marched in comparative safety, but a short distance beyond they were exposed to the Confederate sharpshooters, who had only rifles and muskets to depend on; their artillery had long since been silenced. Near this house was constructed "Coonskin's" Tower; it was built of railway iron and cross-ties under the direction of Second Lieutenant Henry C. Foster, of Company B, Twenty-third Indiana. A backwoodsman and dead-shot, he was particularly active in paying the Confederate sharpshooters in their own coin. He habitually wore a cap of raccoon fur, which gave him his nickname and christened the tower, from which the interior of the Confederate works could be seen.

decisive repulse. His loss was nearly two thousand men; the Confederate loss was scarcely two hundred.

Two hundred feet above the bayou, beyond where the Federals were approaching, towered the Chickasaw Bluffs, to which Pemberton hastened troops from Vicksburg as soon as he learned Sherman's object. At the base of the bluff, and stretching away to the north and west were swamps and forests intersected by deep sloughs, overhung with dense tangles of vines and cane-brakes. Federal valor vied with Confederate pluck in this fight among the marshes and fever-infested jungle-land.

One of Sherman's storming parties, under General G. W. Morgan, came upon a broad and deep enlargement of the bayou, McNutt Lake, which interposed between it and the Confederates in the rifle-pits on the slopes and crest of the bluff. In the darkness of the night of December 28th, the Federal pontoniers labored to construct a passage-way across the lake. When morning dawned the weary pontoniers were chagrined to discover their well-built structure spanning a slough leading in another direction than toward the base of the bluff. The bridge was quickly taken up, and the Federals recommenced their labors, this time in daylight and within sight and range of the Southern regiments on the hill. The men in blue worked desperately to complete the span before driven away by the foe's cannon; but the fire increased with every minute, and the Federals finally withdrew.

Another storming party attempted to assail the Confederates from across a sandbar of the bayou, but was halted at the sight and prospect of overcoming a fifteen-foot bank on the farther side. The crumbling bank was surmounted with a levee three feet high; the steep sides of the barrier had crumbled away, leaving an overhanging shelf, two feet wide. Two companies of the Sixth Missouri regiment volunteered to cross the two hundred yards of exposed passage, and to cut a roadway through the rotten bank to allow their comrades a free

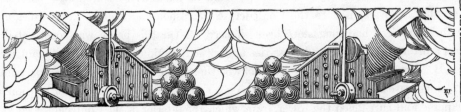

THE FIRST MONUMENT AT THE MEETING PLACE

Independence Day, 1863, was a memorable anniversary of the nation's birth; it brought to the anxious North the momentous news that Meade had won at Gettysburg and that Vicksburg had fallen in the West. The marble shaft in the picture was erected to mark the spot where Grant and Pemberton met on July 3d to confer about the surrender. Under a tree, within a few hundred feet of the Confederate lines, Grant greeted his adversary as an old acquaintance. They had fought in the same division for a time in the Mexican War. Each spoke but two sentences as to the surrender, for Grant lived up to the nickname he gained at Donelson, and Pemberton's pride was hurt. The former comrades walked and talked awhile on other things, and then returned to their lines. Next day the final terms were arranged by correspondence, and the Confederates marched out with colors flying; they stacked their arms and, laying their colors upon them, marched back into the city to be paroled. Those who signed the papers not to fight until exchanged numbered 29,391. The tree where the commanders met was soon carried away, root and branch, by relic-hunters. Subsequently the monument which replaced it was chipped gradually into bits, and in 1866 a 64-pounder cannon took its place as a permanent memorial.

VICKSBURG IN POSSESSION OF THE FEDERALS

path to the bluff beyond. To add to the peril of the crossing, the sandbar was strewn with tangles of undergrowth and fallen trees, and the Confederate shells and bullets were raining upon the ground. Still, the gallant troops began their dash. From the very start, a line of wounded and dead Missourians marked the passage of the volunteers. The survivors reached the bank and desperately sought to dig the roadway. From the shrubbery on the bank suddenly appeared Confederate sharpshooters who poured their fire into the laboring soldiers; the flame of the discharging muskets burned the clothing of the Federals because the hostile forces were so close. Human endurance could not stand before this carnage, and the brave Missourians fled from the inferno. Sherman now found the northern pathway to Vicksburg impassable, and withdrew his men to the broad Mississippi.

Earlier in the same month had occurred two other events which, with the defeat of Chickasaw, go to make up the triple disaster to the Federals. On the 11th, General Nathan Forrest, one of the most brilliant cavalry leaders on either side, began one of those destructive raids which characterize the Civil War. With twenty-five hundred horsemen, Forrest dashed unopposed through the country north of Grant's army, tore up sixty miles of railroad and destroyed all telegraph lines.

Meantime, on December 20th, the day on which Sherman left Memphis, General Van Dorn pounced upon Holly Springs, in Mississippi, like an eagle on its prey, capturing the guard of fifteen hundred men and burning the great store of supplies, worth $1,500,000, which Grant had left there. Through the raids of Forrest and Van Dorn, Grant was left without supplies and for eleven days without communication with the outside world. He marched northward to Grand Junction, in Tennessee, a distance of eighty miles, living off the country. It was not until January 8, 1863, that he heard, through Washington, of the defeat of Sherman in his assault on Chickasaw Bluffs.

SHIRLEY'S RESIDENCE, "THE WHITE HOUSE"

Illinois sent into the war Grant, Logan, McClernand, Grierson, and other prominent leaders in the Vicksburg campaign. It was one of the few States which furnished troops in excess of their quota. The Seventy-second Illinois Infantry, whose synonym was "First Board of Trade," together with other Illinois regiments, saw severe active service along the Mississippi and at Vicksburg; it served in General McArthur's division of the Seventeenth Corps, and distinguished itself on November 30th of the following year in the battle of Franklin, Tenn.

BARRACKS OF FIFTH U. S. COLORED HEAVY ARTILLERY

VICKSBURG IN FEDERAL HANDS

Shirley's "White House," on the Jackson road, stood between the opposing lines; although a target for both sides, it remained practically uninjured. General Lieb's colored regiment was recruited in Louisiana and Mississippi and organized at Vicksburg in August, 1863. It suffered a heavy loss in deaths from fever, being stationed along the river. In the assault on Port Hudson colored troops were first used by the Federals in a general engagement — the First Louisiana Native Guard of the "Corps d'Afrique," organized by General Butler.

HEADQUARTERS 72ND ILLINOIS VOLUNTEERS

Grant and Sherman had no thought of abandoning Vicksburg because of this failure. But a month of unfortunate military dissension over rank in the command of Sherman's army resulted in General John A. McClernand, armed with authority from Washington, coming down from Illinois and superseding Sherman. On January 11, 1864, he captured Arkansas Post, a stronghold on the Arkansas River. But Grant, having authority to supersede McClernand in the general proceedings against Vicksburg, did so, on January 30th, and arguments on military precedence were forgotten.

Grant was determined to lead his Army of the Tennessee below Vicksburg and approach the city from the south, without breaking with his base of supplies up the river. Two projects, both of which were destined to fail, were under way during the winter and spring months of 1863. One of these was to open a way for the river craft through Lake Providence, west of the Mississippi, through various bayous and rivers into the Red River, a detour of four hundred miles.

Another plan was to cut a channel through the peninsula of the great bend of the Mississippi, opposite Vicksburg. For six weeks, thousands of men worked like marmots digging this ditch; but, meantime, the river was rising and, on March 8th, it broke over the embankment and the men had to run for their lives. Many horses were drowned and a great number of implements submerged. The " Father of Waters " had put a decisive veto on the project and it had to be given up. Still another plan that failed was to cut through the Yazoo Pass and approach from the north by way of the Coldwater, the Tallahatchie, and the Yazoo rivers.

Failure with Grant only increased his grim determination. He *would* take Vicksburg. His next plan was destined to bring success. It was to transfer his army by land down the west bank of the Mississippi to a point below the city and approach it from the south and west. This necessitated the running of the batteries by Porter's fleet—an extremely

[206]

THE CONFEDERACY CUT IN TWAIN

The Levee at Vicksburg, February, 1864.   For seven months the Federals had been in possession of the city, and the Mississippi—now open through its entire course—cut off the struggling Confederacy in the East from the South and Southwest, the storehouses of their resources and their main dependence in continuing the struggle.   But even such a blow as this, coming on top of Gettysburg, did not force the brave people of the South to give up the struggle.   In the picture the only remaining warlike signs are the tents on the opposite shore.   But on both sides of the river the Confederates were still desperately striving to reunite their territory.   In the East another year and more of the hardest kind of fighting was ahead; another severing in twain of the South was inevitable before peace could come, and before the muskets could be used to shoot the crows, and before their horses could plough the neglected fields.

GUNS THAT HELPED TO REDUCE PORT HUDSON

This picture is another example of the accuracy and completeness with which Lytle, the Confederate Secret Service photographer at Baton Rouge, recorded the numbers and equipment of the Federal forces operating in Louisiana. This body of artillery first enlisted as the Twenty-first Volunteers in 1861, and sustained the heavy loss of one hundred and twenty-six men while acting as infantry in the battle of Baton Rouge, August 5, 1862. It served with distinction throughout the war, its number of veteran reënlistments being five hundred and three—the largest in any body of Indiana troops. In March, 1863, the regiment was changed to artillery; and in Augur's division of the Nineteenth Corps it accompanied General Banks in his first expedition against Port Hudson, as well as in the final investment of that place. Banks, who had been sent with between fifteen thousand and twenty thousand troops to suc-

FIRST INDIANA HEAVY ARTILLERY, 1863

ceed General Butler in command of the Department of the Gulf, arrived at New Orleans in the middle of December, 1862, with orders from Halleck to advance up the Mississippi, and (in coöperation with Grant) to hold an unbroken line of communication by land from New Orleans to Vicksburg. When this was accomplished he was to occupy the Red River country as a basis for future operations against Texas. During the winter, Banks confined his attention to operations west of the Mississippi, with varying success. Early in March, at the request of Farragut, who had determined to run past the Port Hudson batteries with his fleet, Banks moved forward with about seventeen thousand men to make a demonstration against that place with his artillery. He did not get near enough to do this, however, and was still building bridges when near midnight of March 14th Farragut's guns began to boom from the river.

THE LAST STRONGHOLD ON THE MISSISSIPPI

Confederate Fortifications on the bluff overlooking the Mississippi at Port Hudson, Louisiana. At Port Hudson the east bank of the river rises steeply in a bluff eighty feet high, forming a perfect natural fortress. When Breckinridge failed in his attempt to recapture Baton Rouge in 1862, he retired to Port Hudson, thirty miles farther up the river, and by the middle of August the fortifying of that place was well advanced, the object being to hold the Mississippi between this point and Vicksburg, so that supplies coming from Arkansas by way of the Red River would not be cut off from the Confederacy. Within the heavy parapets, twenty feet thick, the Confederates mounted twenty siege-guns along the bluff, completely commanding the river. It was therefore no light task that Farragut took upon himself when on the night of March 14th he attempted to run by these batteries with his fleet. Five of his seven vessels were disabled, the *Mississippi* running aground and being abandoned and burned by her commander. Farragut, in the famous *Hartford*, with the *Albatross* lashed to her side, barely escaped running aground under the guns of the batteries in the darkness. Finally he got safely by, and the object of the gallant fight was accomplished.

THE WELL–PLANTED BATTERIES

Confederate Siege-gun Mounted in the River Fortifications at Port Hudson. Twenty of these great pieces thundered at Farragut's fleet till long after midnight on March 14, 1863. Although the objective was not so important to the Federals as in the famous fight at New Orleans, the engagement at Port Hudson was scarcely less brilliant, and its outcome was more costly to the navy, which lost the valuable steam corvette *Mississippi*, mounting nineteen guns. The fleet lost 113 men in action. Farragut had the superiority in number and weight of metal, but this was more than offset by the advantageous position of the Confederates. A successful shot from the ship could do little more than tear up the earth in the fortifications on the bluff, while every shot from the shore that told might mean the piercing of a boiler or the disabling of a rudder, rendering a ship helpless. To add to the disadvantages, Farragut's intention was discovered at the outset. A river steamer approached with flaring lights and tooting whistles and ran through the fleet, up to the *Hartford*, merely bringing the word that Banks was within five miles of Port Hudson. Thus the fleet was discovered and the Confederates, illuminating the river with piles of blazing pine-knots, trained their guns with deadly precision on the advancing vessels.

perilous enterprise. The army was divided into four corps, commanded respectively by Sherman, McClernand, McPherson, and Hurlbut. The latter was stationed at Memphis. On March 29th, the movement of McClernand from Milliken's Bend to a point opposite Grand Gulf was begun. He was soon followed by McPherson and a few weeks later by Sherman. It required a month for the army, with its heavy artillery, to journey through the swamps and bogs of Louisiana.

While this march was in progress, something far more exciting was taking place on the river. Porter ran the batteries of Vicksburg with his fleet. After days of preparation the fleet of vessels, protected by cotton bales and hay about the vital parts of the boats, with heavy logs slung near the water-line—seven gunboats, the ram *General Price,* three transports, and various barges were ready for the dangerous journey on the night of April 16th. Silently in the darkness, they left their station near the mouth of the Yazoo, at a quarter past nine. For an hour and a half all was silence and expectancy. The bluffs on the east loomed black against the night sky. Suddenly, the flash of musketry fire pierced the darkness.

In a few minutes every battery overlooking the river was a center of spurting flame. A storm of shot and shell was rained upon the passing vessels. Not one escaped being struck many times. The water of the river was lashed into foam by the shots and shell from the batteries. The gunboats answered with their cannon. The air was filled with flying missiles. Several houses on the Louisiana shore burst into flame and the whole river from shore to shore was lighted with vivid distinctness. A little later, a giant flame leaped from the bosom of the river. A vessel had caught fire. It was the transport *Henry Clay.* It burned to the water's edge, nearly all its crew escaping to other vessels. Grant described the scene as " magnificent, but terrible "; Sherman pronounced it " truly sublime."

By three in the morning, the fleet was below the city and ready to cooperate with the army. One vessel had been

WITHIN THE PARAPET AT PORT HUDSON IN THE SUMMER OF 1863

These fortifications withstood every attack of Banks' powerful army from May 24 to July 9, 1863. Like Vicksburg, Port Hudson could be reduced only by a weary siege. These pictures, taken within the fortifications, show in the distance the ground over which the investing army approached to the two unsuccessful grand assaults they made upon the Confederate defenders. The strength of the works is apparent. A continuous line of parapet, equally strong, had been thrown up for the defense of Port Hudson, surrounding the town for a distance of three miles and more, each end terminating on the riverbank. Four powerful forts were located at the salients, and the line throughout was defended by thirty pieces of field artillery. Brigadier-General Beall, who commanded the post in 1862, constructed these works. Major-General Frank Gardner succeeded him in command at the close of the year.

THE WELL–DEFENDED WORKS

CONFEDERATE FORTIFICATIONS BEFORE PORT HUDSON

Gardner was behind these defenses with a garrison of about seven thousand when Banks approached Port Hudson for the second time on May 24th. Gardner was under orders to evacuate the place and join his force to that of Johnston at Jackson, Mississippi, but the courier who brought the order arrived at the very hour when Banks began to bottle up the Confederates. On the morning of May 25th Banks drove in the Confederate skirmishers and outposts and, with an army of thirty thousand, invested the fortifications from the eastward. At 10 A.M., after an artillery duel of more than four hours, the Federals advanced to the assault of the works. Fighting in a dense forest of magnolias, amid thick undergrowth and among ravines choked with felled timber, the progress of the troops was too slow for a telling attack. The battle has been described as "a gigantic bushwhack." The Federals at the center reached the ditch in front of the Confederate works but were driven off. At nightfall the attempt was abandoned. It had cost Banks nearly two thousand men.

destroyed, several others were crippled; thirteen men had been wounded, but Grant had the assistance he needed. About a week later, six more transports performed the same feat and ran the batteries; each had two barges laden with forage and rations in tow.

Grant's next move was to transfer the army across the river and to secure a base of supplies. There, on the bluff, was Grand Gulf, a tempting spot. But the Confederate guns showed menacingly over the brow of the hill. After a fruitless bombardment by the fleet on April 29th, it was decided that a more practical place to cross the river must be sought below.

Meanwhile, Sherman was ordered by his chief to advance upon the formidable Haynes' Bluff, on the Yazoo River, some miles above the scene of his repulse in the preceding December. The message had said, "Make a demonstration on Haynes' Bluff, and make all the *show* possible." Sherman's transports, and three of Porter's gungoats, were closely followed by the Confederate soldiers who had been stationed at the series of defenses on the range of hills, and when they arrived at Snyder's Mill, just below Haynes' Bluff, on April 30th, General Hébert and several Louisiana regiments were awaiting them. On that day and the next the Confederates fiercely engaged the Union fleet and troops, and on May 2d Sherman withdrew his forces to the western bank of the Mississippi and hastened to Grant. The feint had been most successful. The Confederates had been prevented from sending reenforcements to Grand Gulf, and Grant's crossing was greatly facilitated.

The fleet passed the batteries of Grand Gulf and stopped at Bruinsburg, six miles below. A landing was soon made, the army taken across on April 30th, and a march to Port Gibson, twelve miles inland, was begun. General Bowen, Confederate commander at Grand Gulf, came out and offered battle. He was greatly outnumbered, but his troops fought gallantly throughout most of the day, May 1st, before yielding

THE GUN THAT FOOLED THE FEDERALS

A "Quaker gun" that was mounted by the Confederates in the fortifications on the bluff at the river-front before Port Hudson. This gun was hewn out of a pine log and mounted on a carriage, and a black ring was painted around the end facing the river. Throughout the siege it was mistaken by the Federals for a piece of real ordnance.

To such devices as this the beleaguered garrison was compelled constantly to resort in order to impress the superior forces investing Port Hudson with the idea that the position they sought to capture was formidably defended. The ruse was effective. Port Hudson was not again attacked from the river after the passing of Farragut's two ships.

WITHIN "THE CITADEL"

This bastion fort, near the left of the Confederate line of defenses at Port Hudson, was the strongest of their works, and here Weitzel and Grover's divisions of the Federals followed up the attack (begun at daylight of June 14th) that Banks had ordered all along the line in his second effort to capture the position. The only result was simply to advance the Federal lines from fifty to two hundred yards nearer. In front of the "citadel" an advance position was gained from which a mine was subsequently run to within a few yards of the fort.

the field. Port Gibson was then occupied by the Union army, and Grand Gulf, no longer tenable, was abandoned by the Confederates.

Grant now prepared for a campaign into the interior of Mississippi. His first intention was to cooperate with General Banks in the capture of Port Hudson, after which they would move together upon Vicksburg. But hearing that Banks would not arrive for ten days, Grant decided that he would proceed to the task before him without delay. His army at that time numbered about forty-three thousand. That under Pemberton probably forty thousand, while there were fifteen thousand Confederate troops at Jackson, Mississippi, soon to be commanded by General Joseph E. Johnston, who was hastening to that capital.

The Federal leader now determined on the bold plan of making a dash into the interior of Mississippi, beating Johnston and turning on Pemberton before their forces could be joined. This campaign is pronounced the most brilliant in the Civil War. It was truly Napoleonic in conception and execution. Grant knew that his base of supplies at Grand Gulf would be cut off by Pemberton as soon as he moved away from it. He decided, therefore, against the advice of his generals, to abandon his base altogether.

A more daring undertaking could scarcely be imagined. With a few days' rations in their haversacks the troops were to make a dash that would possibly take several weeks into the heart of a hostile country. This was certainly defying fate. When General Halleck heard of Grant's daring scheme he wired the latter from Washington, ordering him to move his army down the river and cooperate with Banks. Fortunately, this order was received too late to interfere with Grant's plans.

As soon as Sherman's divisions joined the main army the march was begun, on May 7th. An advance of this character must be made with the greatest celerity and Grant's army showed amazing speed. McPherson, who commanded the right

FIFTY-ONE PIECES OF ARTILLERY FELL INTO THE HANDS OF THE FEDERALS AT THE SURRENDER OF PORT HUDSON, MANY OF THEM BATTERED INTO SILENCE BY THE LONG BOMBARDMENT KEPT UP BY THREE FEDERAL FIELD-BATTERIES AND AN ENTIRE REGIMENT OF HEAVY ARTILLERY (THE FIRST IN-DIANA) ON THE FEDERAL SIDE.

THE CONFEDERATES HAD ONLY FIELD-PIECES WITH WHICH TO DEFEND THEIR WORKS AGAINST THE INVESTING ARMY. THE BATTERED GUNS SHOWN IN THE PICTURES WERE MOUNTED IN THE CAMP OF DURYEA'S AND BAINBRIDGE'S BAT-TERIES. THESE WORKS WERE GAR-RISONED BY THE FIFTEENTH ARKANSAS CONFEDERATE INFANTRY

wing, proceeded toward Jackson by way of Raymond and at the latter place encountered five thousand Confederates, on May 12th, who blocked his way and were prepared for fight. The battle of Raymond lasted two hours. McPherson was completely successful and the Confederates hastened to join their comrades in Jackson.

McPherson lost no time. He moved on toward Jackson, and as the last of his command left Raymond the advance of Sherman's corps reached it. That night, May 13th, Grant ordered McPherson and Sherman to march upon Jackson next morning by different roads, while McClernand was held in the rear near enough to reenforce either in case of need. The rain fell in torrents that night and, as Grant reported, in places the water was a foot deep in the road. But nothing could daunt his determined army. At eleven o'clock in the morning of the 14th, a concerted attack was made on the capital of Mississippi. A few hours' brisk fighting concluded this act of the drama, and the Stars and Stripes were unfurled on the State capitol. Among the spoils were seventeen heavy guns. That night, Grant slept in the house which Johnston had occupied the night before.

Meantime, Johnston had ordered Pemberton to detain Grant by attacking him in the rear. But Pemberton considered it more advisable to move toward Grand Gulf to separate Grant from his base of supplies, not knowing that Grant had abandoned his base. And now, with Johnston's army scattered, Grant left Sherman to burn bridges and military factories, and to tear up the railroads about Jackson while he turned fiercely on Pemberton. McPherson's corps took the lead. Grant called on McClernand to follow without delay. Then, hearing that Pemberton was marching toward him, he called on Sherman to hasten from Jackson. At Champion's Hill (Baker's Creek) Pemberton stood in the way, with eighteen thousand men.

The battle was soon in progress—the heaviest of the

THE NAVY HELPS ON LAND

A View within Federal Battery No. 10. One of the investing works before Port Hudson. Farragut's fleet of gunboats and mortar-boats assisted materially from the river above and below Port Hudson. Guns were also taken ashore from the gunboats and placed in position to assist in the bombardment which quickly laid the little hamlet of Port Hudson in ruins. This battery was situated on a wooded height about a mile to the east of the town; its 9-inch Dahlgren guns were kept warm hurling shells at the Confederate forti-fications throughout the siege. Lieutenant Terry, of the "Richmond," was in command of this battery with a detachment from his vessel, which in the effort to run past Port Hudson in March had received a shot in her safety-valves, rendering her engines useless and forcing her to turn back. The "Richmond" mounted twenty such guns as are seen in the picture, besides two heavy rifles.

campaign. It continued for seven or eight hours. The Confederates were defeated with a loss of nearly all their artillery and about half their force, including four thousand men who were cut off from the main army and failed to rejoin it. On the banks of the Big Black River, a few miles westward, the Confederates made another stand, and here the fifth battle of the investment of Vicksburg took place. It was short, sharp, decisive. The Confederates suffered heavy losses and the remainder hastened to the defenses of Vicksburg. They had set fire to the bridge across the Big Black, and Grant's army was detained for a day—until the Confederates were safely lodged in the city.

The Federal army now invested Vicksburg, occupying the surrounding hills. It was May 18th when the remarkable campaign to reach Vicksburg came to an end. In eighteen days, the army had marched one hundred and eighty miles through a hostile country, fought and won five battles, captured a State capital, had taken twenty-seven heavy cannon and sixty field-pieces, and had slain or wounded six thousand men and captured as many more. As Grant and Sherman rode out on the hill north of the city, the latter broke into enthusiastic admiration of his chief, declaring that up to that moment he had felt no assurance of success, and pronouncing the campaign one of the greatest in history.

The great problem of investing Vicksburg was solved at last. Around the doomed city gleamed the thousands of bayonets of the Union army. The inhabitants and the army that had fled to it as a city of refuge were penned in. But the Confederacy was not to yield without a stubborn resistance. On May 19th, an advance was made on the works and the besieging lines drew nearer and tightened their coils. Three days later, on May 22nd, Grant ordered a grand assault by his whole army. The troops, flushed with their victories of the past three weeks, were eager for the attack. All the corps commanders set their watches by Grant's in order to begin

THE GUNS THAT WORKED AT CLOSE RANGE

In advance of Lieutenant Terry's naval battery, at the edge of another wooded height, stood Federal Battery No. 9 (Cox's), within about 300 yards of the Confederate fortifications, its two 12-pounder rifles doing telling work against the Confederate forts in their front. The Federals pushed their entrenchments nearest to the works of the defenders at this part of the line—so near that a duplicate of Grant's message to Banks announcing the surrender of Vicksburg was thrown within the Confederate lines on July 7th. This picture shows the method of constructing field fortifications, the parapet here being revetted with cotton-bales.

the assault at all points at the same moment—ten o'clock in the morning. At the appointed time, the cannon from the encircling lines burst forth in a deafening roar. Then came the answering thunders from the mortar-boats on the Louisiana shore and from the gunboats anchored beneath the bluff. The gunboats' fire was answered from within the bastions protecting the city. The opening of the heavy guns on the land side was followed by the sharper crackle of musketry—thousands of shots, indistinguishable in a continuous roll.

The men in the Federal lines leaped from their hiding places and ran to the parapets in the face of a murderous fire from the defenders of the city, only to be mowed down by hundreds. Others came, crawling over the bodies of their fallen comrades—now and then they planted their colors on the battlements of the besieged city, to be cut down by the galling Confederate fire. Thus it continued hour after hour, until the coming of darkness. The assault had failed. The Union loss was about three thousand brave men; the Confederate loss was probably not much over five hundred.

Grant had made a fearful sacrifice; he was paying a high price but he had a reason for so doing—Johnston with a re-enforcing army was threatening him in the rear; by taking Vicksburg at this time he could have turned on Johnston, and could have saved the Government sending any more Federal troops; and, to use his own words, it was needed because the men "would not have worked in the trenches with the same zeal, believing it unnecessary, as they did after their failure, to carry the enemy's works."

On the north side of the city overlooking the river, were the powerful batteries on Fort Hill, a deadly menace to the Federal troops, and Grant and Sherman believed that if enfiladed by the gunboats this position could be carried. At their request Admiral Porter sent the *Cincinnati* on May 27th to engage the Confederate guns, while four vessels below the town did the same to the lower defenses. In half an hour five

WHERE MEN WORKED LIKE MOLES

In burrows such as these the Federal soldiers worked incessantly from June 14th until the surrender of Port Hudson in an effort to undermine "the citadel," the strongest fortification in the Confederate lines near the Jackson road. Cotton-bales roped about were used as sap-rollers to protect the men from sharpshooters. The heat under the semi-tropical sun was terrible, drying up the brooks and distilling miasma from the pestilential swamp near by. The illness and mortality among the Federals were enormous, and yet the men worked on the saps uncomplainingly, and by July 7th the central one had been carried within seventeen feet of the ditch of the fort, and a storming party of a thousand volunteers had been organized to assault the works as soon as the two heavily charged mines should be sprung. That very day came the word that Vicksburg had fallen, and the work of the sappers and miners was useless.

THE SAP AGAINST "THE CITADEL"

of the *Cincinnati's* guns were disabled; and she was in a sinking condition. She was run toward the shore and sank in three fathoms of water.

The army now settled down to a wearisome siege. For six weeks, they encircled the city with trenches, approaching nearer and nearer to the defending walls; they exploded mines; they shot at every head that appeared above the parapets. One by one the defending batteries were silenced. The sappers slowly worked their way toward the Confederate ramparts. Miners were busy on both sides burrowing beneath the fortifications. At three o'clock on the afternoon of June 25th a redoubt in the Confederate works was blown into the air, breaking into millions of fragments and disclosing guns, men, and timber. With the mine explosion, the Federal soldiers before the redoubt began to dash into the opening, only to meet with a withering fire from an interior parapet which the Confederates had constructed in anticipation of this event. The carnage was appalling to behold; and when the soldiers of the Union finally retired they had learned a costly lesson which withheld them from attack when another mine was exploded on July 1st.

Meantime, let us take a view of the river below and the life of the people within the doomed city. Far down the river, two hundred and fifty miles from Vicksburg, was Port Hudson. The place was fortified and held by a Confederate force under General Gardner. Like Vicksburg, it was besieged by a Federal army, under Nathaniel P. Banks, of Cedar Mountain fame. On May 27th, he made a desperate attack on the works and was powerfully aided by Farragut with his fleet in the river. But aside from dismounting a few guns and weakening the foe at a still heavier cost to their own ranks, the Federals were unsuccessful. Again, on June 10th, and still again on the 14th, Banks made fruitless attempts to carry Port Hudson by storm. He then, like Grant at Vicksburg, settled down to a siege. The defenders of Port Hudson proved their courage by enduring every hardship.

THE USES OF ADVERSITY

War brings out more strongly than anything else the ruth of the trite old adage that necessity is the mother of invention. In the operations on the James River a locomotive mounted on a flat-boat was used as an extemporized stationary engine for working a pile-driver. The Confederates at Port Hudson put one to as strange a use. Lifted free from the rails and with a belt attac ed to the driving-wheels, it was used to operate a grist-mill that ground the corn into rough meal, which was their substitute for flour. It did the work in a very satisfactory manner. There were large quantities of grain and corn that had been brought into Port Hudson before it was invested, and the Red River country, as long as it was kept open and accessible, provided the garrison with supplies. But at the time of the investment the Confederate quartermaster was hard put to it to answer the demands made upon him to feed the overworked and hungry men that night and day toiled and slept at the guns. Powder and shell were also running short. Despite the privations suffered by the garrison, they, being used to the climate, suffered less from sickness than did the Federal troops, many detachments of which were encamped along the low-lying and swampy ground that lay at the bend of the river to the north.

THE CHURCH USED AS A GRANARY

At Vicksburg, during the whole six weeks of the siege, the men in the trenches worked steadily, advancing the coils about the city. Grant received reenforcement and before the end of the siege his army numbered over seventy thousand. Day and night, the roar of artillery continued. From the mortars across the river and from Porter's fleet the shrieking shells rose in grand parabolic curves, bursting in midair or in the streets of the city, spreading havoc in all directions. The people of the city burrowed into the ground for safety. Many whole families lived in these dismal abodes, their walls of clay being shaken by the roaring battles that raged above the ground. In one of these dens, sixty-five people found a home. The food supply ran low, and day by day it became scarcer. At last, by the end of June, there was nothing to eat except mule meat and a kind of bread made of beans and corn meal.

It was ten o'clock in the morning of July 3d. White flags were seen above the parapet. The firing ceased. A strange quietness rested over the scene of the long bombardment. On the afternoon of that day, the one, too, on which was heard the last shot on the battlefield of Gettysburg, Grant and Pemberton stood beneath an oak tree, in front of McPherson's corps, and opened negotiations for the capitulation. On the following morning, the Nation's birthday, about thirty thousand soldiers laid down their arms as prisoners of war and were released on parole. The losses from May 1st to the surrender were about ten thousand on each side.

Three days later, at Port Hudson, a tremendous cheer arose from the besieging army. The Confederates within the defenses were at a loss to know the cause. Then some one shouted the news, "Vicksburg has surrendered!"

The end had come. Port Hudson could not hope to stand alone; the greater fortress had fallen. Two days later, July 9th, the gallant garrison, worn and weary with the long siege, surrendered to General Banks. The whole course of the mighty Mississippi was now under the Stars and Stripes.

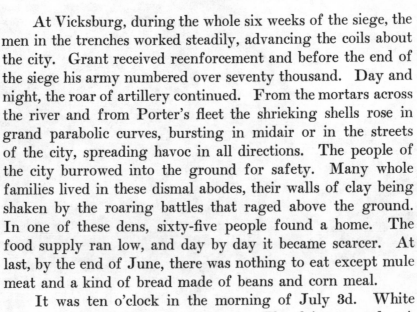

PART III
THE CRISIS

———

GETTYSBURG

———

AFTER THE BATTLE—A SHARPSHOOTER

FEELING FOR LEE'S ARMY

Battery D, Second United States Artillery, Going into Action, June 5, 1863. This was part of the reconnaissance in force under Sedgwick, whom Hooker ordered to cross three miles below Fredericksburg on June 3d and find out if Lee's army still held its old position. The cavalry had brought in reports of some new movement by the Army of Northern Virginia, and Hooker believed that another invasion of the North was impending. It was imperative that this should be checked at once. Every effort was made to discover the real position of the Confederates in order to give battle. Lee, on his side, was equally anxious for a decisive engagement. The

THE NORTH AGAIN THREATENED

It was this Virginia village (seventy-five miles from Washington, on the Orange & Alexandria Railroad) that Lee chose as the point of concentration for his forces preparatory to his last daring invasion of the North, which ended at Gettysburg. Culpeper was no stranger to war's alarms. Two brigades of Pleasonton's cavalry were sent off by Hooker on June 7th to definitely determine Lee's position. Riding in the direction of Culpeper, they ran into a similar force of the Confederates under Stuart, which proved too strong for the

SPARRING BEFORE GETTYSBURG

victory at Chancellorsville had elated the Confederacy with hopes of early recognition by Europe. Exaggerated reports of disaffection at the North led the Government at Richmond to urge an immediate advance. Lee promptly complied. His strongest hope was that he might draw Hooker into a position where the Federals could be advantageously attacked and a blow struck that would end the war. So cleverly was Lee's movement masked by the resistance of Hill's Corps to Howe's division of the Sixth Corps on June 5th that Sedgwick was deceived into reporting that the greater portion of Lee's force still held their old positions.

CULPEPER COURT HOUSE

Federals. The encounter left no doubt in Hooker's mind that Lee was preparing for an aggressive movement either against Washington or into Maryland. On June 13th it was clear that Lee was massing his forces in the direction of Culpeper. Hooker at once began throwing his lines out toward Culpeper, with the purpose of keeping abreast of Lee by advancing south of the Blue Ridge—and the race for the Potomac was on. This picture was taken in November, 1863, when Culpeper was occupied by the Federals.

THE HIGH-WATER MARK OF THE CONFEDERACY

Just as we see it here, the Confederates first saw Gettysburg. Down these roads and past these houses they marched to the high-water mark of their invasion of the North. It was quite by accident that the little town became the theater of the crucial contest of the Civil War. On the morning of June 30th Heth's division of General D. H. Hill's Corps was marching upon the town from the west. It came on confidently, expecting no resistance, meaning only to seize a supply of shoes much needed by the footsore Army of Northern Virginia, which had marched triumphantly from Culpeper to the heart of Pennsylvania. Between Heth's men and their goal lay two brigades of Federal cavalry under Buford. Riding into the town from the opposite direction came Major Kress, sent by General Wadsworth to get these same shoes for his division of the Federals. Before the tavern Kress found Buford and explained his errand. "You

THE LITTLE TOWN OF GETTYSBURG, PENNSYLVANIA

had better return immediately to your command," said Buford. "Why, what is the matter, General?" asked Kress. At that instant a single gun boomed in the distance, and Buford, mounting, replied as he spurred his horse to the gallop, "That's the matter." The world had never seen a finer body of fighting men than Lee's Army of Northern Virginia, then massing rapidly toward Gettysburg. More than seventy-three thousand five hundred strong they came, every man a veteran, contemptuous of adversaries whose superior numbers had never yet been made to count completely against them. In the center of the panorama rises Cemetery Ridge, where the defeated First and Eleventh Federal Corps slept on their arms on the night of July 1st, after having been driven back through the town by the superior forces of Hill and Ewell. The lower eminence to the right of it is Culp's Hill. At the extreme right of the picture stands Round Top.

THE CRISIS BRINGS FORTH THE MAN

Major-General George Gordon Meade and Staff. Not men, but a man is what counts in war, said Napoleon; and Lee had proved it true in many a bitter lesson administered to the Army of the Potomac. At the end of June, 1863, for the third time in ten months, that army had a new commander. Promptness and caution were equally imperative in that hour. Meade's fitness for the post was as yet undemonstrated; he had been advanced from the command of the Fifth Corps three days before the army was to engage in its greatest battle. Lee must be turned back from Harrisburg and Philadelphia and kept from striking at Baltimore and Washington, and the somewhat scattered Army of the Potomac must be concentrated. In the very first flush of his advancement, Meade exemplified the qualities of sound generalship that placed his name high on the list of Federal commanders.

GETTYSBURG—WHERE STIRRING DEEDS BROUGHT FORTH IMMORTAL WORDS

This is Gettysburg, the sleepy little Pennsylvania town that leaped into the focus of the world's eye on those scorching death-ridden days of July, 1863, and down the street comes swaying in cadenced steps a marching regiment. We are looking at them just as the inhabitants, gathered here in their quaint old costumes, saw them. Here are the defenders returned again to the place whose name spells victory and glorious memories on their tattered battle-flags. It is the 19th of November, 1863. Lincoln is here to speak those glowing words that every schoolboy knows, and dedicate the National Cemetery, where lie the Blue and Gray, and where their children's children make yearly pilgrimages.

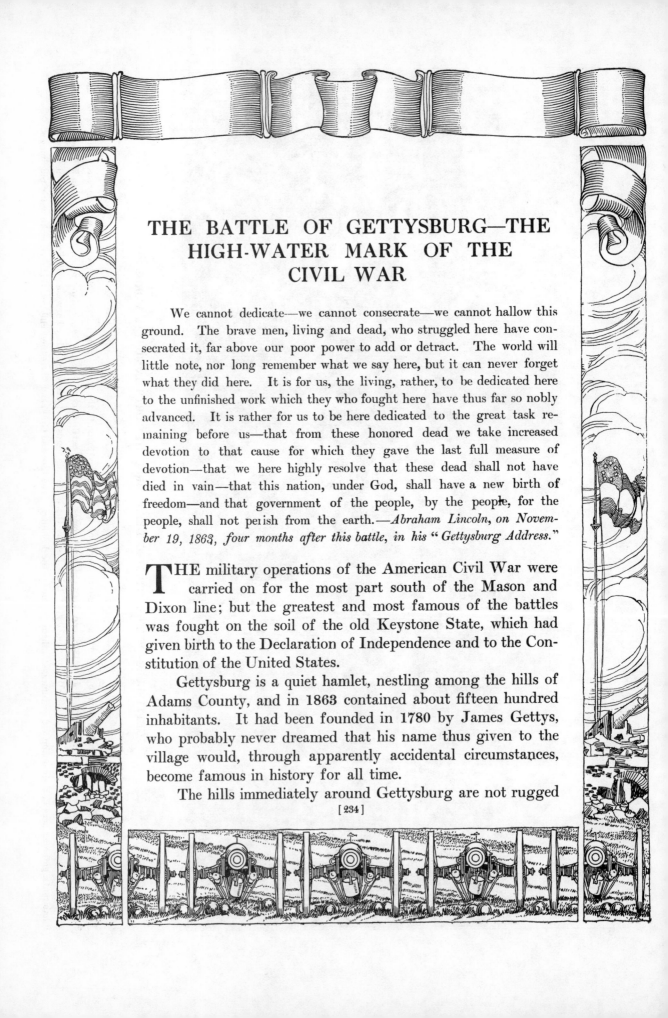

THE BATTLE OF GETTYSBURG—THE HIGH-WATER MARK OF THE CIVIL WAR

We cannot dedicate—we cannot consecrate—we cannot hallow this ground. The brave men, living and dead, who struggled here have consecrated it, far above our poor power to add or detract. The world will little note, nor long remember what we say here, but it can never forget what they did here. It is for us, the living, rather, to be dedicated here to the unfinished work which they who fought here have thus far so nobly advanced. It is rather for us to be here dedicated to the great task remaining before us—that from these honored dead we take increased devotion to that cause for which they gave the last full measure of devotion—that we here highly resolve that these dead shall not have died in vain—that this nation, under God, shall have a new birth of freedom—and that government of the people, by the people, for the people, shall not perish from the earth.—*Abraham Lincoln, on November 19, 1863, four months after this battle, in his " Gettysburg Address."*

THE military operations of the American Civil War were carried on for the most part south of the Mason and Dixon line; but the greatest and most famous of the battles was fought on the soil of the old Keystone State, which had given birth to the Declaration of Independence and to the Constitution of the United States.

Gettysburg is a quiet hamlet, nestling among the hills of Adams County, and in 1863 contained about fifteen hundred inhabitants. It had been founded in 1780 by James Gettys, who probably never dreamed that his name thus given to the village would, through apparently accidental circumstances, become famous in history for all time.

The hills immediately around Gettysburg are not rugged

ROBERT E. LEE IN 1863

It was with the gravest misgivings that Lee began his invasion of the North in 1863. He was too wise a general not to realize that a crushing defeat was possible. Yet, with Vicksburg already doomed, the effort to win a decisive victory in the East was imperative in its importance. Magnificent was the courage and fortitude of Lee's maneuvering during that long march which was to end in failure. Hitherto he had made every one of his veterans count for two of their antagonists, but at Gettysburg the odds had fallen heavily against him. Jackson, his resourceful ally, was no more. Longstreet advised strongly against giving battle, but Lee unwaveringly made the tragic effort which sacrificed more than a third of his splendid army.

or precipitous; they are little more than gentle swells of ground, and many of them were covered with timber when the hosts of the North and the legions of the South fought out the destiny of the American republic on those memorable July days in 1863.

The village is the radiating point of several important roads, known by the names of the respective towns to which they lead. The one leading directly into the town from the north is known as the Carlisle road. It passes through the village and deflects to the southeast, becoming the Baltimore turnpike. East of the Carlisle road is the Harrisburg road, and west of it the Mummasburg road. This latter crosses a wooded ridge known as Oak Hill, and this hill became the center of operations on the first day of the battle. West of the village about half a mile a Lutheran theological seminary is situated on a ridge which extends north and south and is called Seminary Ridge. Directly south of Gettysburg, almost parallel with Seminary Ridge and about a mile from it, lies Cemetery Ridge. Three miles from the town, Cemetery Ridge culminates in a bold, rocky peak, with steep, rugged slopes several hundred feet in height, which is called Round Top. North of Round Top, and quite near it, is a similar peak about half as high, called Little Round Top. About five hundred yards west of Little Round Top another rugged peak, known as the Devil's Den, rises from the lowland marshes at the junction of a small creek which runs along the western base of Cemetery Ridge, and is known as Plum Run, with a smaller tributary. The Devil's Den is about one hundred feet lower than Little Round Top, and its slopes are covered with huge boulders and seamed with crevasses. The largest of these pits, and the one from which the hill took its name, is on the slope facing toward Little Round Top, and formed a natural breastwork of solid rock.

The valley between Cemetery Ridge and Seminary Ridge was rolling farm-land, with cultivated fields and orchards

HANCOCK, "THE SUPERB"

Every man in this picture was wounded at Gettysburg. Seated, is Winfield Scott Hancock; the boy-general, Francis C. Barlow (who was struck almost mortally), leans against the tree. The other two are General John Gibbon and General David B. Birney. About four o'clock on the afternoon of July 1st a foam-flecked charger dashed up Cemetery Hill bearing General Hancock. He had galloped thirteen miles to take command. Apprised of the loss of Reynolds, his main dependence, Meade knew that only a man of vigor and judgment could save the situation. He chose wisely, for Hancock was one of the best all-round soldiers that the Army of the Potomac had developed. It was he who re-formed the shattered corps and chose the position to be held for the decisive struggle.

spreading across the landscape. At the southern end of the valley to the west of Round Top the lowland was covered with heavy timber, and the ground was strewn with huge rocks. Near the northwestern base of the Devil's Den there was a broad wheat-field, with the grain ripening in the summer sun. A short distance to the north of the wheat-field, on a slight elevation, stood the farmhouse and barns of the Trostle farm. To the west and slightly to the south of the Trostle farm the land rises gradually to a low hill which stands midway between the Trostle farm and the crest of Seminary Ridge. On the eastern slope of this hill, and reaching to its crest, there was an extensive peach orchard. The western side of the orchard bordered on the broad Emmitsburg road, which stretched away from Gettysburg to the southwest to Emmitsburg, a short distance over the Maryland line. A mile and a half west of Gettysburg flows Willoughby Run, while at about the same distance on the east and nearly parallel to the run flows a somewhat larger stream called Rock Creek. Between Rock Creek and the northern extremity of Cemetery Ridge is situated Culp's Hill, on whose sides the armies in blue and gray struggled heroically during the three days' fight. The area of the entire battle-ground is something over twenty-five square miles, all of which may be seen at a glance from any one of the five observatories which have since been erected on the ground by the Government.

Lee's army was flushed with victory after Chancellorsville and was strengthened by the memory of Fredericksburg. Southern hopes were high after Hooker's defeat on the Rappahannock, in May, 1863, and public opinion was unanimous in demanding an invasion of Northern soil. On the other hand, the Army of the Potomac, under its several leaders, had met with continual discouragement, and, with all its patriotism and valor, its two years' warfare showed but few bright pages to cheer the heart of the war-broken soldier, and to inspire the hopes of the anxious public in the North.

MUTE PLEADERS IN THE CAUSE OF PEACE

There was little time that could be employed by either side in caring for those who fell upon the fields of the almost uninterrupted fighting at Gettysburg. On the morning of the 4th, when Lee began to abandon his position on Seminary Ridge, opposite the Federal right, both sides sent forth ambulance and burial details to remove the wounded and bury the dead in the torrential rain then falling. Under cover of the hazy atmosphere, Lee was get-ting his whole army in motion to retreat. Many an unfinished shallow grave, like the one above, had to be left by the Confederates. In this lower picture some men of the Twenty-fourth Michigan infantry are lying dead on the field of battle. This regiment—one of the units of the Iron Brigade—left seven distinct rows of dead as it fell back from battle-line to battle-line, on the first day. Three-fourths of its members were struck down.

MEN OF THE IRON BRIGADE

Leaving General Stuart with ten thousand cavalry and a part of Hill's corps to prevent Hooker from pursuing, Lee crossed the Potomac early in June, 1863, concentrated his army at Hagerstown, Maryland, and prepared for a campaign in Pennsylvania, with Harrisburg as the objective. His army was organized in three corps, under the respective commands of Longstreet, Ewell, and A. P. Hill. Lee had divided his army so as to approach Harrisburg by different routes and to assess the towns along the way for large sums of money. Late in June, he was startled by the intelligence that Stuart had failed to detain Hooker, and that the Federals had crossed the Potomac and were in hot pursuit.

Lee was quick to see that his plans must be changed. He knew that to continue his march he must keep his army together to watch his pursuing antagonist, and that such a course in this hostile country would mean starvation, while the willing hands of the surrounding populace would minister to the wants of his foe. Again, if he should scatter his forces that they might secure the necessary supplies, the parts would be attacked singly and destroyed. Lee saw, therefore, that he must abandon his invasion of the North or turn upon his pursuing foe and disable him in order to continue his march. But that foe was a giant of strength and courage, more than equal to his own; and the coming together of two such forces in a mighty death-struggle meant that a great battle must be fought, a greater battle than this Western world had hitherto known.

The Army of the Potomac had again changed leaders, and George Gordon Meade was now its commander. Hooker, after a dispute with Halleck, resigned his leadership, and Meade, the strongest of the corps commanders, was appointed in his place, succeeding him on June 28th. The two great armies—Union and Confederate—were scattered over portions of Maryland and southern Pennsylvania. Both were marching northward, along almost parallel lines. The Confederates

THE FIRST DAY'S TOLL

The lives laid down by the blue-clad soldiers in the first day's fighting made possible the ultimate victory at Gettysburg. The stubborn resistance of Buford's cavalry and of the First and Eleventh Corps checked the Confederate advance for an entire day. The delay was priceless; it enabled Meade to concentrate his army upon the heights to the south of Gettysburg, a position which proved impregnable. To a Pennsylvanian, General John F. Reynolds, falls the credit of the determined stand that was made that day. Commanding the advance of the army, he promptly went to Buford's support, bringing up his infantry and artillery to hold back the Confederates.

McPHERSON'S WOODS

At the edge of these woods General Reynolds was killed by a Confederate sharpshooter in the first vigorous contest of the day. The woods lay between the two roads upon which the Confederates were advancing from the west, and General Doubleday (in command of the First Corps) was ordered to take the position so that the columns of the foe could be enfiladed by the infantry, while contending with the artillery posted on both roads. The Iron Brigade under General Meredith was ordered to hold the ground at all hazards. As they charged, the troops shouted: "If we can't hold it, where will you find the men who can?" On they swept, capturing General Archer and many of his Confederate brigade that had entered the woods from the other side. As Archer passed to the rear, Doubleday, who had been his classmate at West Point, greeted him with "Good morning! I'm glad to see you!"

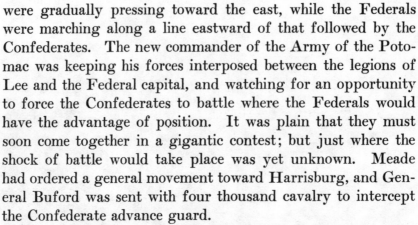

were gradually pressing toward the east, while the Federals were marching along a line eastward of that followed by the Confederates. The new commander of the Army of the Potomac was keeping his forces interposed between the legions of Lee and the Federal capital, and watching for an opportunity to force the Confederates to battle where the Federals would have the advantage of position. It was plain that they must soon come together in a gigantic contest; but just where the shock of battle would take place was yet unknown. Meade had ordered a general movement toward Harrisburg, and General Buford was sent with four thousand cavalry to intercept the Confederate advance guard.

On the night of June 30th Buford encamped on a low hill, a mile west of Gettysburg, and here on the following morning the famous battle had its beginning.

On the morning of July 1st the two armies were still scattered, the extremes being forty miles apart. But General Reynolds, with two corps of the Union army, was but a few miles away, and was hastening to Gettysburg, while Longstreet and Hill were approaching from the west. Buford opened the battle against Heth's division of Hill's corps. Reynolds soon joined Buford, and three hours before noon the battle was in progress on Seminary Ridge. Reynolds rode out to his fighting-lines on the ridge, and while placing his troops, a little after ten o'clock in the morning, he received a sharpshooter's bullet in the brain. The gallant Federal leader fell dead. John F. Reynolds, who had been promoted for gallantry at Buena Vista in the Mexican War, was one of the bravest and ablest generals of the Union army. No casualty of the war brought more widespread mourning to the North than the death of Reynolds.

But even this calamity could not stay the fury of the battle. By one o'clock both sides had been greatly reenforced, and the battle-line extended north of the town from Seminary Ridge to the bank of Rock Creek. Here for hours the roar

FEDERAL DEAD AT GETTYSBURG, JULY 1, 1863

All the way from McPherson's Woods back to Cemetery Hill lay the Federal soldiers, who had contested every foot of that retreat until nightfall. The Confederates were massing so rapidly from the west and north that there was scant time to bring off the wounded and none for attention to the dead. There on the field lay the shoes so much needed by the Confederates, and the grim task of gathering them began. The dead were stripped of arms, ammunition, caps, and accoutrements as well—in fact, of everything that would be of the slightest use in enabling Lee's poorly equipped army to continue the internecine strife. It was one of war's awful expedients.

SEMINARY RIDGE, BEYOND GETTYSBURG

Along this road the Federals retreated toward Cemetery Hill in the late afternoon of July 1st. The success of McPherson's Woods was but temporary, for the Confederates under Hill were coming up in overpowering numbers, and now Ewell's forces appeared from the north. The First Corps, under Doubleday, "broken and defeated but not dismayed," fell back, pausing now and again to fire a volley at  the pursuing Confederates. It finally joined the Eleventh Corps, which had also been driven back to Cemetery Hill. Lee was on the field in time to watch the retreat of the Federals, and advised Ewell to follow them up, but Ewell (who had lost 3,000 men) decided upon discretion. Night fell with the beaten Federals, reënforced by the Twelfth Corps and part of the Third, facing nearly the whole of Lee's army.

THE PRICE OF VICTORY

Such scenes as these marked every one of the detached battle-fields at Gettysburg. The lower picture is a result of the first day's fighting near McPherson's Woods, through which the Iron Brigade swept with the cry, "We've come to stay!" The picture above was taken near the spot where the First Minnesota was sacrificed to stem the advance of the Confederates after their victory at the Peach Orchard. Hancock, while patching up a second line to protect Sickles' retreating troops, saw a heavy column of Confederates emerge from a clump of trees and advance toward a weak point in his line. Dashing up to Colonel Colvill, Hancock shouted: "Do

THE MEN WHO "CAME TO STAY"

WHERE A SHELL DROPPED

you see those colors? Take them!" And the First Minnesota, in five minutes, captured the colors and stemmed the advance. Of the 262 officers and men who obeyed that order, half a hundred lay dead on the field and 174 others were wounded. The regiment's total mortality from that charge was 75, more than 28 per cent. of the number engaged—the highest known short of an Indian massacre. The Federals lost at Gettysburg 3,063 killed, 14,492 wounded, and 5,435 missing (Fox's figures). The Confederate loss was 3,903 killed, 18,735 wounded, and 5,425 missing (Livermore's figures). Total loss on both sides, 51,053.

NEAR THE BLOODY ANGLE

of the battle was unceasing. About the middle of the afternoon a breeze lifted the smoke that had enveloped the whole
battle-line in darkness, and revealed the fact that the Federals
were being pressed back toward Gettysburg. General Carl
Schurz, who after Reynolds' death directed the extreme right
near Rock Creek, leaving nearly half of his men dead or
wounded on the field, retreated toward Cemetery Hill, and
in passing through the town the Confederates pursued and captured a large number of the remainder. The left wing, now
unable to hold its position owing to the retreat of the right,
was also forced back, and it, too, took refuge on Cemetery
Hill, which had been selected by General O. O. Howard;
and the first day's fight was over. It was several hours before night, and had the Southerners known of the disorganized
condition of the Union troops, they might have pursued and
captured a large part of the army. Meade, who was still some
miles from the field, hearing of the death of Reynolds, had
sent Hancock to take general command until he himself should
arrive.

Hancock had ridden at full speed and arrived on the field
between three and four o'clock in the afternoon. His presence
soon brought order out of chaos. His superb bearing, his air
of confidence, his promise of heavy reenforcements during the
night, all tended to inspire confidence and to renew hope in the
ranks of the discouraged army. Had this day ended the affair
at Gettysburg, the usual story of the defeat of the Army of
the Potomac would have gone forth to the world. Only the
advance portions of both armies had been engaged; and yet
the battle had been a formidable one. The Union loss was
severe. A great commander had fallen, and the rank and file
had suffered the fearful loss of ten thousand men.

Meade reached the scene late in the night, and chose to
make this field, on which the advance of both armies had acci-
dentally met, the place of a general engagement. Lee had
come to the same decision, and both called on their outlying

THE CARNAGE OF BLOODY ANGLE

Trostle's House, Sickles' headquarters at the beginning of the second day. The house stood some distance back from the Emmitsburg road, overlooking the Peach Orchard, from which the Confederates finally drove the sturdy men of the Third Corps. Whether or not it was a tactical error for Sickles to post his command along the road so far in advance of the line is a subject of discussion. The result cost many lives, and nearly lost to the Federals the key to their position. Back from the Peach Orchard Sickles' men were driven, past Trostle's House, where Bigelow's Ninth Massachusetts battery made its glorious stand, and near which Sickles himself lost his leg. All the way back to Round Top the ground was strewn with dead.

legions to make all possible speed to Gettysburg. Before morning, nearly all the troops of both armies had reached the field. The Union army rested with its center on Cemetery Ridge, with its right thrown around to Culp's Hill and its left extended southward toward the rocky peak called Round Top. The Confederate army, with its center on Seminary Ridge, its wings extending from beyond Rock Creek on the north to a point opposite Round Top on the south, lay in a great semicircle, half surrounding the Army of the Potomac. But Lee was at a disadvantage. First, "Stonewall" Jackson was gone, and second, Stuart was absent with his ten thousand cavalry. Furthermore, Meade was on the defensive, and had the advantage of occupying the inner ring of the huge half circle. Thus lay the two mighty hosts, awaiting the morning, and the carnage that the day was to bring. It seemed that the fate of the Republic was here to be decided, and the people of the North and the South watched with breathless eagerness for the decision about to be made at Gettysburg.

The dawn of July 2d betokened a beautiful summer day in southern Pennsylvania. The hours of the night had been spent by the two armies in marshaling of battalions and maneuvering of corps and divisions, getting into position for the mighty combat of the coming day. But, when morning dawned, both armies hesitated, as if unwilling to begin the task of bloodshed. They remained inactive, except for a stray shot here and there, until nearly four o'clock in the afternoon.

The fighting on this second day was chiefly confined to the two extremes, the centers remaining comparatively inactive. Longstreet commanded the Confederate right, and opposite him on the Union left was General Daniel E. Sickles. The Confederate left wing, under Ewell, was opposite Slocum and the Union right stationed on Culp's Hill.

The plan of General Meade had been to have the corps commanded by General Sickles connect with that of Hancock and extend southward near the base of the Round Tops.

IN THE DEVIL'S DEN

Upon this wide, steep hill, about five hundred yards due west of Little Round Top and one hundred feet lower, was a chasm named by the country folk "the Devil's Den." When the position fell into the hands of the Confederates at the end of the second day's fighting, it became the stronghold of their sharpshooters, and well did it fulfill its name. It was a most dangerous post to occupy, since the Federal batteries on the Round Top were constantly shelling it in an effort to dislodge the hardy riflemen, many of whom met the fate of the one in the picture. Their deadly work continued, however, and many a gallant officer of the Federals was picked off during the fighting on the afternoon of the second day. General Vincent was one of the first victims; General Weed fell likewise; and as Lieutenant Hazlett bent over him to catch his last words, a bullet through the head prostrated that officer lifeless on the body of his chief.

Sickles found this ground low and disadvantageous as a fighting-place. In his front he saw the high ground along the ridge on the side of which the peach orchard was situated, and advanced his men to this position, placing them along the Emmitsburg road, and back toward the Trostle farm and the wheat-field, thus forming an angle at the peach orchard. The left flank of Hancock's line now rested far behind the right flank of Sickles' forces. The Third Corps was alone in its position in advance of the Federal line. The Confederate troops later marched along Sickles' front so that Longstreet's corps overlapped the left wing of the Union army. The Northerners grimly watched the bristling cannon and the files of men that faced them across the valley, as they waited for the battle to commence.

The boom of cannon from Longstreet's batteries announced the beginning of the second day's battle. Lee had ordered Longstreet to attack Sickles in full force. The fire was quickly answered by the Union troops, and before long the fight extended from the peach orchard through the wheat-field and along the whole line to the base of Little Round Top. The musketry commenced with stray volleys here and there—then more and faster, until there was one continuous roar, and no ear could distinguish one shot from another. Longstreet swept forward in a magnificent line of battle, a mile and a half long. He pressed back the Union infantry, and was seriously threatening the artillery.

At the extreme left, close to the Trostle house, Captain John Bigelow commanded the Ninth Battery, Massachusetts Light Artillery. He was ordered to hold his position at all hazards until reenforced. With double charges of grape and canister, again and again he tore great gaps in the advancing line, but it re-formed and pressed onward until the men in gray reached the muzzles of the Federal guns. Again Bigelow fired, but the heroic band had at last to give way to the increased numbers of the attack, which finally resulted in a hand-

THE UNGUARDED LINK

Little Round Top, the key to the Federal left at Gettysburg, which they all but lost on the second day —was the scene of hand-to-hand fighting rarely equaled since long-range weapons were invented. Twice the Confederates in fierce conflict fought their way near to this summit, but were repulsed. Had they gained it, they could have planted artillery which would have enfiladed the left of Meade's line, and Gettysburg might have been turned into an overwhelming defeat. Beginning at the right, the Federal line stretched in the form of a fish-hook, with the barb resting on Culp's Hill, the center at the bend in the hook on Cemetery Hill, and the left (consisting of General Sickles' Third Corps) forming the shank to the southward as far as Round Top. On his own responsibility Sickles had advanced a portion of his line, leaving Little Round Top unprotected. Upon this advanced line of Sickles, at the Peach Orchard on the Emmitsburg road, the Confederates fell in an effort to turn what they supposed to be Meade's left flank. Only the promptness of General Warren, who discovered the gap and remedied it in time, saved the key.

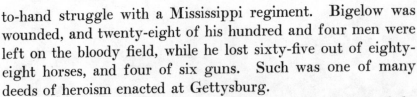

to-hand struggle with a Mississippi regiment. Bigelow was wounded, and twenty-eight of his hundred and four men were left on the bloody field, while he lost sixty-five out of eighty-eight horses, and four of six guns. Such was one of many deeds of heroism enacted at Gettysburg.

But the most desperate struggle of the day was the fight for the possession of Little Round Top. Just before the action began General Meade sent his chief engineer, General G. K. Warren, to examine conditions on the Union left. The battle was raging in the peach orchard when he came to Little Round Top. It was unoccupied at the time, and Warren quickly saw the great importance of preventing its occupation by the Confederates, for the hill was the key to the whole battle-ground west and south of Cemetery Ridge. Before long, the engineer saw Hood's division of Longstreet's corps moving steadily toward the hill, evidently determined to occupy it. Had Hood succeeded, the result would have been most disastrous to the Union army, for the Confederates could then have subjected the entire Union lines on the western edge of Cemetery Ridge to an enfilading fire. Warren and a signal officer seized flags and waved them, to deceive the Confederates as to the occupation of the height. Sykes' corps, marching to the support of the left, soon came along, and Warren, dashing down the side of the hill to meet it, caused the brigade under Colonel Vincent and a part of that under General Weed to be detached, and these occupied the coveted position. Hazlett's battery was dragged by hand up the rugged slope and planted on the summit.

Meantime Hood's forces had come up the hill, and were striving at the very summit; and now occurred one of the most desperate hand-to-hand conflicts of the war—in which men forgot that they were human and tore at each other like wild beasts. The opposing forces, not having time to reload, charged each other with bayonets—men assaulted each other with clubbed muskets—the Blue and the Gray grappled in

THE SECOND DAY'S FIGHT

The battle of Gettysburg was a crescendo of carnage—each day marked by a special climax more dramatic and deadly than the preceding one. That of the second day was the struggle for Little Round Top. It began with the thrilling charge by Longstreet's men of Hood's division. Turning Ward's flank, on they swept from Devil's Den up the ravine between the Round Tops, confident that Little Round Top was undefended. Near the crest Vincent's brigade, posted in the nick of time by General Warren, burst upon them with the bayonet. Up and down the slope the struggling lines undulated, broken rapidly by the trees and boulders into single-handed combats; men and muskets in a moment were scattered all about. Just as Vincent's right was about to be overwhelmed, the 140th New York came upon the crest, led by the gallant young Colonel O'Rorke, who fell dead at the first volley. The regiment, rallied by Vincent, held their ground, but there Vincent, too, was killed. Meanwhile Hazlett's regular battery had

THE BATTLE–FIELD AMID THE TREES

dragged its guns with great difficulty to the crest, where Generals Weed and Hazlett soon fell together. Colonel Rice, of the Forty-fourth New York (now in command in place of Vincent), had repulsed the assaults on his right and center. There was a lull, during which the Confederates stole around from the woods and fell with fury on the left of the line. Here Chamberlain's regiment, the Twentieth Maine, rapidly swinging around the rear of the mountain to meet the attack, was forced over the crest. Rallying, they drove back the Confederates in their turn. Twice more the struggling men fought back and forth over the summit, strewing the slopes with the fallen. Then a brigade of the Pennsylvania reserves and one from the Fifth Corps dashed over the hill. Chamberlain's brave men who were left greeted the reënforcements with a shout, dashed forward in a final charge, and drove the Confederates through the valley between the Round Tops. The Twentieth Maine had lost a third of its men and spent its last round of ammunition.

THE WOODED SLOPE OF LITTLE ROUND TOP

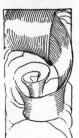
mortal combat and fell dead, side by side. The privates in the front ranks fought their way onward until they fell, the officers sprang forward, seized the muskets from the hands of the dying and the dead, and continued the combat. The furious struggle continued for half an hour, when Hood's forces gave way and were pressed down the hillside. But they rallied and advanced again by way of a ravine on the left, and finally, after a most valiant charge, were driven back at the point of the bayonet.

Little Round Top was saved to the Union army, but the cost was appalling. The hill was covered with hundreds of the slain. Scores of the Confederate sharpshooters had taken position among the crevasses in the Devil's Den, where they could overlook the position on Little Round Top, and their unerring aim spread death among the Federal officers and gunners. Colonel O'Rourke and General Vincent were dead. General Weed was dying; and, as Hazlett was stooping to receive Weed's last message, a sharpshooter's bullet laid him—dead— across the body of his chief.

During this attack, and for some hours thereafter, the battle continued in the valley below on a grander scale and with demon-like fury. Here many thousands were engaged. Sickles' whole line was pressed back to the base of the hill from which it had advanced in the morning. Sickles' leg was shattered by a shell, necessitating amputation, while scores of his brave officers, and thousands of his men, lay on the field of battle when the struggle ceased at nightfall. This valley has been appropriately named the "Valley of Death."

Before the close of this main part of the second day's battle, there was another clash of arms, fierce but of short duration, at the other extreme of the line. Lee had ordered Ewell to attack Cemetery Hill and Culp's Hill on the north, held by Slocum, who had been weakened by the sending of a large portion of the Twelfth Corps to the assistance of the left wing. Ewell had three divisions, two of which were commanded by

MEN WHO HELD LITTLE ROUND TOP

When General Warren discovered the defenseless condition of Little Round Top, he spied the division of Brigadier-General James Barnes marching to the relief of their comrades fighting along the Emmitsburg road. Warren, on his own responsibility, rode over to General Barnes and detached Vincent's brigade, hurrying it back to guard Little Round Top. It was not long before the men of the Forty-fourth New York were engaged in a fierce hand-to-hand combat with the determined Confederates of Hood, worming their way from tree to tree and boulder to boulder, in a running fight up the slope. The men of the Forty-fourth New York were among the finest in the service; they were enlisted from every county in their native State, and were selected in accordance with strict requirements as to fitness. The average age of the regiment was twenty-two; its heaviest battle loss (one hundred and eleven), occurred in the defense of Little Round Top at Gettysburg. The ground seemed impregnable, but the Southerners, rushing on from their victory at "the bloody angle," climbed the slopes in such a desperate onslaught that the Federals, not having time to load, advanced to repel the attack with the bayonet. The hillside after the battle was literally strewn with the dead and wounded. To the prompt and brave work of Vincent's brigade, in which fought the Forty-fourth New York, was due, in part, the fact that Little Round Top was not taken in that first assault. The repulse of the Confederates gave the Federals time to bring up a battery and strengthen the position against the repeated charges of the afternoon.

WHERE THE SECOND DAY'S ATTACK ENDED

Generals Early and Johnson. It was nearly sunset when he sent Early to attack Cemetery Hill. Early was repulsed after an hour's bloody and desperate hand-to-hand fight, in which muskets and bayonets, rammers, clubs, and stones were used. Johnson's attack on Culp's Hill was more successful. After a severe struggle of two or three hours General Greene, who alone of the Twelfth Corps remained on the right, succeeded, after reenforcement, in driving the right of Johnson's division away from its entrenchments, but the left had no difficulty in taking possession of the abandoned works of Geary and Ruger, now gone to Round Top and Rock Creek to assist the left wing.

Thus closed the second day's battle at Gettysburg. The harvest of death had been frightful. The Union loss during the two days had exceeded twenty thousand men; the Confederate loss was nearly equal. The Confederate army had gained an apparent advantage in penetrating the Union breastworks on Culp's Hill. But the Union lines, except on Culp's Hill, were unbroken. On the night of July 2d, Lee and his generals held a council of war and decided to make a grand final assault on Meade's center the following day. Against this decision Longstreet protested in vain. His counsel was that Lee withdraw to the mountains, compel Meade to follow, and then turn and attack him. But Lee was encouraged by the arrival of Pickett's division and of Stuart's cavalry, and Longstreet's objections were overruled. Meade and his corps commanders had met and made a like decision—that there should be a fight to the death at Gettysburg.

That night a brilliant July moon shed its luster upon the ghastly field on which thousands of men lay, unable to rise. Many of them no longer needed help. Their last battle was over, and their spirits had fled to the great Beyond. But there were great numbers, torn and gashed with shot and shell, who were still alive and calling for water or for the kindly touch of a helping hand. Nor did they call wholly in vain. Here and

THE GROUND THAT WAS REGAINED

The indomitable photographer, Brady, in his famous duster, is sitting amid the battered trees on Culp's Hill, whose scars mark the scene of the recent crucial contest. The possession of the hill at nightfall of July 2d encouraged Lee to renew the general assault next day. This was the extreme right of the Federal position. Hancock, arriving on the afternoon of the first day, had seen its importance and sent a shattered brigade of Doubleday's First Corps to hold it. The marvelous fighting of Longstreet's men on the 2d had laid low 6,000 Federals before the Round Tops at the Federal left, and by nightfall Johnson's division of Ewell's Corps drove the defenders of Culp's Hill from their entrenchments. But Ewell, owing to the darkness, did not perceive the value of his new position. A short musket-shot beyond Culp's Hill, the artillery reserves and the supply trains of the Union army lay almost unprotected. At daylight of the 3d, Johnson's lines were attacked by the Second Massachusetts and the Twentieth Indiana, but these regiments were almost annihilated. But after seven hours of fighting the Confederates retreated.

there in the moonlight little rescuing parties were seeking out whom they might succor. They carried many to the improvised hospitals, where the surgeons worked unceasingly and heroically, and many lives were saved.

All through the night the Confederates were massing artillery along the crest of Seminary Ridge. The sound horses were carefully fed and watered, while those killed or disabled were replaced by others. The ammunition was replenished and the guns were placed in favorable positions and made ready for their work of destruction.

On the other side, the Federals were diligently laboring in the moonlight, and ere the coming of the day they had planted batteries on the brow of the hill above the town as far as Little Round Top. The coming of the morning revealed the two parallel lines of cannon, a mile apart, which signified only too well the story of what the day would bring forth.

The people of Gettysburg, which lay almost between the armies, were awakened on that fateful morning—July 3, 1863 —by the roar of artillery from Culp's Hill, around the bend toward Rock Creek. This knoll in the woods had, as we have seen, been taken by Johnson's men the night before. When Geary and Ruger returned and found their entrenchments occupied by the Confederates they determined to recapture them in the morning, and began firing their guns at daybreak. Seven hours of fierce bombardment and daring charges were required to regain them. Every rod of space was disputed at the cost of many a brave man's life. At eleven o'clock this portion of the Twelfth Corps was again in its old position.

But the most desperate onset of the three days' battle was yet to come—Pickett's charge on Cemetery Ridge—preceded by the heaviest cannonading ever heard on the American continent.

With the exception of the contest at Culp's Hill and a cavalry fight east of Rock Creek, the forenoon of July 3d

THE HEIGHT OF THE BATTLE-TIDE

Near this gate to the local cemetery of Gettysburg there stood during the battle this sign: "All persons found using firearms in these grounds will be prosecuted with the utmost rigor of the law." Many a soldier must have smiled grimly at these words, for this gateway became the key of the Federal line, the very center of the cruelest use of firearms yet seen on this continent. On the first day Reynolds saw the value of Cemetery Hill in case of a retreat. Howard posted his reserves here, and Hancock greatly strengthened the position. One hundred and twenty Confederate guns were turned against it that last afternoon. In five minutes every man of the Federals had been forced to cover; for an hour and a half the shells fell fast, dealing death and laying waste the summer verdure in the little graveyard. Up to the very guns of the Federals on Cemetery Hill, Pickett led his devoted troops. At night of the 3d it was one vast slaughter-field. On this eminence, where thousands were buried, was dedicated the soldiers' National Cemetery.

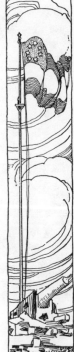

passed with only an occasional exchange of shots at irregular intervals. At noon there was a lull, almost a deep silence, over the whole field. It was the ominous calm that precedes the storm. At one o'clock signal guns were fired on Seminary Ridge, and a few moments later there was a terrific outburst from one hundred and fifty Confederate guns, and the whole crest of the ridge, for two miles, was a line of flame. The scene was majestic beyond description. The scores of batteries were soon enveloped in smoke, through which the flashes of burning powder were incessant.

The long line of Federal guns withheld their fire for some minutes, when they burst forth, answering the thunder of those on the opposite hill. An eye-witness declares that the whole sky seemed filled with screaming shells, whose sharp explosions, as they burst in mid-air, with the hurtling of the fragments, formed a running accompaniment to the deep, tremendous roar of the guns.

Many of the Confederate shots went wild, passing over the Union army and plowing up the earth on the other side of Cemetery Ridge. But others were better aimed and burst among the Federal batteries, in one of which twenty-seven out of thirty-six horses were killed in ten minutes. The Confederate fire seemed to be concentrated upon one point between Cemetery Ridge and Little Round Top, near a clump of scrub oaks. Here the batteries were demolished and men and horses were slain by scores. The spot has been called "Bloody Angle."

The Federal fire proved equally accurate and the destruction on Seminary Ridge was appalling. For nearly two hours the hills shook with the tremendous cannonading, when it gradually slackened and ceased. The Union army now prepared for the more deadly charge of infantry which it felt was sure to follow.

They had not long to wait. As the cannon smoke drifted away from between the lines fifteen thousand of Longstreet's

The Now-or-never Charge of Pickett's Men. When the Confederate artillery opened at one o'clock on the afternoon of July 3d, Meade and his staff were driven from their headquarters on Cemetery Ridge. Nothing could live exposed on that hillside, swept by cannon that were being worked as fast as human hands could work them. It was the beginning of Lee's last effort to wrest victory from the odds that were against him. Longstreet, on the morning of the 3d, had earnestly advised against renewing the battle against the Gettysburg heights. But Lee saw that in this moment the fate of the South hung in the balance; that if the Army of Northern Virginia did not win, it would never again become the aggressor. Pickett's division,

PICKETT—THE MARSHALL NEY OF GETTYSBURG

asked of Longstreet if he should go forward. Longstreet merely bowed in answer. "Sir, I shall lead my division forward," said Pickett at last, and the heavy-hearted Longstreet bowed his head. As the splendid column swept out of the woods and across the plain the Federal guns reopened with redoubled fury. For a mile Pickett and his men kept on, facing a deadly greeting of round shot, canister, and the bullets of Hancock's resolute infantry. It was magnificent—but every one of Pickett's brigade commanders went down and their men fell by scores and hundreds around them. A hundred led by Armistead, waving his cap on his sword-point, actually broke through and captured a battery, Armistead falling beside a gun.

as yet not engaged, was the force Lee designated for the assault; every man was a Virginian, forming a veritable Tenth Legion in valor. Auxiliary divisions swelled the charging column to 15,000. In the middle of the afternoon the Federal guns ceased firing. The time for the charge had come. Twice Pickett

It was but for a moment. Longstreet had been right when he said: "There never was a body of fifteen thousand men who could make that attack successfully." Before the converging Federals the thinned ranks of Confederates drifted wearily back toward Seminary Ridge. Victory for the South was not to be.

MEADE'S HEADQUARTERS ON CEMETERY RIDGE

corps emerged in grand columns from the wooded crest of
Seminary Ridge under the command of General Pickett on
the right and General Pettigrew on the left. Longstreet had
planned the attack with a view to passing around Round Top,
and gaining it by flank and reverse attack, but Lee, when he
came upon the scene a few moments after the final orders had
been given, directed the advance to be made straight toward
the Federal main position on Cemetery Ridge.

The charge was one of the most daring in warfare. The
distance to the Federal lines was a mile. For half the distance
the troops marched gayly, with flying banners and glittering
bayonets. Then came the burst of Federal cannon, and the
Confederate ranks were torn with exploding shells. Pettigrew's columns began to waver, but the lines re-formed and
marched on. When they came within musket-range, Hancock's
infantry opened a terrific fire, but the valiant band only quick-
ened its pace and returned the fire with volley after volley.
Pettigrew's troops succumbed to the storm. They broke ranks
and fell back in great disorder. Federal troops from all parts
of the line now rushed to the aid of those in front of Pickett.
The batteries which had been sending shell and solid shot
changed their ammunition, and double charges of grape and
canister were hurled into the column as it bravely pressed into
the sea of flame. The Confederates came close to the Federal
lines and paused to close their ranks. Each moment the fury
of the storm from the Federal guns increased.

" Forward," again rang the command along the line of
the Confederate front, and the Southerners dashed on. The
first line of the Federals was driven back. A stone wall behind them gave protection to the next Federal force. Pickett's
men rushed upon it. Riflemen rose from behind and hurled a
death-dealing volley into the Confederate ranks. A defiant
cheer answered the volley, and the Southerners placed their
battle-flags on the ramparts. General Armistead grasped the
flag from the hand of a falling bearer, and leaped upon the

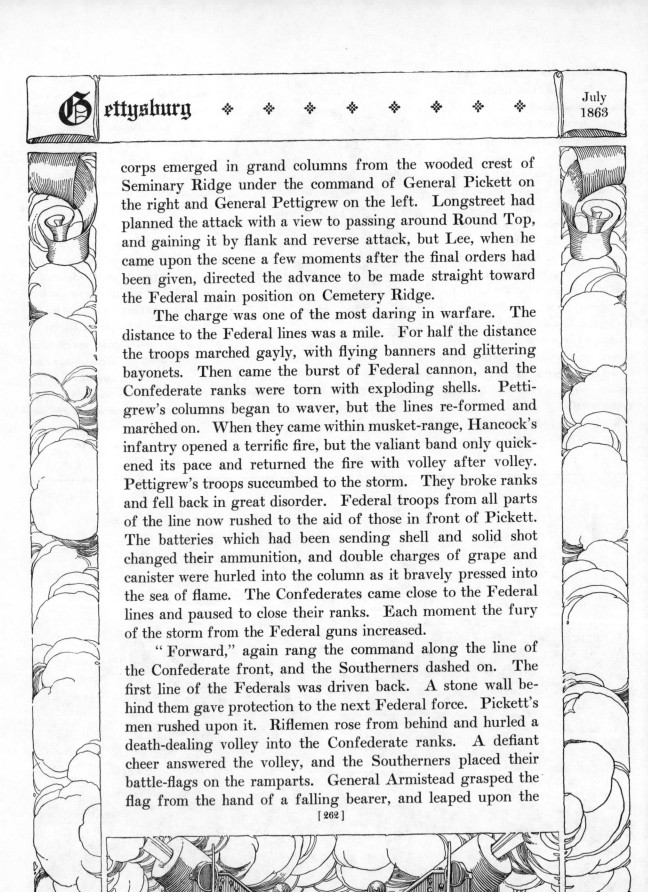

The prelude to Pickett's magnificent charge was a sudden deluge of shells from 159 long-range Confederate guns trained upon Cemetery Ridge. General Meade and his staff were instantly driven from their headquarters (already illustrated) and within five minutes the concentrated artillery fire had swept every unsheltered position on Cemetery Ridge clear of men. In the woods, a mile and a half distant, Pickett and his men watched the effect of the bombardment, expecting the order to "Go Forward" up the slope (shown in the picture). The Federals had instantly opened with their eighty available guns, and for three hours the most terrific artillery duel of the war was kept up. Then the Federal fire slackened, as though the batteries were silenced. The Confederates' artillery ammunition also was now low. "For God's sake, come on!" was the word to Pickett. And at Longstreet's reluctant nod the commander led his 14,000 Virginians across the plain in their tragic charge up Cemetery Ridge.

WHERE PICKETT CHARGED

In that historic charge was Armistead, who achieved a momentary victory and met a hero's death. On across the Emmitsburg road came Pickett's dauntless brigades, coolly closing up the fearful chasms torn in their ranks by the canister. Up to the fence held by Hays' brigade dashed the first gray line, only to be swept into confusion by a cruel enfilading fire. Then the brigades of Armistead and Garnett moved forward, driving Hays' brigade back through the batteries on the crest. Despite the death-dealing bolts on all sides, Pickett determined to capture the guns; and, at the order, Armistead, leaping the fence and waving his cap on his sword-point, rushed forward, followed by about a hundred of his men. Up to the very crest they fought the Federals back, and Armistead, shouting, "Give them the cold steel, boys!" seized one of the guns. For a moment the Confederate flag waved triumphantly over the Federal battery. For a brief interval the fight raged fiercely at close quarters. Armistead was shot down beside the gun he had taken, and his men were driven back. Pickett, as he looked around the top of the ridge he had gained, could see his men fighting all about with clubbed muskets and even flag-staffs against the troops that were rushing in upon them from all sides. Flesh and blood could not hold the heights against such terrible odds, and with a heart full of anguish Pickett ordered a retreat. The despairing Longstreet, watching from Seminary Ridge, saw through the smoke the shattered remnants drift sullenly down the slope and knew that Pickett's glorious but costly charge was ended.

GENERAL L. A. ARMISTEAD, C.S.A.

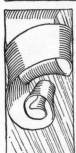

wall, waving it in triumph. Almost instantly he fell among the Federal troops, mortally wounded. General Garnett, leading his brigade, fell dead close to the Federal line. General Kemper sank, wounded, into the arms of one of his men.

Pickett had entered a death-trap. Troops from all directions rushed upon him. Clubbed muskets and barrel-staves now became weapons of warfare. The Confederates began surrendering in masses and Pickett ordered a retreat. Yet the energy of the indomitable Confederates was not spent. Several supporting brigades moved forward, and only succumbed when they encountered two regiments of Stannard's Vermont brigade, and the fire of fresh batteries.

As the remnant of the gallant division returned to the works on Seminary Ridge General Lee rode out to meet them. His demeanor was calm. His features gave no evidence of his disappointment. With hat in hand he greeted the men sympathetically. "It was all my fault," he said. "Now help me to save that which remains."

The battle of Gettysburg was over. The cost in men was frightful. The losses of the two armies reached fifty thousand, about half on either side. More than seven thousand men had fallen dead on the field of battle.

The tide could rise no higher; from this point the ebb must begin. Not only here, but in the West the Southern cause took a downward turn; for at this very hour of Pickett's charge, Grant and Pemberton, a thousand miles away, stood under an oak tree on the heights above the Mississippi and arranged for the surrender of Vicksburg.

Lee could do nothing but lead his army back to Virginia. The Federals pursued but feebly. The Union victory was not a very decisive one, but, supported as it was by the fall of Vicksburg, the moral effect on the nation and on the world was great. The period of uncertainty was ended. It required but little prophetic vision to foresee that the Republic would survive the dreadful shock of arms.

THE MAN WHO HELD THE CENTER

Headquarters of Brigadier-General Alexander S. Webb. It devolved upon the man pictured here (booted and in full uniform, before his headquarters tent to the left of the picture) to meet the shock of Pickett's great charge. In command of three Pennsylvania regiments (the Seventy-First, Seventy-Second, and One Hundred and Sixth) of Hancock's Second Corps, Webb was equal to the emergency. Stirred to great deeds by the example of a patriotic ancestry, he felt that upon his holding his position depended the outcome of the day. His front had been the focus of the Confederate artillery fire. Batteries to right and left of his line were practically silenced. Young Lieutenant Cushing, mortally wounded, fired the last serviceable gun and fell dead as Pickett's men came on. Wheeler's First New York Battery dashed up to take Cushing's place and was captured by the men of Armistead. Webb at the head of the Seventy-second Pennsylvania fought back the on-rush, posting a line of slightly wounded in his rear. Webb himself fell wounded but his command checked the assault till Hall's brilliant charge turned the tide at this point.

THE GOLDEN OPPORTUNITY

The Potomac from Berlin Heights, July, 1863. Instead of a wall of steel in his rear, as might have happened, Lee met only open roads in his retreat after Gettysburg. After the failure of Pickett's charge, Lee and his generals began rallying their troops behind the guns as a protection against the counter-charge which all felt sure was bound to come. Hancock, lying in an ambulance, severely wounded, argued that as he had been struck by a ten-penny nail the Confederate ammunition must be exhausted. His deduction was correct, but although he summoned his waning strength to dictate an approval of the charge, should it be ordered, no advance was made. Meade could have sent forward an entire corps (Sedgwick's) which had not been engaged. By the afternoon of July 4th, Lee's shattered forces were in full retreat toward the Potomac, beyond which lay safety.

THE LEISURELY PURSUIT

Meade's army crossing the Potomac at Berlin, eighteen days after the battle of Gettysburg. Lincoln never ceased to regret that he had not gone in person to Gettysburg to push the pursuit of Lee. Not till July 5th did Meade put his army in motion to follow the Confederates, who had marched all afternoon and all night in the pouring rain, impeded with heavy trains of ammunition which might easily have been captured. Lee found the pontoon bridges which he had left at Falling Waters destroyed by a Federal raiding party sent by General French from Frederick, and drew up his army for the battle that he anticipated must be fought before recrossing the Potomac. Not till the night of July 13th did Meade determine upon an attack. Meanwhile Lee had gained the time necessary to repair his bridges and retreat into Virginia. Meade could not follow directly. Only after a long march through the neighborhood of Harper's Ferry did he get his army across. Before he could strike the Confederates again, Lee was strongly posted along the line of the Rapidan.

CHAPTER ONE

PART IV
ALONG THE TENNESSEE

CHICKAMAUGA—A
CONFEDERATE VICTORY

1864
UNION STOREHOUSES AT BRIDGEPORT, TENNESSEE RIVER

LEE & GORDON'S MILLS ON THE CHICKAMAUGA, SEPTEMBER, 1863

Dozing in the autumn sunlight of 1863, this obscure building, bearing by chance the patronymics of two great Southern generals, was suddenly to mark a strategic point in the most sanguinary of the battles of the West. It stood on the west branch of Chickamauga Creek, which flowed through the fertile valley between Missionary Ridge and Pigeon Mountain. Through the passes of the one the Federals under Rosecrans were advancing on September 12th, while the Confederates under Bragg held the approaches at the other. Between them flowed the little stream, undoubtedly the scene of some prehistoric conflict, for the Indians had named it Chickamauga, "River of Death." In 1863 the word was about to be written into American history to designate a two-days' battle in which the South lost more in killed and wounded than at Gettysburg and the North almost the same number as at Chancellorsville. The storm center

THE BLOODIEST BATTLE-FIELD OF THE WAR

of the mighty conflict had shifted to the West.   After Gettysburg the Army of Northern Virginia and the Army of the Potomac lay warily watching each other, each disinclined to become the aggressor.   Lincoln had been urging Rosecrans to move his Army of the Cumberland on from Murfreesboro and attack Bragg's entrenched position in south central Tennessee so as to prevent Bragg from detaching troops to raise the siege of Vicksburg.   At last, on June 24, 1863, he took the initiative, and then, with what is considered by some military writers the war's masterpiece of strategy, he drove Bragg out of Tennessee into Georgia.   Rosecrans' advance was in Bragg's abandoned works around Tullahoma on July 3d and in Chattanooga on September 9th, all without a battle.   Burnside, with the Army of the Ohio, captured Knoxville on September 3d.   But Tennessee was not to be abandoned by the Confederates without a fight.

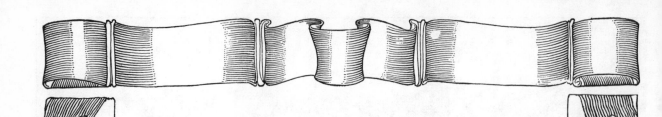

CHICKAMAUGA—THE BLOODIEST CONFLICT IN THE WEST

In its dimensions and its murderousness the battle of Chickamauga was the greatest battle fought by our Western armies, and one of the greatest of modern times. In our Civil War it was exceeded only by Gettysburg and the Wilderness; in European history we may compare with it such battles as Neerwinden, or Malplaquet, or Waterloo.—John Fiske in "The Mississippi Valley in the Civil War."

THE town of Chattanooga, Tennessee, lies in a great bend of the Tennessee River and within a vast amphitheater of mountains, ranging in a general southwesterly direction, and traversed at intervals by great depressions or valleys. These passes form a natural gateway from the mid-Mississippi valley to the seaboard States. To dislodge the Confederate army under General Bragg from this natural fortress would remove the last barrier to the invading Federals, and permit an easy entry upon the plains of Georgia. The importance of this position was readily apparent to the Confederate Government, and any approach by the Federal forces toward this point was almost certain to be met by stubborn resistance.

Rosecrans' forward movement from Murfreesboro, in the early summer of 1863, forced Bragg over the Cumberland Mountains and across the Tennessee. The Confederate leader destroyed the railroad bridge at Bridgeport and entrenched himself in and around Chattanooga. The advanced portion of the Federal army had made its way as far as Stevenson, Alabama, when circumstances compelled a halt. It was found impossible to transport needed forage and supplies over the terrible roads of eastern Tennessee. Rosecrans could go no

[272]

ON THE WAY TO CHICKAMAUGA

To the Elk River Bridge (near Decherd, Tennessee) the enterprising army photographer who was recording Rosecrans' advance had followed the Army of the Cumberland in July, 1863. The two distinct maneuvers that led to Chickamauga fully sustained the reputation of Rosecrans as one of the greatest strategic generals of the war. The first movement was executed in nine days, during which time the troops struggled with their heavy trains along roads little better than bogs. Torrential rains, such as Tennessee had rarely known before, fell incessantly; the artillery had to be dragged through the mire by hand. Despite such difficulties, Rosecrans succeeded in flanking Bragg, compelling him to retreat from his strong position at Tullahoma. South of that place, on the Nashville & Chattanooga Railroad, this bridge was made the objective of Wilder's mounted infantry, which swept around in Bragg's rear, striking the railroad at Decherd, destroying the commissary depot and cutting the rail connection with Chattanooga. A detachment pushed forward to the bridge, but it was too strongly guarded to be destroyed. The Confederates burnt it in their retreat to Chattanooga, but was rebuilt by Rosecrans; it was completed by the Federal engineers on July 13th.

further until the Nashville and Chattanooga Railroad was repaired as far as Stevenson and Bridgeport, and storage depots established at these and neighboring places. Consequently it was not until August 16th that the movement over the Cumberland Mountains began. Rosecrans had the choice of approaching Chattanooga from the north side of the river, a seventy-mile march through a rough, mountainous country, ill supplied with water and forage, or of crossing the Tennessee on the southwest and moving on the town over Sand and Lookout mountains. He chose the latter for all but a small portion of his force, although it was the more hazardous.

Between August 29th and September 4th Crittenden, Thomas, and McCook got their corps over at various places between Shellmound and Caperton's Ferry. General Granger, with the reserve corps, took charge of the rear. When Crittenden received orders for crossing the river he was commanded to leave the brigades of Hazen and Wagner behind to threaten Chattanooga from the north. For some days Wagner had been shelling the town, and Bragg, fully expecting the early approach of the Army of the Cumberland from this direction, had concentrated his forces at and above Chattanooga. Rosecrans, consequently, was able to accomplish the difficult crossing of the Tennessee without interference.

He found the Confederates in possession of the north end of Lookout Mountain and decided to dislodge his adversary by endangering his line of communication from the south and east. McCook on the Federal right was sent across Lookout Mountain at Winston's Gap, forty-six miles south of Chattanooga to occupy Alpine, east of the mountains. Thomas went to McLemore's Cove, east of Missionary Ridge, while Crittenden, on the left, was stationed in Lookout Valley to keep his eye on Chattanooga. The cavalry was sent forward to destroy the Western and Atlantic Railroad near Dalton, Georgia. On September 8th, before all these moves had been accomplished, Bragg abandoned his stronghold.

WHERE THE PONTOONS RAN SHORT

The Railroad Bridge over the Tennessee River at Bridgeport, Alabama, August, 1863. In the movement against Chattanooga, Rosecrans chose the Tennessee River for his line. Feinting strongly with Crittenden's command to the north of Bragg's position, he crossed the main body of his army to the south. There was much impatience in Washington that the movement was not more promptly executed, but serious difficulties delayed it. It took three weeks to repair the railroad, and on August 25th the first supply-train was pushed through Stevenson, Alabama, where the new commissary base was established. Meanwhile the Tennessee, greatly swollen by recent rains, presented a formidable barrier. There were not enough pontoons, and at Bridgeport Sheridan had to piece out the bridge with trestle-work.

Crittenden the next day marched around the north end of Lookout and entered the town, while Hazen and Wagner crossed over from the opposite bank of the Tennessee.

Rosecrans believed that Bragg was in full retreat toward Rome, Georgia, and Crittenden, leaving one brigade in Chattanooga, was ordered to pursue. Bragg encouraged his adversary in the belief that he was avoiding an engagement and sent spies as deserters into the Federal ranks to narrate the details of his flight. Meanwhile, he was concentrating at Lafayette, about twenty-five miles south of Chattanooga. Hither General S. B. Buckner, entirely too weak to cope with Burnside's heavy column approaching from Kentucky, brought his troops from Knoxville. Breckinridge and two brigades arrived from Mississippi, while twelve thousand of Lee's veterans, under Lee's most trusted and illustrious lieutenant, Longstreet, were hastening from Virginia to add their numbers to Bragg's Army of Tennessee.

The three corps of the Union army, as we have seen, were now separated over a wide extent of territory by intervening ridges, so intent was Rosecrans on intercepting the vanished Bragg. But the latter, by no means vanished, and with his face toward Chattanooga, considered the position of his antagonist and discovered his own army almost opposite the Federal center. Crittenden was advancing toward Ringgold, and the remoteness of Thomas' corps on his right precluded any immediate union of the Federal forces.

Bragg was quick to grasp the opportunity made by Rosecrans' division of the army in the face of his opponent. He at once perceived the possibilities of a master-stroke; to crush Thomas' advanced divisions with an overwhelming force.

The attempt failed, owing to a delay in the attack, which permitted the endangered Baird and Negley to fall back. Bragg then resolved to throw himself upon Crittenden, who had divided his corps. Polk was ordered to advance upon that portion of it at Lee and Gordon's Mills, but when Bragg came

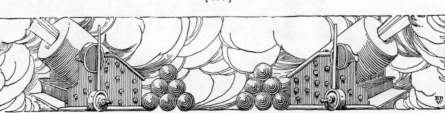

THE FIRST TO REACH THE BATTLE–FIELD

General James S. Negley and Staff.   General Negley (standing uncovered in this picture) formed with his division the advance-guard in the forward movement from the Tennessee against Bragg.   This picture (taken at Cove Spring, near Stevenson, Alabama, before the advance) shows the arduous character of the country through which the march was made.   Crossing the Tennessee at Caperton's Ferry, Negley's division pressed forward, and on September 9th held the passes of Lookout Mountain.   Next day, crossing Missionary Ridge, he took up position in McLemore's Cove.   This was destined to become the battle-field of Chickamauga, and here Negley's advance was checked.   Bragg, instead of being in retreat, was concentrating in his front, eager to crush the corps of Thomas, which he knew had come up too confidently, unsupported by the rest of Rosecrans' army.   On the 11th Negley's position became precarious; Bragg was sending against him such a superior force that he was in great danger of losing his train.   With great energy and skill, supported by Baird's division, he succeeded in falling back to a strong position in front of Stevens' Gap without the loss of a single wagon.   Negley, who was made a major-general for his bravery at Stone's River, was censured by the irascible Rosecrans for his supposed disobedience of orders at Chickamauga.   Subsequent investigation completely exonerated him.   With only a handful of his men he had saved fifty guns in the rout of the 20th.

to the front early on the 13th, expecting to witness the annihilation of the Twenty-first Corps, he found to his bitter disappointment that the bishop-general had made no move and that Crittenden had reunited his divisions and was safe on the west bank of the Chickamauga. Thus his splendid chances of breaking up the Army of the Cumberland were ruined.

When Bragg's position became known to Rosecrans, great was his haste to effect the concentration of his army. Couriers dashed toward Alpine with orders for McCook to join Thomas with the utmost celerity. The former started at once, shortly after midnight on the 13th, in response to Thomas's urgent call. It was a real race of life and death, attended by the greatest hardships. Ignorant of the roads, McCook submitted his troops to a most exhausting march, twice up and down the mountain, fifty-seven miles of the most arduous toil, often dragging artillery up by hand and letting it down steep declines by means of ropes. But he closed up with Thomas on the 17th, and the Army of the Cumberland was saved from its desperate peril.

Crittenden's corps now took position at Lee and Gordon's Mills on the left bank of Chickamauga Creek, and the Federal troops were all within supporting distance. In the Indian tongue Chickamauga means "The River of Death," a name strangely prophetic of that gigantic conflict soon to be waged by these hostile forces throughout this beautiful and heretofore peaceful valley.

The Confederate army, its corps under Generals Polk, D. H. Hill, and Buckner, was stationed on the east side of the stream, its right wing below Lee and Gordon's Mills, and the left extending up the creek toward Lafayette. On the Federal side Thomas was moved to the left, with Crittenden in the center and McCook on the right. The strength of the army was about fifty-seven thousand men. On the 18th of September, Longstreet's troops were arriving from Virginia, and by the morning of the 19th the greater part of the Confederate army

THE LEADER OF THE RIGHT WING

General Alexander McD. McCook at Chickamauga. While Thomas, preceded by Negley, was pressing forward to McLemore's Cove, McCook advanced the right wing of the army to the southward within twenty miles of Lafayette, where Bragg had his headquarters. Crittenden, meanwhile, with the left wing, was advancing from Chattanooga on the north. It was the opportunity to strike one of these widely separated corps that Bragg missed. At midnight on September 13th McCook received the order to hurry back and make junction with Thomas. Then began a race of life and death over fifty-seven miles of excruciating marching, back across Lookout Mountain and northward through Lookout Valley to Stevens' Gap, where he arrived on the 17th. After a brief rest the right wing marched through half the night to its designated position on the battle-field, and by the morning of the 18th Rosecrans' army was at last concentrated. General McCook (of a family that sent a father and five sons into the war) had distinguished himself at Shiloh and Corinth, and with the First Corps of the Army of the Ohio had borne the brunt of the battle at Perryville. At Stone's River he commanded the right wing of the army, which suffered such severe disaster. Again at Chickamauga the right wing, after sending reënforcements to Thomas at the left, was driven back in rout.

had crossed the Chickamauga. The two mighty armies were now face to face, and none could doubt that the impending struggle would be attended by frightful loss to both sides.

It was Bragg's intention to send Polk, commanding the right wing, in a flanking movement against the Federal left under Thomas, and thus intervene between it and Chattanooga. The first encounter, at 10 o'clock in the morning of the 19th, resulted in a Confederate repulse, but fresh divisions were constantly pushed forward under the deadly fire of the Federal artillery. The Federals were gradually forced back by the incessant charge of the Confederates; but assailed and assailant fought with such great courage and determination that any decided advantage was withheld from either. Meanwhile, the Federal right was hard pressed by Hood, commanding Longstreet's corps, and a desperate battle ensued along the entire line. It seemed, however, more like a struggle between separate divisions than the clash of two great armies. When night descended the Federals had been forced back from the creek, but the result had been indecisive.

Disaster to the Union army had been averted by the use of powerful artillery when the infantry seemed unable to withstand the onslaught. Rosecrans had assumed the defensive, and his troops had so far receded as to enable the Confederates to form their lines on all the territory fought over on that day. During the night preparations were made in both camps for a renewal of the battle on the following morning, which was Sunday. A fresh disposition of the troops was made by both leaders. Near midnight General Longstreet arrived on the field, and was at once placed in command of the Confederate left, Polk retaining the right. Not all of Longstreet's troops arrived in time for the battle, but Bragg's whole force now amounted to seventy thousand.

Thomas was given command of the Union left, with McCook at his right, while Crittenden's forces occupied the center, but to the rear of both Thomas and McCook. Thomas had

THE CONFEDERATE LEADER AT CHICKAMAUGA

Major-General Braxton Bragg, C.S.A.   Born, 1815; West Point, 1837;
Died, 1876.   Bragg's name before 1861 was perhaps better known in military annals than that of any other Southern leader because of his brilliant
record in the Mexican War.   In the Civil War he distinguished himself
first at Shiloh and by meritorious services thereafter.   But his delays rendered him scarcely a match for Rosecrans, to say nothing of Grant and
Sherman.   Flanked out of two strong positions, he missed the opportunity
presented by Rosecrans' widely separated forces and failed to crush the
Army of the Cumberland in detail, as it advanced to the battle of Chickamauga.   The error cost the Confederates the loss of Tennessee, eventually.

spent the night in throwing up breastworks on the brow of Snodgrass Hill, as it was anticipated that the Confederates would concentrate their attack upon his position.

Hostilities began with a general movement of the Confederate right wing in an attempt to flank the Union left. General Bragg had ordered Polk to begin the attack at daybreak, but it was nearly ten o'clock in the morning before Breckinridge's division, supported by General Cleburne, advanced upon Thomas' entrenchments. Fighting desperately, the Confederates did not falter under the heavy fire of the Federals, and it seemed as if the latter must be driven from their position. Rosecrans, in response to urgent requests for reenforcements, despatched troops again and again to the aid of Thomas, and the assault was finally repulsed. Cleburne's division was driven back with heavy loss, and Breckinridge, unable to retain any advantage, was forced to defend his right, which was being seriously menaced. The battle at this point had been desperately waged, both sides exhibiting marked courage and determination. As on the previous day, the Confederates had been the aggressors, but the Federal troops had resisted all attempts to invade their breastworks.

However, the fortunes of battle were soon to incline to the side of the Southern army. Bragg sent Stewart's division forward, and it pressed Reynolds' and Brannan's men back to their entrenchments. Rosecrans sent Wood word to close up on Reynolds. Through some misunderstanding in giving or interpreting this order, General Wood withdrew his division from its position on the right of Brannan. By this movement a large opening was left almost in the center of the battle-line. Johnson's, Hindman's, and Kershaw's divisions rushed into the gap and fell upon the Union right and center with an impetus that was irresistible. The Confederate general, Bushrod Johnson, has given us an unforgetable picture of the thrilling event: " The resolute and impetuous charge, the rush of our heavy columns sweeping out from the shadow and gloom of the forest

THE TOO–ADVANCED POSITION

Crawfish Spring, to the South of the Chickamauga Battle-field. Rosecrans, in concentrating his troops on the 18th of September, was still possessed of the idea that Bragg was covering his retreat upon his railroad connections at Dalton. Instead, the Confederate commander had massed his forces on the other side of Chickamauga and was only awaiting the arrival of Longstreet to assume the aggressive. On the morning of the 19th, McCook's right wing at Crawfish Spring was strongly threatened by the Confederates, while the real attack was made against the left in an effort to turn it and cut Rosecrans off from a retreat upon Chattanooga. All day long, brigade after brigade was marched from the right of the Federal line in order to extend the left under Thomas and withstand this flanking movement. Even after nightfall, Thomas, trying to re-form his lines and carry them still farther to the left for the work of the morrow, brought on a sharp conflict in the darkness. The Confederates had been held back, but at heavy cost. That night, at the Widow Glenn's house, Rosecrans consulted his generals. The exhausted Thomas, when roused from sleep for his opinion, invariably answered, "I would strengthen the left." There seemed as yet to be no crisis at hand, and the council closed with a song by the debonair McCook.

into the open fields flooded with sunlight, the glitter of arms, the onward dash of artillery and mounted men, the retreat of the foe, the shouts of the hosts of our army, the dust, the smoke, the noise of fire-arms—of whistling balls, and grape-shot, and of bursting shell—made up a battle-scene of unsurpassed grandeur. Here, General Hood gave me the last order I received from him on the field, 'Go ahead and keep ahead of everything.'" A moment later, and Hood fell, severely wounded, with a minie ball in his thigh.

Wood's right brigade was shattered even before it had cleared the opening. Sheridan's entire division, and part of Davis' and Van Cleve's, were driven from the field. Longstreet now gave a fine exhibition of his military genius. The orders of battle were to separate the two wings of the opposing army. But with the right wing of his opponents in hopeless ruin, he wheeled to the right and compelled the further withdrawal of Federal troops in order to escape being surrounded. The brave soldier-poet, William H. Lytle, fell at the head of his brigade as he strove to re-form his line. McCook and Crittenden were unable, in spite of several gallant efforts, to rally their troops and keep back the onrushing heroes of Stone's River and Bull Run. The broken mass fled in confusion toward Chattanooga, carrying with it McCook, Crittenden, and Rosecrans. The latter telegraphed to Washington that his army had been beaten. In this famous charge the Confederates took several thousand prisoners and forty pieces of artillery.

Flushed with victory, the Confederates now concentrated their attack upon Thomas, who thus far, on Horseshoe Ridge and its spurs, had repelled all attempts to dislodge him. The Confederates, with victory within their grasp, and led by the indomitable Longstreet, swarmed up the slopes in great numbers, but they were hurled back with fearful slaughter. Thomas was looking anxiously for Sheridan, whom, as he knew, Rosecrans had ordered with two brigades to his support.

WHERE THE LINES WERE SWEPT BACK

Lee & Gordon's mill, seen in the picture, marked the extreme right of the Federal line on the second day at Chickamauga. From it, northward, were posted the commands of McCook and Crittenden, depleted by the detachments of troops the day before to strengthen the left. All might have gone well if the main attack of the Confederates had continued to the left, as Rosecrans expected. But hidden in the woods, almost within a stone's throw of the Federal right on that misty morning, was the entire corps of Longstreet, drawn up in columns of brigades at half distance—"a masterpiece of tactics," giving space for each column to swing right or left. Seizing a momentous opportunity which would have lasted but thirty minutes at the most, Longstreet hurled them through a gap which, owing to a misunderstanding, had been left open, and the entire Federal right was swept from the field.

But in Longstreet's rout of the right wing Sheridan, with the rest, had been carried on toward Chattanooga, and he found himself completely cut off from Thomas, as the Confederates were moving parallel to him. Yet the indomitable Sheridan, in spite of his terrible experience of the morning, did not give up the attempt. Foiled in his efforts to get through McFarland's Gap, he moved quickly on Rossville and came down the Lafayette road toward Thomas' left flank.

Meanwhile, advised by the incessant roar of musketry, General Gordon Granger, in command of the reserve corps near Rossville, advanced rapidly with his fresh troops. Acting with promptness and alacrity under orders, Granger sent Steedman to Thomas' right.

Directly across the line of Thomas' right was a ridge, on which Longstreet stationed Hindman with a large command, ready for an attack on Thomas' flank—a further and terrible menace to the nearly exhausted general, but it was not all. In the ridge was a small gap, and through this Kershaw was pouring his division, intent on getting to Thomas' rear. Steedman, with two brigades, drove Kershaw back and swept Hindman from the ridge. This was done in twenty minutes of terrific conflict and frightful slaughter.

The fighting grew fiercer, and at intervals was almost hand to hand. The casualties among the officers, who frequently led their troops in person, were mounting higher and higher as the moments passed. For six long hours the assaults continued, but the Union forces stood their ground. Ammunition ran dangerously low, but Steedman had brought a small supply, and when this was distributed each man had about ten rounds. Finally, as the sun was setting in the west, the Confederate troops advanced in a mighty concourse. The combined forces of Kershaw, Law, Preston, and Hindman once more rushed forward, gained possession of their lost ridge at several points, but were unable to hold their ground. The Union lines stood firm, and the Confederates retired to their

THE HOUSE WHENCE HELP CAME

Here, at his headquarters, holding the Federal line of retreat at Rossville Gap (the Confederate objective in the battle), General Gordon Granger heard with increasing anxiety the sounds of the conflict, three miles away, growing more and more ominous. Finally, in disobedience of orders, he set in motion his three brigades to the relief of Thomas, pushing forward two of them under Steedman. These arrived upon the field early in the afternoon, the most critical period of the battle, as Longstreet charged afresh on Thomas' right and rear. Seizing a battle-flag, Steedman (at the order of General Granger) led his command in a counter-charge which saved the Army of the Cumberland. This old house at Rossville was built by John Ross, a chief of the Cherokee Ind'ns, and he lived in it till 1832, giving his name to the hamlet. Half-breed descendants of the Cherokees who had intermarried with both whites and Negroes were numerous in the vicinity of Chickamauga, and many of them fought with their white neighbors on the Confederate side.

original position at the foot of the slope. Thomas was saved. The onslaught on the Federal left of the battlefield was one of the heaviest attacks made on a single point during the war.

History records no grander spectacle than Thomas' stand at Chickamauga. He was ever afterwards known as " The Rock of Chickamauga." Under the cover of darkness, Thomas, having received word from Rosecrans to withdraw, retired his army in good order to Rossville, and on the follow-ing day rejoined Rosecrans in Chattanooga. The battle of Chickamauga, considering the forces engaged, was one of the most destructive of the Civil War. The Union army lost approximately sixteen thousand men, and while the loss to the Confederate army is not definitely known, it was probably nearly eighteen thousand. The personal daring and tenacious courage displayed in the ranks of both armies have never been excelled on any battlefield. The Confederate generals, Helm, Deshler, and Preston Smith were killed; Adams, Hood, Brown, Gregg, Clayton, Hindman, and McNair were wounded. The Federal side lost Lytle. The battle is generally considered a Confederate victory, and yet, aside from the terrible loss of human life, no distinct advantage accrued to either side. The Federal army retained possession of Chattanooga, but the Confederates had for the time checked the Army of the Cum-berland from a further occupation of Southern soil.

It is a singular coincidence that the generals-in-chief of both armies exercised but little supervision over the movements of their respective troops. The brunt of the battle fell, for the most part, upon the commanders of the wings. To the subor-dinate generals on each side were awarded the highest honors. Longstreet, because of his eventful charge, which swept the right wing of the Union army from the field, was proclaimed the victor of Chickamauga; and to General Thomas, who by his firmness and courage withstood the combined attack of the Confederate forces when disaster threatened on every side, is due the brightest laurels from the adherents of the North.

PART IV
ALONG THE TENNESSEE

———

THE BATTLES
AT CHATTANOOGA

———

ON LOOKOUT MOUNTAIN—1864

IN THE BELEAGUERED CITY

In the parlor of this little dwelling sat Ulysses S. Grant on the evening of October 23, 1863.   Muddy and rain-soaked from his long ride, he was gravely consulting with General Thomas and his officers.   The Army of the Cumberland was in a serious predicament, summed up by Thomas' reply to Grant's first order from Nashville: "We will hold the town till we starve."   Grant had starved a Confederate army out of Vicksburg; and now Bragg's army, reënforced by troops from Johnston, had settled down before Chattanooga to starve out, in turn, what was then the most important Federal force in the West.   Strongly posted on Missionary Ridge and Lookout Mountain and in Chattanooga Valley to the south and southeast of the town, Bragg controlled the railroad, making it impossible for supplies to come over it from Bridgeport, Ala.   Everything had to be brought into Chattanooga by wagon-trains over a roundabout route of nearly

HEADQUARTERS OF GENERAL THOMAS AT CHATTANOOGA

thirty miles. The passage of wagons over the roads was difficult even in good weather, and they were rapidly becoming impassable from the autumn rains. Bragg's forces had fallen upon and burned some three hundred Federal wagons, and with those that were left it was impossible to bring in more than the scantiest supplies. The men had been for weeks on half-rations; all the artillery horses had starved to death; an occasional herd of beef cattle was driven down from Nashville through the denuded country and upon arrival would be aptly characterized by the soldiers as "beef dried on the hoof." This and hard bread were their only sustenance. Grant, now in command of all the Federal forces from the Alleghanies to the Mississippi, was first confronted by the necessity of hastening the delivery of supplies. Either the Army of the Cumberland must be fed or Bragg would regain the ground that had been lost in Tennessee.

THE ATTACK THAT HAD TO WAIT

Near this spot General Sherman crossed his advance column in boats on the night of November 23d and captured all the Confederate pickets along the river except one. Grant, after seizing Brown's Ferry and thus opening a new route for his supplies, ordered Sherman to join him by forced marches. Immediately upon arrival the wearied soldiers of the Army of the Tennessee were assigned the task of opening the main attack upon Bragg's line to the southeast of Chattanooga on Missionary Ridge. Grant did not consider the Army of the Cumberland strong enough to attack Bragg alone, and consequently had postponed such a movement until Sherman could come up. By the 23d of November Sherman's divisions lay in camp, concealed behind the hills near the river bank, at the right of this structure, all ready to cross on a pontoon-bridge which had already been laid higher up the stream.

THE UNEXPECTED VICTORY

The Northeast Slope of Lookout Mountain. This photograph was taken from the hill to the north, where Hooker directed his troops in their "battle above the clouds" on the morning of November 24, 1863. Up this mountain-side Hooker's men fought their way to Pulpit Rock, a height of 2,400 feet. Grant's plan was for nothing more than a demonstration by Hooker to drive the Confederates back from reënforcing their right, where Sherman was to do the heavy work. Hooker's divisions had never before fought together, but with fine ardor they drove Stevenson's six brigades up this slope, and, fighting in the mist, swept them from their entrenchments on the mountain-top. Thus victory first came at the farther end of the line.

THE BATTLES ON LOOKOUT MOUNTAIN AND MISSIONARY RIDGE

AFTER CHATTANOOGA: "The Confederate lines . . . could not be rebuilt. The material for reconstructing them was exhausted. The blue-crested flood which had broken these lines was not disappearing. The fountains which supplied it were exhaustless. It was still coming with an ever increasing current, swelling higher and growing more resistless. This triune disaster [Vicksburg, Gettysburg, Missionary Ridge] was especially depressing to the people because it came like a blight upon their hopes which had been awakened by recent Confederate victories."—*General John B. Gordon, C. S. A., in "Reminiscences of the Civil War."*

FOLLOWING the defeat of Rosecrans' army at Chickamauga, in September, 1863, Bragg at once took strong positions on Missionary Ridge and Lookout Mountain. From these heights he was able to besiege the entire Army of the Cumberland in Chattanooga and obstruct the main arteries of supply to the Federal troops. Rosecrans was forced to abandon the route along the south bank of the Tennessee River, which led from Bridgeport, in Alabama, and to depend exclusively upon a long and mountainous wagon road on the north side of the river for the transportation of supplies. The Confederate cavalry, crossing the Tennessee above Chattanooga, fell upon the trains entangled in the mud of the Sequatchie valley, destroying in one day three hundred wagons, and killing or capturing about eighteen hundred mules. Within a short time the wisdom of Bragg's plan became apparent; famine threatened the Union army and several thousand horses and mules had already died from starvation. By his relentless vigil, the Confederate leader seemed destined to achieve a greater victory over his opponent than had hitherto attended his efforts in actual conflict.

[294]

THE BESIEGED

At this point, where Citico Creek joins the Tennessee, the left of the Eleventh Corps of the Army of the Cumberland rested on the river bank, the limit of the Federal line of defense, east of Chattanooga. Here, on high ground overlooking the stream, was posted Battery McAloon to keep the Confederates back from the river, so that timber and firewood could be rafted down to the besieged army. In the chill of autumn, with scanty rations, the soldiers had a hard time keeping warm, as all fuel within the lines had been consumed. The Army of the Cumberland was almost conquered by hardship. Grant feared that the soldiers "could not be got out of their trenches to assume the offensive." But it was these very men who achieved the most signal victory in the battle of Chattanooga.

Meanwhile, a complete reorganization of the Federal forces in the West was effected. Under the title of the Military Division of the Mississippi, the Departments of the Ohio, the Cumberland, and the Tennessee were united with Grant as general commanding, and Rosecrans was replaced by Thomas at the head of the Army of the Cumberland.

A hurried concentration of the Federal forces was now ordered by General Halleck. Hooker with fifteen thousand men of the Army of the Potomac came rapidly by rail to Bridgeport. Sherman, with a portion of his army, about twenty thousand strong, was summoned from Vicksburg and at once embarked in steamers for Memphis. General Grant decided to assume personal charge of the Federal forces; but before he reached his new command, Thomas, ably assisted by his chief engineer, General W. F. Smith, had begun to act on a plan which Rosecrans had conceived, and which proved in the end to be a brilliant conception. This was to seize a low range of hills known as Raccoon Mountain on the peninsula made by a bend of the river, on its south side and west of Chattanooga, and establish a wagon road to Kelly's Ferry, a point farther down the river to which supplies could be brought by boat from Bridgeport, and at the same time communication effected with Hooker.

A direct line was not only secured to Bridgeport, but Hooker advanced with a portion of his troops into Lookout Valley and after a short but decisive skirmish drove the Confederates across Lookout Creek, leaving his forces in possession of the hills he had gained. The route was now opened between Bridgeport and Brown's Ferry; abundant supplies were at once available and the Army of the Cumberland relieved of its perilous position.

Unlike the condition which had prevailed at Chickamauga, reenforcements from all sides were hastening to the aid of Thomas' army; Hooker was already on the ground; Sherman was advancing rapidly from Memphis, and he arrived in

OPENING "THE CRACKER LINE"

The U. S. S. *Chattanooga* was the first steamboat built by the Federals on the upper Tennessee River. Had the gunboats on the Ohio been able to come up the Tennessee River nearly three hundred miles, to the assistance of Rosecrans, Bragg could never have bottled him up in Chattanooga. But between Florence and Decatur, Alabama, Muscle Shoals lay in the stream, making the river impassable. While Bragg's pickets invested the railroad and river, supplies could not be brought up from Bridgeport; and besides, with the exception of one small steamboat (the *Dunbar*), the Federals had no boats on the river. General W. F. Smith, Chief Engineer of the Army of the Cumberland, had established a saw-mill with an old engine at Bridgeport for the purpose of getting out lumber from logs rafted down the river, with which to construct pontoons. Here Captain Arthur Edwards, Assistant Quartermaster, had been endeavoring since the siege began to build a steamboat consisting of a flat-bottom scow, with engine, boiler, and stern-wheel mounted upon it. On October 24th, after many difficulties and discouragements had been overcome, the vessel was launched successfully and christened the *Chattanooga*. On the 29th she made her trial trip. That very night, Hooker, in the battle of Wauhatchie, definitely established control of the new twelve-mile "Cracker Line" from Kelley's Ferry, which Grant had ordered for the relief of the starving army. The next day the little *Chattanooga*, with steam up, was ready to start from Bridgeport with a heavy load of the much-needed supplies, and her arrival was anxiously awaited at Kelley's Ferry, where the wagon-trains were all ready to rush forward the rations and forage to Chattanooga. The mechanics were still at work upon the little vessel's unfinished pilot-house and boiler-deck while she and the two barges she was to tow were being loaded, and at 4 A.M. on November 30th she set out to make the 45-mile journey against unfavorable head-winds.

person on November 15th, while Burnside's forces at Knoxville offered protection to the left flank of the Federal army.

The disposition of the Confederate troops at this time was a formidable one; the left flank rested on the northern end of Lookout Mountain and the line extended a distance of twelve miles across Chattanooga Valley to Missionary Ridge. This position was further strengthened by entrenchments throughout the lowlands. Despite the danger which threatened his army from the converging Union forces, General Bragg determined to attack Burnside and despatched Longstreet with twenty thousand of his best troops to Knoxville. His army materially weakened, the Confederate general continued to hold the same extended position, although his combined force was smaller than had opposed Rosecrans alone at Chickamauga.

On the 23d of November, after a long and fatiguing march over roads almost impassable by reason of continuous rains, Sherman crossed the Tennessee by the pontoon bridge at Brown's Ferry, recrossed it above Chattanooga, and was assigned a position to the left of the main army near the mouth of Chickamauga Creek. Grant had now some eighty thousand men, of whom sixty thousand were on the scene of the coming battle, and, though fearful lest Burnside should be dislodged from his position at Knoxville, he would not be diverted from his purpose of sweeping the Confederates from the front of Chattanooga. It had been Grant's plan to attack on the 24th, but information reached him that Bragg was preparing a retreat. He, therefore, on the 23d, ordered Thomas to advance upon Bragg's center.

Preparations for the movement were made in full view of the Confederates; from the appearance of the troops, clad in their best uniforms, the advance line of the Southern army was content to watch this display, in the belief that the maneuvering army was parading in review. Suddenly, the peaceful pageant turned into a furious charge, before which the

THE WELCOME NEWCOMER

The home-made little steamboat *Chattanooga* was beset with difficulties and dangers on her memorable voyage of November 30th. She made but slow progress against the wind and the rapid current of the tortuous Tennessee. Fearful of breaking a steam pipe or starting a leak, she crawled along all day, and then was enveloped in one of the darkest of nights, out of which a blinding rain stung the faces of her anxious crew. Assistant Quartermaster William G. Le Duc, in command of the expedition, helped the pilot to feel his way through the darkness. At last the camp-fires of the Federals became guiding beacons from the shore and soon the *Chattanooga* tied up safely at Kelley's Ferry. The "Cracker Line" was at last opened—in the nick of time, for there were but four boxes of hard bread left in the commissary at Chattanooga, where four cakes of hard bread and one-quarter of a pound of pork were being issued as a three-days' ration.

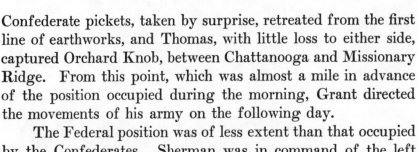

Confederate pickets, taken by surprise, retreated from the first line of earthworks, and Thomas, with little loss to either side, captured Orchard Knob, between Chattanooga and Missionary Ridge. From this point, which was almost a mile in advance of the position occupied during the morning, Grant directed the movements of his army on the following day.

The Federal position was of less extent than that occupied by the Confederates. Sherman was in command of the left wing, while Thomas held the center, and "Fighting Joe" Hooker, with the Union right in Lookout Valley, threatened Lookout Mountain. The plan of battle was for Sherman to engage the Confederate right and sever communications between Bragg and Longstreet; Hooker was to carry out an assault on the Southern left flank, and at the same time maintain connection with Bridgeport. With both wings assailed by a superior force, it was believed that Bragg must reenforce these positions and permit Thomas, with overwhelming numbers, to concentrate upon the center.

On the 24th, two distinct movements were in progress. Sherman met with but little opposition in his initial attack upon the Confederate right and promptly seized and occupied the north end of Missionary Ridge. The Confederates, late in the afternoon, fought desperately to regain the hill but were finally repulsed, and Sherman fortified the position he had gained. In the mean time, Hooker, early in the day, had begun his operations against Lookout Mountain. Standing like a lone sentinel above the surrounding valleys, its steep, rocky, and deeply furrowed slopes, rising into a high, palisaded crest, frowned defiance upon the advancing troops, while a well-constructed line of defenses completed the imposing barrier.

Hooker had in addition to his own troops a division of Sherman's army (Osterhaus') which, owing to damage to the pontoon bridge at Brown's Ferry, had been prevented from joining its own leader. As ordered by Hooker, General Geary took his division up the valley to Wauhatchie, crossed the creek

WHERE AN ARMY GAVE ITS OWN ORDERS

At Missionary Ridge (seen in the distance in the lower picture) the Army of the Cumberland removed forever from Grant's mind any doubt of its fighting qualities. Grant, anxious to develop Bragg's strength, ordered Thomas, on November 23d, to demonstrate against the forces on his front. Moving out as if on parade, the troops under Gordon Granger drove back the Confederates and captured Orchard Knob (or Indian Hill) a day before it had been planned to do so. Still another surprise awaited Grant on the 25th, when from this eminence he watched the magnificent spectacle of the battle of Chattanooga. Thomas' men again pressed forward in what was ordered as a demonstration against Missionary Ridge. Up and over it they drove the Confederates from one entrenchment after another, capturing the guns parked in the lower picture. "By whose orders are those troops going up the hill?" "Old Pap" Thomas, who knew his men better than did Grant, replied that it was probably by their own orders. It was the most signal victory of the day.

THE CAPTURED CONFEDERATE GUNS

and marched down the east bank, sweeping the Confederate outposts before him. The remainder of the command got across by bridges lower down. Gaining the slopes of the mountain the Federal troops rushed on in their advance. From the high palisaded summit, invisible in the low-hanging clouds, the guns of General Stevenson's brigades poured an iron deluge upon them. But on they went, climbing over ledges and boulders, up hill and down, while the soldiers of the South with musket and cannon tried in vain to check them. Position after position was abandoned to the onrushing Federals, and by noon Geary's advanced troops had rounded the north slope of the mountain and passed from the sight of General Hooker, who was watching the contest from a vantage point to the west. Grant and Thomas from the headquarters on Orchard Knob were likewise eager witnesses of the struggle, although the haze was so dense that they caught a glimpse only now and then as the clouds would rise.

Reenforcements came to the Confederates and they availed nothing. Geary's troops had been ordered to halt when they reached the foot of the palisades, but fired by success they pressed impetuously forward. From its higher position at the base of the cliff Cobham's brigade showered volley after volley upon the Confederate main line of defense, while that of Ireland gradually rolled up the flank. The Federal batteries on Moccasin Point across the river were doing what they could to clear the mountain. The Southerners made a last stand in their walls and pits around the Craven house, but were finally driven in force over rocks and precipices into Chattanooga Valley.

Such was the "battle in the clouds," a wonderful spectacle denied the remainder of Hooker's troops holding Lookout Valley. That general says, "From the moment we had rounded the peak of the mountain it was only from the roar of battle and the occasional glimpses our comrades in the valley could catch of our lines and standards that they knew of the

THE MEN WHO COMPLETED THE VICTORY

General Hooker and Staff at Lookout Mountain. Hooker's forces of about 9,700 men had been sent from the East to reënforce Rose-crans, but until the arrival of Grant they were simply so many more mouths to feed in the besieged city. In the battle of Wauhatchie, on the night of October 20th, they drove back the Confederates and established the new line of communication. On November 24th they, too, had a surprise in store for Grant. Their part in the triple conflict was also ordered merely as a "demonstration," but they astounded the eyes and ears of their comrades with the spectacular fight by which they made their way up Lookout Mountain. The next day, pushing on to Rossville, the daring Hooker attacked one of Bragg's divisions and forced it into precipitate retreat.

HOOKER'S CAMP AT THE BASE OF LOOKOUT MOUNTAIN

strife or its progress, and when from these evidences our true condition was revealed to them their painful anxiety yielded to transports of joy which only soldiers can feel in the earliest moments of dawning victory."

By two in the afternoon the clouds had settled completely into the valley and the ensuing darkness put an end to further operations. Hooker established and strengthened a new position and waited for reenforcements, which General Carlin brought from Chattanooga at five o'clock. Until after midnight an irregular fire was kept up, but the Confederates could not break the new line. Before dawn General Stevenson abandoned the summit, leaving behind twenty thousand rations and the camp equipage of his three brigades. Hooker, anticipating this move, sent several detachments to scale the palisades. A party of six men from the Eighth Kentucky regiment, by means of ladders, was the first to reach the summit, and the waving Stars and Stripes greeted the rising sun of November 25th on Lookout Mountain, amid the wild and prolonged cheers of " Fighting Joe's " valiant troops.

The fighting of Sherman and Hooker on the 24th secured to Grant's army a distinct advantage in position. From the north end of Lookout Mountain across Chattanooga Valley to the north end of Missionary Ridge the Union forces maintained an unbroken front.

The morning of the 25th dawned cold, and an impenetrable mist which lay deep in the valleys was soon driven away. From Orchard Knob, a point almost in the center of the united Federal host, General Grant watched the preparations for the battle. At sunrise, Sherman's command was in motion. In his front, an open space intervened between his position and a ridge held by the Confederates, while just beyond rose a much higher hill. Toward the first ridge the attacking column, under General Corse, advanced rapidly and in full view of the foe. For a time it seemed as if the Confederates must recede before the terrific onslaught, but the advance was abruptly

THE BATTLE–FIELD ABOVE THE CLOUDS

Entrenchments on Lookout Mountain.   Up such rugged heights as these, heavily timbered and full of chasms, Hooker's men fought their way on the afternoon of November 24th.   Bridging Lookout Creek, the troops crossed, hidden by the friendly mist, and began ascending the mountain-sides, driving the Confederates from one line of rifle-pits and then from another.   The heavy musketry fire and the boom of the Confederate battery on the top of the mountain apprised the waiting Federals before Chattanooga that the battle had begun.   Now and again the fitful lifting of the mist disclosed to Grant and Thomas, watching from Orchard Knob, the men of Hooker fighting upon the heights.   Then all would be curtained once more.   At two o'clock in the afternoon the mist became so heavy that Hooker and his men could not see what they were doing, and paused to entrench.   By four o'clock, however, he had pushed on to the summit and reported to Grant that his position was impregnable.   Direct communication was then established and reënforcements sent.

checked after a very close and stubborn struggle, when within a short distance of the entrenchment.

Unmindful of the numbers which opposed him, General Hardee not only succeeded in repulsing the attack, but, assuming the offensive, drove back the forces under General John E. Smith, who had sought to turn his left, and captured several hundred prisoners. The Federals, quickly re-forming their lines, renewed the assault and for several hours the fighting was desperate on both sides. A general advance of the Northern forces had been withheld, awaiting the arrival of Hooker who, under orders from Grant, was sweeping down Chickamauga Valley, and was to operate against the Confederate left and rear, in the expectation that Bragg would further weaken his line by massing at those points. But Hooker's army had been delayed several hours by repairs to the bridge crossing Chattanooga Creek. Although Sherman had failed in his attempt to turn the Confederate right he had forced Bragg to draw heavily upon his center for reenforcements. Grant, satisfied that Hooker was not far off, ordered the signal—six guns fired in rapid succession from the battery on Orchard Knob—for a general advance of Thomas' army upon the Confederate center.

It was now three o'clock in the afternoon. The four division commanders of the Army of the Cumberland, Sheridan, Wood, Baird, and Johnson, gave the word to advance. Between Orchard Knob and the base of Missionary Ridge, a mile away, is a broad valley covered for the most part with heavy timber. This had to be crossed before the entrenchments at the foot of the hill could be assaulted. Scarcely were the Cumberland troops in motion when fifty pieces of artillery on the crest of Missionary Ridge opened a terrific fire upon them. But the onward rush of the Federals was not checked in the slightest degree. The line of entrenchments at the base was carried with little opposition. Most of Breckinridge's men abandoned the ditches as the Federal skirmishers approached

THE PEAK OF VICTORY—THE MORNING AFTER THE BATTLE

Pulpit Rock, the Summit of Lookout Mountain. Before dawn of November 25th, Hooker, anticipating the withdrawal of the Confederates, sent detachments to seize the very summit of the mountain, here 2,400 feet high. Six volunteers from the Eighth Kentucky Regiment scaled the palisades by means of the ladders seen in this picture, and made their way to the top. The rest of the regiment quickly followed; then came the Ninety-sixth Illinois. The rays of the rising sun disclosed the Stars and Stripes floating in triumph from the lofty peak "amid the wild and prolonged cheers of the men whose dauntless valor had borne them to that point."

and sought refuge up the hill, breaking and throwing into confusion other troops as they passed through.

At the foot of Missionary Ridge Thomas' army had reached its goal. Its orders carried it no further. But, as General Wood has related, " the enthusiasm and impetuosity of the troops were such that those who first reached the entrenchments at the base of the ridge bounded over them and pressed on up the ascent. . . . Moreover the entrenchments were no protection against the artillery on the ridge. To remain would be destruction—to return would be both expensive in life, and disgraceful. Officers and men, all seemed impressed with this truth. . . . Without waiting for an order the vast mass pressed forward in the race for glory, each man anxious to be the first on the summit. . . . Artillery and musketry could not check the impetuous assault. The troops did not halt to fire. To have done so would have been ruinous. Little was left to the commanders of the troops than to cheer on the foremost—to encourage the weaker of limb and to sustain the very few who seemed to be faint-hearted."

Midway up the slope was a small line of rifle-pits, but these proved of no use in stemming the Federal tide. In the immediate front, however, Major Weaver of the Sixtieth North Carolina rallied a sufficient number of the demoralized Confederates to send a well-directed and effective fire upon the advancing troops. At this point the first line of oncoming Federals was vigorously repulsed, and thrown back to the vacated Confederate trenches. General Bragg, noticing this, rode along the ridge to spread his good news among the troops, but he had not gone far when word was brought that the right flank was broken and that the Federal standard had been seen on the summit. A second and a third flag appeared in quick succession. Bragg sent General Bate to drive the foe back, but the disaster was so great that the latter was unable to repair it. Even the artillery had abandoned the infantry. The Confederate flank had gone, and within an hour of the start from

THE FLANKING PASS

The Gap in Missionary Ridge at Rossville. Through this Georgia mountain-pass runs the road to Ringgold. Rosecrans took advantage of it when he turned Bragg's flank before the battle of Chickamauga; and on November 25, 1863, Thomas ordered Hooker to advance from Lookout Mountain to this point and strike the Confederates on their left flank, while in their front he (Thomas) stood ready to attack. The movement was entirely successful, and in a brilliant battle, begun by Hooker, Bragg's army was swept from Missionary Ridge and pursued in retreat to Georgia.

THE SKIRMISH LINE

Multiply the number of these men by ten, strike out the tents, and we see vividly how the advancing line of Thomas' Army of the Cumberland appeared to the Confederates as they swept up the slope at Missionary Ridge to win the brilliant victory of November 25th. This view of drilling Federal troops in Chattanooga preserves the exact appearance of the line of battle only a couple of months before the picture was taken. The skirmishers, thrown out in advance of the line, are "firing" from such positions as the character of the ground makes most effective. The main line is waiting for the order to charge.

CONQUERING THE CURRENT

The "Suck" in the Tennessee River below Chattanooga. Through this narrow gorge in Raccoon Mountain the water rushes with such force that vessels cannot stem the current under their own steam. The little *Chattanooga* could not be rendered the customary assistance of windlass and shore-lines while Bragg's forces invested the river, consequently she could ascend it only so far as Kelly's Ferry. In the picture one of the river steamers is being warped through this difficult part of the stream.

THE RIVER OPENED

The success of the little *Chattanooga* spurred the Federal saw-mill at Bridgeport to renewed activity. Captain Edwards' shipyard was greatly enlarged after the defeat of Bragg, and in a remarkably short time thirteen staunch transports and four light-draft gunboats were built. Their trial trips during the spring and summer of 1864 were watched with interest because of the difficulties of navigation at "the Suck," where the current of the Tennessee River prevented the small craft from ascending under their own steam.

THE READY RIVER ROUTE

Here, waiting to get through the "Suck," below Chattanooga, are some of the light-draft river steamers which enabled Grant to establish communications almost immediately after his successful encounter with Bragg. The smoke of the Chattanooga battles had scarely cleared away when the two little steamboats then at the disposal of the Federals were loaded with supplies for Burnside, besieged in Knoxville. They were to steam up the Tennessee, abreast of the troops, as far as the mouth of the Holston River, so that their freight might reach Burnside's famished troops as soon as the reënforcements drove off Longstreet. When this was done the river steamers plying between Knoxville and Chattanooga were kept busy and the former became a secondary base. Preparations for the Spring campaign were now set afoot. There were two objectives in Grant's mind. General Joseph E. Johnston had succeeded Bragg in

FEDERAL TRANSPORTS IN THE TENNESSEE, WINTER OF 1863-4

command of the Confederate forces, and to vanquish his army and obtain possession of Atlanta were the important things. But Grant looked further into the future. An expedition against Mobile was seriously considered, and from Nashville, to which place Grant had returned, the telegraph wires were kept busy. Every effort was made to strengthen the Federal positions and prepare for the important movements that were to follow. Early in January, 1864, the Commander-in-Chief, with his staff, returned to Chattanooga, and, boarding one the little river steamers, proceeded up the Tennessee as far as its junction with the Clinch River, up to which point the tedious repairs of the railroad from Knoxville to Chattanooga had progressed. From Knoxville Grant and his staff rode out over the frozen and difficult road to inspect the line of communication from Cumberland Gap that it was necessary to abandon or improve.

PREPARING FOR PERMANENT OCCUPATION

Bragg was now definitely driven from Tennessee, and his beaten army lay in winter quarters at Dalton, Georgia, holding the rail-road to Atlanta Longstreet had failed at Knoxville, and after a winter of hardship in the unfriendly mountain regions was to make his way back to Lee for the final struggle. This bridge was the last link in the connection by rail between Nashville and Chatta-nooga, and the Federal engineers at once set about rebuilding it so that trains might be run into the latter city, which was now made

MILITARY RAILROAD BRIDGE OVER CHATTANOOGA CREEK, DECEMBER, 1863

a military post. The original structure was destroyed by Bragg September 7, 1863, when he withdrew from Chattanooga, outflanked by Rosecrans. Grant had saved the Army of the Cumberland and Chattanooga, and Sherman had pressed forward to the relief of Burnside at Knoxville, driving off Longstreet. Chattanooga and Knoxville, now occupied by the Federals, were to become new bases for still greater and more aggressive operations by Sherman against the Confederate army in Georgia the following year.

COUNTRY HARD TO HOLD

Whiteside Valley, Tennessee. Over such difficult ground as this the Army of the Cumberland had to make its way in the Chattanooga campaign. Therein lay one valid reason why the Confederates were not sooner swept from eastern Tennessee, as President Lincoln and the War Department at Washington impatiently expected. Only the men who marched over the mountain roads knew to the full the hardships that the task involved. Railroad communications were constantly threatened and interrupted and, when this happened, the daily bread of the soldiers must be hauled in groaning wagon-trains by long, roundabout routes over the almost impassable mountain roads. On these roads points open to attack had to be properly guarded. Even the crude bridges shown in the picture must be commanded by protecting blockhouses or the army might be without food for days.

COMMUNICATION COMPLETED

Railroad Bridge Across the Ravine of Running Water at Whiteside, Tennessee. In this picture stands one of the most notable of the almost incredible achievements of army engineers in the Civil War. Between Whiteside and Wauhatchie the railroad on its way in Chattanooga curves southward almost along the boundary of Alabama, and the destroyed bridge at Whiteside had to be replaced before trains could be run into Chattanooga, which was to be held as a Federal military post and base for future operations in Georgia. Here, fourteen miles from Chattanooga, the engineers built this four-tier trestle-bridge, 780 feet long and 116 feet high in the center, completing the work in a remarkably short time toward the close of 1863. Plans for Sherman's Atlanta campaign were already formulating and it was necessary that this bridge in its isolated position should be strongly held. The camp of the Federal detachment constantly on guard here is seen in the picture, and two of the four double-cased blockhouses, which served as refuges from any attack.

Orchard Knob the crest of Missionary Ridge was occupied by Federal troops. Sheridan did not stop here. He went down the eastern slope, driving all in front of him toward Chickamauga Creek. On a more easterly ridge he rested until midnight, when he advanced to the creek and took many prisoners and stores.

While the Army of the Cumberland accomplished these things, Hooker was advancing his divisions at charging pace from the south. Cruft was on the crest, Osterhaus in the eastern valley, and Geary in the western—all within easy supporting distance. Before Cruft's onrush the left wing of Bragg's army was scattered in all directions from the ridge. Many ran down the eastern slope into Osterhaus' column and the very few who chose a way of flight to the west, were captured by Geary. The bulk of them, however, fell back from trench to trench upon the crest until finally, as the sun was sinking, they found themselves surrounded by Johnson's division of the Army of the Cumberland. Such was the fate of Stewart's division; only a small portion of it got away.

On the Confederate right Hardee held his own against Sherman, but with the left and center routed and in rapid flight Bragg realized the day was lost. He could do nothing but cover Breckinridge's retreat as best he might and order Hardee to retire across Chickamauga Creek.

Thus ended the battle of Chattanooga. Bragg's army had been wholly defeated, and, after being pursued for some days, it found a resting place at Dalton among the mountains of Georgia. The Federal victory was the result of a campaign carefully planned by Generals Halleck and Grant and ably carried out by the efforts of the subordinate generals.

The losses in killed and wounded sustained by Grant were over fifty-eight hundred and those of Bragg about sixty-six hundred, four thousand being prisoners. But the advantage of the great position had been forever wrested from the Southern army.

PART V

ENGAGEMENTS
OF THE CIVIL WAR

THE SIEGE OF CHARLESTON, JULY–SEPTEMBER, 1863.
A BREACHING BATTERY IN THE MARSHES.   BELOW
ARE FEDERAL MORTARS ON MORRIS ISLAND,
TURNED AGAINST SUMTER

ENGAGEMENTS OF THE CIVIL WAR

WITH LOSSES ON BOTH SIDES

AUGUST, 1862—APRIL, 1864

CHRONOLOGICAL summary and record of historical events, and of important engagements between the Union and the Confederate armies, in the Civil War in the United States, showing troops participating, losses and casualties, collated and compiled by George L. Kilmer from the official records of the Union and Confederate armies filed in the United States War Department. Minor engagements are omitted; also some concerning which statistics, especially Confederate, are not available.

AUGUST, 1862.

3.—Jonesboro', L'Anguille Ferry, Ark. *Union,* 1st Wis. Cav.; *Confed.,* Parsons' Texas Rangers. Losses: *Union,* 11 killed, 33 wounded, 21 missing; *Confed.* *

5.—Baton Rouge, La. *Union,* 14th Me., 6th Mich., 7th Vt., 21st Ind., 30th Mass., 9th Conn., 4th Wis., 2d, 4th, and 6th Mass. Batteries; *Confed.,* Four brigades under command of Gen. John C. Breckinridge, Semmes' Battery and Pond's Partisan Rangers. Losses: *Union,* 82 killed, 255 wounded, 34 missing; *Confed.,* 84 killed, 316 wounded, 78 missing; *Union,* Brig.-Gen. Thomas Williams killed.

—Malvern Hill, Va. *Union,* Portion of Hooker's Div., Third Corps, and Richardson's Div., Second Corps and Cavalry, Army of the Potomac; *Confed.,* Divisions of Longstreet, McLaws, Jones, and Ripley, Army of Northern Virginia, Gen. R. E. Lee commanding. Losses: *Union,* 3 killed, 11 wounded; *Confed.,* 100 captured.

6.—Kirksville, Mo. *Union,* Detachments commanded by Col. John McNeil, 2d Mo. Cav.; *Opponents,* Porter's independent forces. Losses: *Union,* 28 killed, 60 wounded (estimated); Porter's loss, 128 killed, 200 wounded (estimated).

—Matapony or Thornburg, Va. *Union,* Gen. John Gibbons' Brigade; *Confed.,* Stuart's Cav. Losses: *Union,* 1 killed, 12 wounded, 72 missing; *Confed.* *

9.—Cedar Mountain, Va., also called Slaughter Mountain, Southwest Mountain, Cedar Run, and Mitchell's Station. *Union,* Second Corps, Maj.-Gen. Banks; Third Corps, Maj.-Gen. McDowell; Army of Virginia, under command of Maj.-Gen. Pope; *Confed.,* Army commanded by Gen. T. J. ("Stonewall") Jackson as follows: Gen. C. S. Winder's Division; Gen. R. S. Ewell's Division; Gen. A. P. Hill's Division. Losses: *Union,* 450 killed, 660 wounded, 290 missing; *Confed.,* 229 killed, 1,047 wounded, 31 missing; *Union,* Brig.-Gens. Augur, Carroll, and Geary wounded; *Confed.,* Brig.-Gen. C. S. Winder killed.

10 to 13.—Grand River, Lee's Ford, Chariton River, Walnut Creek, Compton Ferry, Switzler's Mills, and Yellow Creek, Mo. *Union,* 9th Mo. Cav.; *Opponents,* Poindexter's Independent forces. Losses: *Union,* 5 wounded. Poindexter lost 150 men killed and wounded, 100 captured [estimated].

11.—Independence, Mo. *Union,* 7th Mo. Cav.; *Confed.,* Col. J. T. Hughes' command. Losses: *Union,* 26 killed, 30 wounded, 256 missing; *Confed.* *

12.—Gallatin, Tenn. *Union,* 28th Ky. (4 co's) surrendered to Morgan's Cavalry.

16.—Lone Jack, Mo. *Union,* 7th Mo. Cav.; *Confed.,* Col. Cockrell's Cav. Losses: *Union,* 43 killed, 54 wounded, 73 missing; *Confed.,* 118 killed and wounded.

* No record found.

THE GENERAL–IN–CHIEF IN 1862

Major-General Henry Wager Halleck; born 1814; West Point 1839; died 1872. Sherman credits Halleck with having first discovered that Forts Henry and Donelson, where the Tennessee and the Cumberland Rivers so closely approach each other, were the keypoints to the defensive line of the Confederates in the West. Succeeding Fremont in November, 1861, Halleck, importuned by both Grant and Foote, authorized the joint expedition into Tennessee, and after its successful outcome he telegraphed to Washington: "Make Buell, Grant, and Pope major-generals of volunteers and give me command in the West. I ask this in return for Donelson and Henry." He was chosen to be General-in-Chief of the Federal Armies at the crisis created by the failure of McClellan's Peninsula Campaign. Halleck held this position from July 11, 1862, until Grant, who had succeeded him in the West, finally superseded him at Washington.

19.—Clarksville, Tenn. *Union*, 71st Ohio (5 co's) surrendered to Confederates commanded by Col. A. R. Johnson. Losses: *Union*, 350 captured.

23.—Big Hill, Madison Co., Ky. *Union*, 3d Tenn. (Houk's Battalion), 7th Ky. Cav.; *Confed.*, 1st La. Cav. Losses: *Union*, 120 killed, wounded, and missing (estimate); *Confed.*, 4 killed, 12 wounded.

23 to 25.—Skirmishes on the Rappahannock at Waterloo Bridge, Lee Springs, Freeman's Ford and Sulphur Springs, Va. *Union*, Milroy's Brigade, Army of Virginia; *Confed.*, Gen. Longstreet's command. Losses: *Confed.*, 27 killed, 94 wounded; *Union*, Brig.-Gen. Bohlen captured.

23 to Sept. 1.—Pope's Campaign in Virginia. *Union*, Army of Virginia, commanded by Gen. John Pope; *Confed.*, Army of Northern Virginia, commanded by Gen. R. E. Lee. Losses: *Union*, 1747 killed, 8452 wounded, and 4623 missing; *Confed.*, 1090 killed, 6154 wounded.

25 and 26.—Fort Donelson and Cumberland Iron Works, Tenn. *Union*, 71st Ohio (4 co's), 5th Ia. Cav.; *Confed.*, Col. Woodward's command. Losses: *Union*, 31 killed and wounded; *Confed.*, 30 killed and wounded.

27.—Bull Run Bridge, Va. *Union*, 11th and 12th Ohio, 1st, 2d, 3d, and 4th N. J.; *Confed.*, Part of Gen. "Stonewall" Jackson's command. Losses:* *Union*, Brig.-Gen. G. W. Taylor mortally wounded.

—Kettle Run, Va. *Union*, Maj.-Gen. Hooker's Div. of Third Corps; *Confed.*, Ewell's Division of Jackson's Corps. Losses: *Union*, 300 killed and wounded; *Confed.*, 300 killed and wounded.

28 and 29.—Groveton and Gainesville, Va. *Union*, First Corps, Maj.-Gen. Sigel, Third Corps, Maj.-Gen. McDowell, Army of Virginia, Hooker's and Kearny's Divisions of Third Corps and Reynolds' Division of First Corps, Army of Potomac, Ninth Corps, Maj.-Gen. Reno, Buford's cavalry brigade (Second Corps); *Confed.*, Army of Northern Virginia commanded by Gen. Robert E. Lee, as follows: Right Wing, Gen. James Longstreet's Corps; Left Wing, Gen. T. J. Jackson's Corps; Cavalry Division, Gen. J. E. B. Stuart. Casualties included in those given for the campaign, Aug. 23 to Sept. 1.

—McMinnville, Tenn. *Union*, 18th Ohio (2 co's) 9th Mich. (1 co); *Confed.*, Forrest's Cav. Losses: *Union*, 9 wounded; *Confed.*, 12 killed, 41 wounded.

30.—Second Battle of Bull Run or Manassas, Va. Same troops as engaged at Groveton and Gainesville on the 28th and 29th, with the addition of Porter's Fifth Corps (*Union*). Casualties included as above.

—Bolivar, Tenn. *Union*, 20th, 78th Ohio, 2d Ill. Cav. (4 co's), 11th Ill. Cav. (2 co's) 9th Ind. Battery; *Confed.*, Armstrong's Cavalry. Losses: *Union*, 5 killed, 18 wounded, 64 missing. *Confed.*, 100 killed and wounded (estimate).

—Richmond, Ky. *Union*, 12th, 16th, 55th, 66th, 69th and 71st Ind., 95th Ohio, 18th Ky., 6th and 7th Ky. Cav., Batteries D and G Mich. Art.; *Confed.*, Four brigades under Generals Kirby Smith and Patrick Cleburne. Losses: *Union*, 200 killed, 700 wounded, 4000 missing; *Confed.*, 250 killed, 500 wounded.

SEPTEMBER, 1862

1.—Britton's Lane, Tenn. *Union*, 20th and 30th Ill., 4th Ill. Cav., Foster's (Ohio) Cav., Battery A 2d Ill. Art. *Confed.*, Gen. F. C. Armstrong's command. Losses: *Union*, 5 killed, 51 wounded, 52 missing; *Confed.*, 179 killed, 100 wounded. (Union Report.)

—Chantilly, Va. *Union*, McDowell's Corps, Army of Virginia. Hooker's and Kearny's Divisions of Third Corps, Army of Potomac, Reno's Ninth Corps; *Confed.*, "Stonewall" Jackson's Corps. Losses: *Union*, 1300 killed, wounded, and missing; *Confed.*, 800 *killed*, wounded, and missing; *Union*, Maj.-Gen. Kearny and Brig.-Gen. Stevens killed.

6.—Washington, N. C. *Union*, 24th Mass., 1st N. C., 3d N. Y. Cav.; *Confed.*, Gen. J. G. Martin's command. Losses: *Union*, 7 killed, 47 wounded; *Confed.*, 30 killed, 100 wounded.

10.—Fayetteville, W. Va. *Union*, 34th, 37th Ohio, 4th W. Va.; *Confed.*, Gen. W. W. Loring's command. Losses: *Union*, 13 killed, 80 wounded.

* No record found.

A DARING MOVE OF SEPTEMBER, 1862

Ruins of the Bridge at Harper's Ferry, Virginia. Lee had invaded Maryland. Boldly dividing his army, which was but two-thirds as strong as that of McClellan, who was confronting him with seventy-five thousand men, he sent the swift and silent Jackson to capture Harper's Ferry, renowned as the place where John Brown was captured. Europe, watching with keen interest the progress of the war, was dazzled by the splendid coöperation of the two great Confederate leaders. By the stroke at Harper's Ferry Lee removed an element of danger from his rear, while his advance into Maryland was causing consternation throughout the North. The Federal garrison of twelve thousand five hundred men at Harper's Ferry, out-numbered and out-maneuvered by Jackson, surrendered on September 15th, after a two-days' defense, and Jackson rejoined Lee in Maryland just in time to stem the tide at Antietam.

Engagements of the Civil War

12 to 15.—Harper's Ferry, Va. *Union,* 39th, 111th, 115th, 125th, and 126th N. Y., 12th N. Y. Militia, 32d, 60th, and 87th Ohio, 9th Vt., 65th Ill., 15th Ind., 1st and 3d Md. Home Brigade, 8th N. Y. Cav., 12th Ill. Cav., 7th Squadron R. I. Cav., five batteries of Artil.; *Confed.,* Gen. T. J. Jackson's Corps; Gen. R. H. Anderson's Division; Gen. J. G. Walker's Division; Gen. Lafayette McLaws' Division. Losses: *Union,* 44 killed, 173 wounded, 12520 missing and captured; *Confed.,* 500 killed and wounded.

14.—Turner's and Crampton's Gap, South Mountain, Md. *Union,* First Corps, Maj.-Gen. Hooker; Sixth Corps, Maj.-Gen. Franklin; Ninth Corps, Maj.-Gen. Reno; *Confed.,* Gen. D. H. Hill's Division; Gen. Lafayette McLaws' Division. Losses: *Union,* 443 killed, 1806 wounded. *Confed.,* 500 killed, 2343 wounded, 1500 captured; *Union,* Maj.-Gen. Reno killed; *Confed.,* Brig.-Gen. Garland killed.

14 to 16.—Mumfordsville, Ky. *Union,* 18th U. S. Inft., 28th and 33d Ky., 17th, 50th, 60th, 67th, 68th, 74th, 78th, and 89th Ind., Conkle's Battery, 13th Ind. Artil., and Louisville Provost Guard; *Confed.,* Army of the Tennessee, commanded by Gen. Braxton Bragg. Losses: *Union,* 50 killed, 3566 captured and missing; *Confed.,* 714 killed and wounded.

17.—Antietam or Sharpsburg, Md. *Union,* Army of the Potomac, commanded by Maj.-Gen. Geo. B. McClellan, as follows: First Corps, Maj.-Gen. Joseph Hooker; Second Corps, Maj.-Gen. E. V. Sumner; Fifth Corps, Maj.-Gen. Fitz-John Porter; Sixth Corps, Maj.-Gen. W. B. Franklin; Ninth Corps, Maj.-Gen. A. E. Burnside; Twelfth Corps, Maj.-Gen. J. K. F. Mansfield, Brig.-Gen. Alpheus Williams; Couch's Div., Fourth Corps; Pleasonton's Cavalry; *Confed.,* Army of Northern Virginia, commanded by Gen. Robert E. Lee, as follows: Maj.-Gen. James Longstreet's Corps; Maj.-Gen. T. J. Jackson's Corps; Reserve Artillery, Gen. W. N. Pendleton, Gen. J. E. B. Stuart's Cavalry. Losses: *Union,* 2010 killed, 9416 wounded, 1043 missing; *Confed.,* total in the campaign, 1890 killed, 9770 wounded, 2304 missing; *Union,* Maj.-Gen. Mansfield killed, Maj.-Gens. Hooker and Richardson, and Brig.-Gens. Rodman, Weber, Sedgwick, Hartsuff, Dana, and Meagher wounded; *Confed.,* Brig.-Gens. Branch, Anderson, and Starke killed, Maj.-Gen. Anderson, Brig.-Gens. Toombs, Lawton, Ripley, Rodes, Gregg, Armistead, and Ransom wounded.

19 and 20.—Iuka, Miss. *Union,* Stanley's and Hamilton's Divisions, Army of the Mississippi, under Maj.-Gen. Rosecrans; *Confed.,* Gen. Sterling Price, Army of the West; Gen. Henry Little's Division, Gen. Frank C. Armstrong's Cavalry. Losses: *Union,* 144 killed, 598 wounded; *Confed.,* 263 killed, 692 wounded, 561 captured; *Confed.,* Brig.-Gens. Little killed and Whitfield wounded.

20.—Blackford's Ford, Shepherdstown, Va. *Union,* Fifth Corps, Griffin's and Barnes' Brigades; *Confed.,* Gen. A. P. Hill's Division. Losses: *Union,* 92 killed, 131 wounded, 103 missing; *Confed.,* 33 killed, 231 wounded.

30.—Newtonia, Mo. *Union,* 1st Brigade Army of Kansas, 4th Brigade Mo. Militia Cav.; *Confed.,* 3000 Indians under Col. D. H. Cooper, Gen. Shelby's Cav. Losses: *Union,* 50 killed, 80 wounded, 115 missing; *Confed.,* 220 killed, 280 wounded.

OCTOBER, 1862.

1.—Shepherdstown, Va. *Union,* 8th Ill., 8th Penna., 3d Ind. Cav., Pennington's Battery; *Confed.,* Stuart's Cav. Losses: *Union,* 12 wounded; *Confed.,* 60 killed.

3 and 4.—Corinth, Miss. *Union,* McKean's, Davies', Hamilton's, and Stanley's Divisions, Army of the Miss.; *Confed.,* Army of West Tennessee, commanded by Gen. Earl Van Dorn, Gen. Price's Corps, and Gen. Mansfield Lovell's Division of Mississippians. Losses: *Union,* 315 killed, 1812 wounded, 232 missing; *Confed.,* 1423 killed, 5692 wounded, 2248 missing. *Union,* Brig.-Gens. Hackleman killed and Oglesby wounded.

5.—Metamora, on Big Hatchie River, Miss. *Union,* Hurlburt's and Ord's Divisions; *Confed.,* Rear-Guard of Van Dorn's Army. Losses: *Union,* 500 killed and wounded; *Confed.,* 400 killed and wounded.

7.—La Vergne, Tenn. *Union,* Palmer's Brigade; *Confed.,* Outposts of Bragg's

THE ABANDONED STRONGHOLD

Maryland Heights, in the rear of Harper's Ferry. The Federal retreat from this position on September 13, 1862, sealed the fate of Harper's Ferry. Colonel Ford was dismissed from the service for yielding it so easily. From this commanding hill and from Loudon Heights (on the Virginia side of the Potomac) the Confederate artillery could enfilade the Federal rifle-pits on Bolivar Heights. These can be seen in the opposite picture, rising amid the houses. McClellan had urged that the garrison be withdrawn, as the position could be easily reoccupied. But when one of Lee's despatches fell into his hands, acquainting him with Jackson's daring movement to capture it, he pushed forward rapidly two divisions under Franklin to prevent its fall—but in vain. Jackson's haul of more than twelve thousand prisoners had been equaled only at Fort Donelson.

Engagements of the Civil War

Army. Losses: *Union,* 5 killed, 9 wounded; *C o n f e d.,* 80 killed and wounded, 175 missing.

8.—Perryville, Ky. *Union,* First Corps, Army of the Ohio, Maj.-Gen. McCook, and Third Corps, Brig.-Gen. Gilbert; *Confed.,* Gen. Braxton Bragg's Army, Gen. B. F. Cheatham's and Simon B. Buckner's Divisions, Gen. J o s e p h Wheeler's Cav. Losses: *Union,* 916 killed, 2943 wounded, 489 missing; *Confed.,* 2500 killed, wounded, and missing. *Union,* Brig.-Gens. J. S. Jackson and Terrill killed; *Confed.,* Brig.-Gens. Cleburne, Wood, and Brown wounded.

10.—Harrodsburg, Ky. *Union,* Troops commanded by Lieut.-Col. Boyle, 9th Ky. Cav.; *Confed.,* same as at Perryville. Losses: *Confed.,* 1600 captured.

17.—Lexington, Ky. *Union,* Detach. 3d and 4th Ohio Cav.; *Confed.,* Gen. J. H. Morgan's Cav. Losses: *Union,* 4 killed, 24 wounded, 350 missing.

22.—Pocotaligo or Yemassee, S. C. *Union,* 47th, 55th, and 76th Penna., 48th N. Y., 6th and 7th Conn., 3d and 4th N. H., 3d R. I., 1st N. Y. Engineers, 1st Mass. Cav., Batteries B, D, and M 1st U. S. Artil. and E 3d U. S. Artil.; *Confed.,* Gen. W. S. Walker's Command. Losses: *Union,* 43 killed, 258 wounded; *Confed.,* 14 killed, 102 wounded.

NOVEMBER, 1862.

1.—Philomont, Va. *Union,* Pleasonton's Cav.; *Confed.,* Stuart's Cav. Losses: *Union,* 1 killed, 14 wounded; *Confed.,* 5 killed, 10 wounded.

2 and 3.—Bloomfield and Union, Loudon Co., Va. *Union,* Pleasonton's Cav.; *Confed.,* Stuart's Cav. Losses: *Union,* 2 killed, 10 wounded; *Confed.,* 3 killed, 15 wounded.

5.—Barbee's Cross Roads and Chester Gap, Va. *Union,* Pleasonton's Cav.; *Confed.,* Gen. J. E. B. Stuart's Cav. Losses, *Union,* 5 killed, 10 wounded; *Confed.,* 36 killed.

—Nashville, Tenn. *Union,* 16th and 51st Ill., 69th Ohio, 14th Mich., 78th Pa., 5th Tenn. Cav., 7th Pa. Cav.; *Confed.,* Cheatham's Division, Wheeler's Cav. Losses: *Union,* 26 wounded; *Confed.,* 23 captured.

7.—Big Beaver Creek, Mo. 10th Ill., two Cos. Mo. Militia Cav.; *Confed.** Losses: *Union,* 300 captured.

—Marianna, Ark. *Union,* 3d and 4th Iowa, 9th Ill. Cav.; *Confed.** Losses: *Union,* 3 killed, 20 wounded; *Confed.,* 50 killed and wounded.

8.—Hudsonville, Miss. *Union,* 7th Kan. Cav., 2d Iowa Cav.; *Confed.** Losses: *Confed.,* 16 killed, 185 captured.

24.—Beaver Creek, Mo. *Union,* 21st Iowa, 3d Mo. Cav.; *Confed.,* Campbell's Cav. Losses: *Union,* 6 killed, 10 wounded; *Confed.,* 5 killed, 20 wounded.

28.—Cane Hill, Boston Mountain, and Boonsboro', Ark. *Union,* 1st Division Army of the Frontier; *Confed.,* Gen. Jno. S. Marmaduke's Cav. Losses: *Union,* 4 killed, 36 wounded; *Confed.,* 75 killed, 300 wounded.

—Hartwood Church, Va. *Union,* 3d Pa. Cav.; *Confed.,* Gen. Hampton's Cav. Losses: *Union,* 4 killed, 9 wounded, 200 missing.

DECEMBER, 1862.

5.—Coffeeville, Miss. *Union,* 1st, 2d, and 3d Cav. Brigades, Army of the Tennessee; *Confed.,* Gen. John C. Pemberton, Army of Vicksburg defense. Losses: *Union,* 10 killed, 54 wounded; *Confed.,* 7 killed, 43 wounded.

7.—Prairie Grove or Fayetteville, Ark. *Union,* 1st, 2d, and 3d Divisions Army of the Frontier; *Confed.,* Gen. T. C. Hindman's command, and Gen. Marmaduke's Cav. Losses: *Union,* 167 killed, 798 wounded, 183 missing; *Confed.,* 300 killed, 1200 wounded and missing.

—Hartsville, Tenn. *Union,* 106th and 108th Ohio, 104th Ill., 2d Ind. Cav., 11th Ky. Cav., 13th Ind. Battery; *Confed.,* Gen. Basil Duke's Cav. Brigade, Hanson's Kentucky Infantry, Cobb's Battery. Losses: *Union,* 58 killed, 204 wounded, 1834 captured; *Confed.,* 21 killed, 114 wounded.

9.—Dobbin's Ferry, Tenn. *Union,* 35th Ind., 51st Ohio, 8th and 21st Ky., 7th Ind. Battery; *Confed.,* Wheeler's Cav. Losses: *Union,* 5 killed, 48 wounded.

12 to 18.—Foster's expedition to G o l d s-boro', N. C. *Union,* 1st, 2d, and 3d Brigades of First Division and Wessell's

* No record found.

IN SOUTH CAROLINA

With his foot on the cannon-ball sits Captain Michael J. Donohoe, commanding at the time—1862—Company C of the Third New Hampshire. On the left is Lieutenant Allen, and on the right Lieutenant Cody. At the battle of Secessionville, Captain Donohoe's company was stationed on the left and received the first fire of the Confederate reënforcements. Both lieutenants were wounded. Thus in June, 1862, these gallant officers first came into notice, and Captain Donohoe rose rapidly to the rank of colonel, commanding the Tenth New Hampshire. At Fredericksburg, on December 17, 1862, the Tenth New Hampshire (organized September, 1862) was under fire for the first time and acquitted itself creditably for raw troops. Colonel Donohoe and his regiment were transferred to the Army of the James, where his old regiment, the Third New Hampshire, was distinguishing itself. On September 29, 1864, Colonel Donohoe was wounded while leading his troops at Fort Harrison, near Richmond. His gallantry was mentioned by General Ord in despatches, and he was brevetted brigadier-general September 27, 1864.

Brigade of Peck's Division, Dep't of North Carolina; *Confed.*, Robertson's, Clingman's and Evans' brigades. Losses: *Union*, 90 killed, 478 wounded; *Confed.*, 71 killed, 268 wounded, 400 missing.

13.—Fredericksburg, Va. *Union*, Army of the Potomac, Maj.-Gen. Burnside; Right Grand Div., Maj.-Gen. Sumner; Second Corps, Maj.-Gen. Couch; Ninth Corps, Maj.-Gen. Wilcox. Left Grand Div., Maj.-Gen. Franklin; First Corps, Gen. Reynolds; Sixth Corps, Maj.-Gen. W. F. Smith. Center Grand Div., Maj.-Gen. Hooker. Third Corps, Maj.-Gen. Stoneman; Fifth Corps, Maj.-Gen. Butterfield. *Confed.*, Army of Northern Virginia, Gen. Robert E. Lee; First Corps, Gen. Longstreet; Second Corps, "Stonewall" Jackson; Artillery Reserve, Gen. W. N. Pendleton; Gen. Stuart's Cavalry. Losses: *Union*, 1180 killed, 9028 wounded, 2145 missing; *Confed.*, 579 killed, 3870 wounded, 127 missing. *Union*, Brig.-Gens. Jackson and Bayard killed and Gibbon and Vinton wounded; *Confed.*, Brig.-Gen. T. R. R. Cobb killed and Maxcy Gregg wounded.

14.—Kingston, N. C. *Union*, 1st, 2d, and 3d Brigades 1st Div. and Wessell's Brigade of Peck's Division, Dep't of North Carolina; *Confed.*, Gen. N. G. Evans' Command. Losses: *Union*, 40 killed, 120 wounded; *Confed.*, 50 killed, 75 wounded, 400 missing.

18.—Lexington, Tenn. *Union*, 11th Ill. Cav., 5th Ohio Cav., 2d Tenn. Cav.; *Confed.*, Forrest's Cav. Losses: *Union*, 7 killed, 10 wounded, 124 missing. *Confed.*, 7 killed, 28 wounded.

20.—Holly Springs, Miss. *Union*, 2d Ill. Cav. (6 co's), 8th Wis., part of 62d Ill.; *Confed.*, Earl Van Dorn's Cav. Losses: *Union*, 9 killed, 39 wounded, 1500 captured.
—Trenton, Tenn. *Union*, Detachments 122d Ill., 7th Tenn. Cav., and convalescents; *Confed.*, Forrest's Cav. Losses: *Union*, 1 killed, 250 prisoners; *Confed.*, 17 killed, 50 wounded.

21.—Davis' Mills, Miss. *Union*, Six Cos. 25th Ind., two Cos. 5th Ohio Cav.; *Confed.*, Earl Van Dorn's Cav. Losses: *Union*, 3 wounded; *Confed.*, 22 killed, 50 wounded, 20 missing.

24.—Middleburg, Tenn. *Union*, 115 men of 12th Mich.; *Confed.*, Griffith's Texas Brigade. Losses: *Union*, 9 wounded; *Confed.*, 9 killed, 11 wounded.

25.—Green's Chapel, Ky. *Union*, Detachment of 4th and 5th Ind. Cav.; *Confed.*, Morgan's Cav. Losses: *Union*, 1 killed; *Confed.*, 9 killed, 22 wounded.

26.—Bacon Creek, Ky. *Union*, 91st Ill.; *Confed.*, Morgan's Cav. Losses: *Union*, 3 wounded, 93 captured.

27.—Elizabethtown, Ky. *Union*, 91st Ill. 500 men captured by Morgan.
—Dumfries, Va. *Union*, 5th, 7th, and 66th Ohio, 12th Ill. Cav., 1st Md. Cav., 6th Maine Battery; *Confed.*, Stuart's Cav. Losses: *Union*, 3 killed, 8 wounded; *Confed.*, 25 killed, 40 wounded.

28.—Bacon Creek, Ky. *Union*, 91st Ill.; Ky. Cav.; *Confed.** Losses: *Confed.*, 30 killed, 176 wounded, 51 missing.

28 and 29.—Chickasaw Bayou, Vicksburg, Miss. *Union*, Thirteenth Army Corps, Maj.-Gen. W. T. Sherman, Brig.-Gens. G. W. Morgan's, Frederick Steele's, M. L. Smith's, and A. J. Smith's Divisions; *Confed.*, Gen. Pemberton's Army, M. L. Smith's and S. D. Lee's Divisions. Losses: *Union*, 191 killed, 982 wounded, 756 missing; *Confed.*, 63 killed, 134 wounded, 10 missing; *Union*, Maj.-Gen. M. L Smith wounded.

30.—Wautauga Bridge and Carter's Station, Tenn. *Union*, 7th Ohio Cav., 9th Pa. Cav.; *Confed.*, Gen. Humphrey Marshall's command. Losses: *Union*, 1 killed, 2 wounded; *Confed.*, 7 killed, 15 wounded, 273 missing.
—Jefferson, Tenn. *Union*, Second Brigade 1st Division Thomas' corps; *Confed.*, Wheeler's Cav. Losses: *Union*, 20 killed, 40 wounded; *Confed.*, 15 killed, 50 wounded.
—Parker's Cross Roads or Red Mound, Tenn. *Union*, 18th, 106th, 119th, and 122d Ill., 27th, 39th, and 63d Ohio, 50th Ind., 39th Iowa, 7th Tenn., 7th Wis. Battery; *Confed.*, Forrest's Cav. Losses: *Union*, 23 killed, 139 wounded, 58 missing; *Confed.*, 50 killed, 150 wounded, 300 missing.

31 to Jan. 2.—Murfreesboro' or Stone's River, Tenn. *Union*, Army of the Cumberland, Maj.-Gen. Rosecrans; Right

* No record found.

A NEW ENGLAND REGIMENT IN THE SOUTH

Company F, Third New Hampshire Volunteers. Organized in August, 1861, this regiment first saw active service in South Carolina. Accompanying the famous Port Royal Expedition, by which a Federal foothold was first gained in Southern territory, the regiment was stationed at Hilton Head, November 4, 1861. While Port Royal was being elaborately equipped as a naval and military base, the troops were constantly coöperating with the gunboats in reconnaissances, the ultimate object being operations against Savannah and Charleston. At the beginning of 1862 Confederate troops were found to be massing for the purpose of shutting up the Federals on Port Royal Island, and General Stevens, determining to nip the attempt in the bud, began active operations which were pushed close to both Savannah and Charleston. The Federals succeeded in occupying the southwestern portion of James' Island on the Stono River, after skirmishes at Pocotaglio, St. John's Island, and James' Island. On June 16th a battle took place at Secessionville, within five or six miles of Charleston, in which the Federals were defeated, and in this the Third New Hampshire, under command of Colonel John H. Jackson, established its reputation for gallantry, losing 104 men.

Wing, McCook's Corps; Center, Thomas' Corps; Left Wing, Crittenden's Corps; *Confed.*, Army of the Tennessee, Gen. Braxton Bragg; L. K. Polk's Corps, W. J. Hardee's Corps, Wheeler's Cav. Losses: *Union,* 1,533 killed, 7245 wounded, 2800 missing; *Confed.,* 1294 killed, 7945 wounded, 1027 missing. *Union,* Brig.-Gens. Sill killed and Kirk wounded; *Confed.,* Brig.-Gens. Rains and Hanson killed and Chalmers and Davis wounded.

JANUARY, 1863.

1.—Galveston, Tex. *Union,* Three Cos. 42d Mass., U. S. Gunboats *Westfield, Harriet Lane, Owasco, Sachem, Clifton* and *Coryphæus; Confed.,* Gen. J. B. Magruder's Command, Gunboats *Bayou City* and *Neptune.* Losses: *Union,* 600 killed, wounded, and missing; *Confed.,* 50 killed and wounded.

7. and 8.—Springfield, Mo. *Union,* Mo. Militia, convalescents and citizens; *Confed.,* Marmaduke's Cav. Losses: *Union,* 14 killed, 144 wounded; *Confed.,* 40 killed, 206 wounded and missing. *Union,* Brig.-Gen. Brown wounded.

11.—Fort Hindman, Ark. *Union,* Thirteenth Corps, Maj.-Gen. McClernand; Fifteenth Corps, Maj.-Gen. Sherman and gunboats Mississippi squadron; *Confed.,* Brig.-Gen. T. J. Churchill's command. Losses: *Union,* 129 killed, 831 wounded; *Confed.,* 100 killed, 400 wounded, 5000 prisoners.

—Hartsville or Wood's Fork, Mo. *Union,* 21st Iowa, 99th Ill., 3d Iowa Cav., 3d Mo. Cav., Battery L, 2d Mo. Artil.; *Confed.,* Marmaduke's Cav. Losses: *Union,* 7 killed, 64 wounded; *Confed.,* Brig.-Gen. McDonald killed.

14.—Bayou Teche, La. *Union,* 8th Vt., 16th and 75th N. Y., 12th Conn., 6th Mich., 21st Ind., 1st La. Cav., 4th and 6th Mass. Battery, 1st Maine Battery, and U. S. Gunboats *Calhoun, Diana, Kinsman,* and *Estrella; Confed.,* Gen. Magruder's Command, Gunboat *Cotton.* Losses: *Union,* 10 killed, 27 wounded; *Confed.,* 15 killed. *Union,* Commodore Buchanan killed. *Confed.,* Gunboat *Cotton* destroyed.

24.—Woodbury, Tenn. *Union,* Second Division Crittenden's Corps; *Confed.,* Gen.

Bragg's Command. Losses: *Union,* 2 killed, 1 wounded; *Confed.,* 35 killed, 100 missing.

30.—Deserted House or Kelly's Store, near Suffolk, Va. *Union,* portion of Maj.-Gen. Peck's forces; *Confed.,* 1st S. C. Losses: *Union,* 24 killed, 80 wounded; *Confed.,* 50 wounded.

31.—Rover, Tenn. *Union,* 4th Ohio Cav.; *Confed.,* 51st Ala., 8th Confed. Losses: *Confed.,* 12 killed, 12 wounded, 300 captured.

—Charleston, S. C. Raid of the *Confed.* Gunboats *Palmetto State* and *Chicora* on the *Union* blockading fleet; *Union,* Mercidita, Quaker City, and Keystone State, Ottawa, Unadilla, Augusta, and Memphis. Losses: *Union,* 30 killed and wounded.

FEBRUARY, 1863.

3.—Fort Donelson or Cumberland Iron Works, Tenn. *Union,* 83d Ill., 2d Ill. Artil., one battalion 5th Iowa Cav.; *Confed.,* Wheeler's, Forrest's, and Wharton's Cav. Losses: *Union,* 16 killed, 60 wounded, 50 missing; *Confed.,* 140 killed, 400 wounded, 130 missing.

24.—Mississippi River below Vicksburg. *Union,* U. S. Gunboat *Indianola; Confed., The Webb* and *Queen of the West.* Losses: *Union,* 1 killed, 1 wounded; *Confed.,* 35 killed.

MARCH, 1863.

4 and 5.—Thompson's Station, also called Spring Hill and Unionville, Tenn. *Union,* 33d and 85th Ind., 22d Wis., 19th Mich., 124th Ohio, 18th Ohio Battery, 2d Mich. Cav., 9th Pa. Cav., 4th Ky. Cav.; *Confed.,* Earl Van Dorn's Cav. Corps, Forrest's, Martin's, and Jackson's Divisions. Losses: *Union,* 100 killed, 300 wounded, 1306 captured; *Confed.,* 150 killed, 450 wounded.

8.—Fairfax C. H., Va. *Union,* Brig.-Gen. Stoughton and thirty-three men captured by Capt. John S. Mosby (*Confed.*) in a midnight raid.

13 to April 5.—Fort Pemberton, Miss. *Union,* Thirteenth Corps, Brig.-Gen. Ross; Seventeenth Corps, Brig.-Gen. Quimby, U. S. Gunboats *Chillicothe* and

WHERE NEW ORLEANS WAS SAVED, JUNE 28, 1863

Donaldsonville, Louisiana. Within the little Fort Butler (the lower picture), Major J. D. Mullen, at half-past one in the morning of June 28th, with 180 men of the Twenty-eighth Maine, gallantly withstood the assault of 14,000 Confederates sent against the place by General Taylor. By daylight the little garrison, assisted by three gunboats in the river, completed the repulse. The Confederates retired, leaving behind them, according to Major Mullen's report, 69 dead and 120 prisoners. This prevented Taylor from capturing New Orleans before the capitulation of Port Hudson would permit Banks to detach a sufficient force to drive off the Confederates, who were threatening his communications down the river. New Orleans would undoubtedly have been retaken had Taylor's request for reënforcements not been overruled by Kirby Smith. As it was, Taylor recruited his own forces to about 3,000 and moved against New Orleans in two detachments, getting within twenty-five miles of New Orleans two weeks before Port Hudson surrendered.

DeKalb; Confed., Garrison under Gen. W. W. Loring. Casualties not recorded.

14.—Port Hudson, La. *Union,* Maj.-Gen. Banks' troops and Admiral Farragut's fleet; *Confed.,* Gen. Frank Gardner's Command. Losses: *Union,* 65 wounded.

16 to 22.—Expedition up Steele's Bayou, and at Deer Creek, Miss. *Union,* 2d Division Fifteenth Corps, Maj.-Gen. Sherman, Gunboat fleet, Admiral Porter; *Confed.,* Troops of Gen. Maury's and Gen. S. D. Lee's commands. Casualties not recorded.

17.—Kelly's Ford, Va. *Union,* 1st and 5th U. S. Regulars, 3d, 4th, and 16th Pa., 1st R. I., 6th Ohio, 4th N. Y. Cav., 6th N. Y. Battery; *Confed.,* Stuart's Cav. Losses: *Union,* 9 killed, 35 wounded; *Confed.,* 11 killed, 88 wounded.

20.—Vaught's Hill, near Milton, Tenn. *Union,* 105th Ohio, 101st Ind., 80th and 123d Ill., 1st Tenn. Cav., 9th Ind. Battery; *Confed.,* Morgan's Cav. Losses: *Union,* 7 killed, 48 wounded; *Confed.,* 63 killed, 300 wounded.

22.—Mt. Sterling, Ky. *Union,* 10th Ky. Cav.; *Confed.,* Morgan's Cav. Losses: *Union,* 4 killed, 10 wounded; *Confed.,* 8 killed, 13 wounded.

24.—Danville, Ky. *Union,* 18th and 22d Mich., 1st Ky. Cav., 2d Tenn. Cav., 1st Ind. Battery; *Confed.,* Morgan's Cav.

25.—Brentwood, Tenn. *Union,* Detachment 22d Wis. and 19th Mich.; *Confed.,* Forrest's Cav. Losses: *Union,* 1 killed, 4 wounded, 300 captured; *Confed.,* 1 killed, 5 wounded.

—Franklin and Little Harpeth, Tenn. *Union,* 4th and 6th Ky. Cav., 9th Pa. Cav., 2d Mich. Cav.; *Confed.,* Forrest's Cav. Losses: *Union,* 4 killed, 19 wounded, 40 missing.

28.—Pattersonville, La. *Union,* Gunboat *Diana* with Detachment of 12th Conn. and 160th N. Y. on board; *Confed.,* Gen. Richard Taylor's Command. Losses: *Union,* 4 killed, 14 wounded, 99 missing.

30.—Dutton's Hill or Somerset, Ky. *Union,* 1st Ky. Cav., 7th Ohio Cav., 44th and 45th Ohio Mounted Vol.; *Confed.,* Gen. John Pegram's Command. Losses: *Union,* 10 killed, 25 wounded; *Confed.,* 290 killed, wounded, and missing.

APRIL, 1863.

2 and 3.—Woodbury and Snow Hill, Tenn. *Union,* 3d and 4th Ohio Cav.; *Confed.,* Morgan's Cav. Losses: *Union,* 1 killed, 8 wounded; *Confed.,* 50 killed and wounded.

7.—Bombardment Fort Sumter, S. C. *Union,* South Atlantic squadron; *Keokuk, Weehawken, Passaic, Montauk, Patapsco, New Ironsides, Catskill, Nantucket,* and *Nahant; Confed.,* S. C. Art. in Batteries Beauregard, Wagner, and Bee, Fort Sumter and Fort Moultrie. Losses: *Union,* 2 killed, 20 wounded; *Confed.,* 4 killed, 10 wounded.

10.—Franklin and Harpeth River, Tenn. *Union,* 40th Ohio and portion of Granger's Cav.; *Confed.,* Forrest's Cav. Losses: *Union,* 100 killed and wounded; *Confed.,* 19 killed, 35 wounded, 83 missing.

12 to 14.—Irish Bend and Bisland, La., also called Indian Ridge and Centreville. *Union,* Nineteenth Corps, Grover's, Emory's, and Weitzel's Divisions; *Confed.,* Gen. Richard Taylor's Command, Gunboat *Diana.* Losses: *Union,* 89 killed, 458 wounded, 30 missing; *Confed.**

12 to May 4.—Siege of Suffolk, Va. *Union,* Troops of the Army of Virginia and Department of North Carolina; *Confed.,* Gen. James Longstreet's Command. Losses: *Union,* 44 killed, 202 wounded; *Confed.,* 500 killed and wounded, 400 captured.

17 to May 2.—Grierson's expedition from La Grange, Tenn., to Baton Rouge, La. *Union,* 6th and 7th Ill. Cav., 2d Iowa Cav.; *Confed.,* detachments of Cav. and Home Guards. Losses: *Union,* 3 killed, 7 wounded, 9 missing; *Confed.,* 100 killed and wounded, 1600 captured (estimated).

26.—Cape Girardeau, Mo. *Union,* 32d Iowa, 1st Wis. Cav., 2d Mo. Cav., Batteries D and L 1st Mo. Lt. Artil.; *Confed.,* Marmaduke's Cav. Losses: *Union,* 6 killed, 6 wounded; *Confed.,* 60 killed, 275 wounded and missing.

27 to May 3.—Streight's Raid, Tuscumbia, Ala., to Rome, Ga., including skirmishes at Day's Gap, April 30th; Black Warrior Creek, May 1, and Blount's Farm,

* No record found.

SUMTER

Searching all history for a parallel, it is impossible to find any defenses of a beleaguered city that stood so severe a bombardment as did this bravely defended and never conquered fortress of Sumter, in Charleston Harbor. It is estimated that about eighty thousand projectiles were discharged from the fleet and the marsh batteries, and yet Charleston, with its battered water-front, was not abandoned until all other Confederate positions along the Atlantic Coast were in Federal hands and Sherman's triumphant army was sweeping in from the West and South. The picture shows Sumter from the Confederate Fort Johnson. The powerful batteries in the foreground played havoc with the Federal fleet whenever it came down the main ship-channel to engage the forts. Protected by almost impassable swamps, morasses, and a network of creeks to the eastward, Fort Johnson held an almost impregnable position; and from its protection by Cummings' Point, on which was Battery Gregg, the Federal fleet could not approach nearer than two miles. Could it have been taken by land assault or reduced by gun-fire, Charleston would have fallen.

Engagements of the Civil War

May 2. *Union,* 3d Ohio, 51st and 73d Ind., 80th Ill., Mounted Inft., two Cos. 1st Ala. Cav.; *Confed.,* Forrest's *Cav.* Losses: *Union,* 12 killed, 69 wounded. 1466 missing and captured; *Confed.,* 12 killed, 73 wounded.

27 to May 8.—Cavalry Raid in Virginia. *Union,* Gen. Stoneman's Corps; *Confed.,* Stuart's Cav., Home Guards and local garrisons. Losses.*

—Grand Gulf, Miss. *Union,* Gunboat fleet; *Confed.;* Gen. Bowen's Command. Losses: *Union,* 26 killed, 54 wounded.

30.—Spottsylvania C. H., Va. *Union,* 6th N. Y. Cav.; *Confed.,* Stuart's Cav. *Union,* 58 killed and wounded.

MAY, 1863.

1.—Port Gibson, Miss. (the first engagement in Grant's Campaign against Vicksburg). *Union,* Thirteenth Corps, Maj.-Gen. McClernand, and 3d Division Seventeenth Corps, Maj.-Gen. McPherson; *Confed.,* Gen. Bowen's Command. Losses: *Union,* 130 killed, 718 wounded; *Confed.,* 68 killed, 380 wounded, 384 missing. *Confed.* Brig.-Gen. T r a c y killed.

1 to 4.—Chancellorsville, Va., i n c l u d i n g battles of Sixth Corps at Fredericksburg and Salem Heights. *Union,* Army of the Potomac, Maj.-Gen. Hooker; First Corps, Maj.-Gen. Reynolds; Second Corps, Maj.-Gen. Couch; Third Corps, Maj.-Gen. Sickles; Fifth Corps, Maj.-Gen. Meade; Sixth Corps, Maj.-Gen. Sedgwick; Eleventh Corps, Maj.-Gen. Howard; Twelfth Corps, Maj.-Gen. Slocum; *Confed.,* Army of Northern Virginia, Gen. R. E. Lee; Second Corps, "Stonewall" Jackson; R. H. Anderson's and McLaws' divisions of Longstreet's First Corps; Pendleton's Art. Battalion; Stuart's Cav. Losses: *Union,* 1512 killed, 9518 wounded, 5000 missing; *Confed.,* 1581 killed, 8700 wounded, 2000 missing. *Union,* Maj.-Gen. Berry and Brig.-Gen. Whipple killed, Devens and Kirby wounded. *Confed.,* Brig.-Gen. Paxton killed, Lieut.-Gen. Jackson, Maj.-Gen. A. P. Hill, Brig.-Gens. Hoke, Nichols, Ramseur, McGowan, Heth, and Pender wounded. Jackson's wound was mortal.

3.—Warrenton Junction, Va. *Union,* 1st W. Va. Cav., 5th N. Y. Cav.; *Confed.,* Stuart's Cav. Losses: *Union,* 1 killed, 16 wounded; *Confed.,* 15 wounded.

4.—Siege of Suffolk, Va., raised. (See April 12.)

11.—Horse Shoe Bend, Ky. *Union,* Detachment commanded by Col. R. T. Jacobs; *Confed.,* Morgan's Cav. Losses: *Union,* 10 killed, 20 wounded, 40 missing; *Confed.,* 100 killed, wounded, and missing.

12.—Raymond, Miss. *Union,* Seventeenth Corps, Maj.-Gen. McPherson. *Union,* 66 killed, 339 wounded, 37 missing; *Confed.,* Gen. Gregg's Command. Losses: *Confed.,* 969 killed and wounded.

14.—Jackson, Miss. *Union,* Fifteenth Corps, Maj.-Gen. Sherman; Seventeenth Corps, Maj.-Gen. McPherson; *Confed.,* Gen. Jos. E. Johnston's Command. Losses: *Union,* 42 killed, 251 wounded, 7 missing; *Confed.,* 450 killed and wounded.

16.—Champion's Hill, Miss. *Union,* Hovey's Div. Thirteenth Corps and Seventeenth Corps; *Confed.,* Army of Defense, commanded by Gen. J. C. Pemberton. Losses: *Union,* 410 killed, 1844 wounded, 187 missing; *Confed.,* 2500 killed and wounded, 1800 missing (estimate). *Confed.,* Gen. Tilghman killed.

17.—Big Black River, Miss. *Union,* Carr's and Osterhaus' divisions, Thirteenth Corps, Maj.-Gen. McClernand; *Confed.,* same as at Champion's Hill on the 16th. Losses: *Union,* 39 killed, 237 wounded, 3 missing; *Confed.,* 600 killed and wounded (estimate), 1751 captured.

18 to July 4.—S i e g e of Vicksburg, Miss. *Union,* Army of the Tennessee, commanded by Maj.-Gen. U. S. Grant; Ninth Corps, Thirteenth Corps, Fifteenth Corps, Sixteenth Corps (detachment), and Seventeenth Corps, and gunboat fleet, commanded by Admiral D. D. Porter; *Confed.,* Army of Defense, Gen. J. C. Pemberton. Assault on Fort Hill on May 19th and general assault on the 20th, in which *Confed.* Brig.-Gen. Green was killed; Loring's (portion), Bowen's, Stevenson's, Forney's, Smith's divisions, forces under Gen. J. E. Johnston and 7 river batteries. Losses: Included in the table for July 4.

* No record found.

[334]

THE NEVER–SURRENDERED FORT MOULTRIE, BESIEGED APRIL 10–SEPTEMBER 6, 1863

This is no hastily constructed battery, but the remains of a fort older than Sumter itself, as is shown by the brick walls and the permanent emplacement of the guns. It may be that this was the very piece of ordnance from which was fired the first shot that staggered humanity in 1861. Like Sumter, Fort Moultrie never surrendered. Protected by the encroaching sand-banks, it presented no such target as the high brick walls of the more historic fortress. Yet it had its place in history. Eighty-five years before, guns placed here had helped to repel the British fleet, and Sergeant Jasper had nailed to the flagstaff the banner of the new republic. Farther down the harbor the Confederates held permanent positions, the efforts to capture which were costly to the blockading fleet and besieging army. Before Fort Wagner there fell more than two thousand Federal soldiers. On Morris Island, to the south, the Federals had effected lodgment and turned their guns upon Sumter, Moultrie, and Wagner. The breaching batteries they erected in the swamps helped to complete the ruin. Tons of iron and exploding shells rained for months upon the bravely defended positions. The Confederate flags at Moultrie and Sumter, shot away a dozen times, were always replaced; and they waved proudly and defiantly until Charleston was threatened from the rear.

20 to 28.—Clendenin's raid, below Fredericksburg, Va. *Union*, 8th Ill. Cav.; *Confed.*, Outposts of Lee's Army. Losses: *Confed.*, 100 prisoners.

23 to July 8.—Siege of Port Hudson, La. Losses: *Union*, 708 killed, 3336 wounded, 319 missing; *Confed.*, 176 killed, 447 wounded, 5500 (estimate) captured.

JUNE, 1863.

4.—Franklin, Tenn. *Union*, 85th Ind., 7th Ky. Cav., 4th and 6th Ky. Cav., 9th Pa. Cav., 2d Mich. Cav.; *Confed.** Losses: *Union*, 25 killed and wounded; *Confed.*, 200 killed and wounded.

5.—Franklin's Crossing, Rappahannock River, Va. *Union*, 26th N. J., 5th Vt., 15th and 50th N. Y. Engineers, supported by 6th Corps; *Confed.*, Outposts of Gen. R. E. Lee's Army. Losses: *Union*, 6 killed, 35 wounded.

6 to 8.—Milliken's Bend, La. *Union*, 23d Iowa and three regts. colored troops, gunboat *Choctaw; Confed.*, Gen. Richard Taylor's Command. Losses: *Union*, 154 killed, 223 wounded, 115 missing; *Confed.*, 125 killed, 400 wounded, 200 missing.

9.—Monticello and Rocky Gap, Ky. *Union*, 2d and 7th Ohio Cav., 1st Ky. Cav., 45th Ohio and 2d Tenn. Mounted Inft.; *Confed.*, Morgan's Cav. Losses: *Union*, 4 killed, 26 wounded; *Confed.*, 20 killed, 80 wounded.

—Beverly Ford and Brandy Station, Va. *Union*, Cavalry Corps, Brig.-Gen. Pleasonton, 2d, 3d, and 7th Wis., 2d and 33d Mass., 6th Maine, 86th and 124th N. Y., 1st, 2d, 5th, and 6th U. S. Cav., 2d, 6th, 8th, 9th, and 10th N. Y. Cav., 1st, 3d, 4th, 6th, 11th, and 17th Pa. Cav, 1st Md., 8th Ill., 3d Ind., 1st N. J., 1st Maine Cav., 1st R. I. Cav., and 3d W. Va. Cav., 8th and 12th Ill.* Cav., 1st Mass. Cav., 6th O. Cav., Batteries B and L, 2d U. S. Art., K, 1st U. S. Art., E, 4th U. S. Art., 6th Bat. N. Y. Light Art.; *Confed.*, Stuart's Cav. Losses: *Union*, 421 killed and wounded, 486 missing; *Confed.*, 301 killed and wounded, 184 missing. First true cavalry battle in the East.

11.—Middletown, Va. *Union*, 87th Pa., 13th Pa. Cav., Battery L, 5th U. S. Artil.; *Confed.*, Gen. Ewell's Command. Losses: *Confed.*, 8 killed, 42 wounded.

13 and 15.—Winchester, Va. *Union*, 2d, 67th and 87th Pa., 18th Conn., 12th W. Va., 110th, 116th, 122d, and 123d Ohio, 3d, 5th, and 6th Md., 12th and 13th Pa. Cav., 1st N. Y. Cav., 1st and 3d W. Va. Cav., Battery L 5th U. S. Artil., 1st W. Va. Battery, Baltimore Battery, one Co. 14th Mass. Heavy Artil.; *Confed.*, Gen. R. S. Ewell's Corps. Losses: *Union*, 95 killed, 443 wounded, and 4443 missing; *Confed.*, 42 killed and 210 wounded.

14.—Martinsburg, Va. *Union*, 106th N. Y., 126th Ohio, W. Va. Battery; *Confed.*, Gen. Ewell's Command. Losses: *Union*, 200 missing; *Confed.*, 1 killed, 2 wounded.

16.—Triplett's Bridge, Ky. *Union*, 15th Mich., 10th and 14th Ky. Cav., 7th and 9th Mich. Cav., 11th Mich. Battery; *Confed.*, Morgan's Cav. Losses: *Union*, 15 killed, 30 wounded.

17.—Aldie, Va. *Union*, Kilpatrick's Cav.; *Confed.*, Stuart's Cav. Losses: *Union*, 24 killed, 41 wounded, 89 missing; *Confed.*, 100 wounded.

—Wassau Sound, Ga. Capture of *Confederate* gunboat *Atlanta* by U. S. ironclad *Weehawken*. Losses: *Confed.*, 1 killed, 17 wounded, 145 prisoners.

20 and 21.—La Fourche Crossing, La. *Union*, Detachments 23d Conn., 176th N. Y., 26th, 42d, and 47th Mass., 21st Ind.; *Confed.*, Gen. Richard Taylor's Command. Losses: *Union*, 8 killed, 40 wounded; *Confed.*, 53 killed, 150 wounded.

21.—Upperville, Va. *Union*, Pleasonton's Cav.; *Confed.*, Stuart's Cav. Losses: *Union*, 94 wounded; *Confed.*, 20 killed, 100 wounded, 60 missing.

22.—Hill's Plantation, Miss. Detachment of 4th Iowa Cav.; *Confed.** Losses: *Union*, 4 killed, 10 wounded, 28 missing.

23.—Brashear City, La. *Union*, Detachments of 114th and 176th N. Y., 23d Conn., 42d Mass., 21st Ind.; *Confed.*, Gen. Taylor's Command. Losses: *Union*, 46 killed, 40 wounded, 300 missing; *Confed.*, 3 killed, 18 wounded.

* No record found.

The lower picture was taken after the war, when relic-hunters had removed the shells, and a beacon light had been erected where once stood the parapet. On September 8, 1863, at the very position in these photographs, the garrison repelled a bold assault with musketry fire alone, causing the Federals severe loss. The flag of the Confederacy floated triumphantly over the position during the whole of the long struggle. Every effort of the Federals to reduce the crumbling ruins into submission was unavailing. It stood the continual bombardment of ironclads until it was nothing but a mass of brickdust, but still the gallant garrison held it.

SCENE OF THE NIGHT ATTACK ON SUMTER,
SEPTEMBER 8, 1863

It is strange that despite the awful destruction the loss of lives within the fort was few. For weeks the bombardment, assisted by the guns of the fleet, tore great chasms in the parapet. Fort Sumter never fell, but was abandoned only on the approach of Sherman's army. It had withstood continuous efforts against it for 587 days. From April, 1863, to September of the same year, the fortress was garrisoned by the First South Carolina Artillery, enlisted as regulars. Afterward the garrison was made up of detachments of infantry from Georgia, North Carolina, and South Carolina. Artillerists also served turns of duty during this period.

WHERE BURNSIDE HELD KNOXVILLE, NOVEMBER 17TH TO DECEMBER 4, 1863

This high ground, commanding Fort Sanders across the Holston River, had just been captured by the Confederates when Longstreet learned of Bragg's defeat at Chattanooga and was compelled to abandon the siege of Knoxville. He had bottled up Burnside. In Fort Sanders the Army of the Ohio was bravely holding on till help should come from Grant; they were eating bread made of pure bran, and their sustenance was almost exhausted. Before dawn on November 29, 1863, they repulsed the second assault which Longstreet's superior numbers made upon them. Longstreet, disheartened by constant disagreements with Bragg and without faith in the generalship of his superior, led the expedition, contrary to his judgment, as a forlorn hope, and his officers prosecuted the movement but half-heartedly. Longstreet himself admits that he was not as energetic as was his wont. Delay and misinformation as to the strength of the Federals cost him a thousand men before Fort Sanders. Baffled and discouraged, he finally abandoned the siege.

FORT SANDERS, KNOXVILLE, WHERE LONGSTREET ATTACKED, NOVEMBER 29, 1863

KNOXVILLE, AND TWO BRIDGES IN THE SIEGE. THE LOWER ONE, AT STRAWBERRY PLAINS, WAS DESTROYED FOUR TIMES DURING THE WAR

Engagements of the Civil War

23 to July 7.—Rosecrans' Campaign. Murfreesboro to Tullahoma, Tenn., including Middleton, Hoover's Gap, Beech Grove, Liberty Gap, and Guy's Gap. Army of the Cumberland: Fourteenth, Twentieth, and Twenty-first Corps, Granger's Reserve Corps, and Stanley's Cavalry; *Confed.*, Army of Tennessee, Gen. Braxton Bragg. Losses: *Union*, 84 killed, 473 wounded, 13 missing; *Confed.*, 1634 (estimate) killed, wounded, and captured.

28.—Donaldsonville, La., and Fort Butler. *Union*, 28th Maine and convalescents, assisted by gunboats; *Confed.*, Gen. Taylor's Command. Losses: *Confed.*, 39 killed, 112 wounded, 150 missing.

30.—Hanover, Pa. *Union*, Kilpatrick's Cavalry Division; *Confed.*, Stuart's Cav. Losses: *Union*, 12 killed, 43 wounded; *Confed.*, 75 wounded, 60 missing.

JULY, 1863.

1 to 3.—Gettysburg, Pa. *Union*, Army of the Potomac, Maj.-Gen. Geo. G. Meade; First Corps, Maj.-Gen. Reynolds; Second Corps, Maj.-Gen. Hancock; Third Corps, Maj.-Gen. Sickles; Fifth Corps, Maj.-Gen. Sykes; Sixth Corps, Maj.-Gen. Sedgwick; Eleventh Corps, Maj.-Gen. Howard; Twelfth Corps, Maj.-Gen. Slocum; Cavalry Corps, Maj.-Gen. Pleasonton, Artillery Reserve under Brig.-Gen. Tyler; *Confed.*, Army of Northern Virginia, Gen. R. E. Lee; First Corps, Gen. Longstreet; Second Corps, Gen. Ewell; Third Corps, Gen. A. P. Hill; Gen. Stuart's Cav., Reserve Artillery under Cols. Walton, Walker, and Brown. Losses: *Union*, 3155 killed, 14529 wounded, 5365 missing; *Confed.*, 3500 killed, 14500 wounded, 13621 missing.

2 to 26.—Morgan's raid into Kentucky, Indiana, and Ohio. At Blennerhasset Island, Ohio River (July 19th), the larger part of Morgan's force was killed, wounded, and captured—820 in all. The remainder, with Morgan himself, surrendered July 26th, near New Lisbon, Ohio. *Union*, Detachments of Rosecrans' Army of the Cumberland, Hobson's and Shackleford's Cav., Home Guard, and Militia; *Confed.*, Gen. John H. Morgan's Cav. Corps. Losses: *Union*, 33 killed, 97 wounded, 805 missing; *Confed.*, about 2500 killed, wounded, and captured.

4.—Helena, Ark. *Union*, Maj.-Gen. Prentiss' Division of Sixteenth Corps and gunboat *Tyler*; *Confed.*, Gen. T. H. Holmes' Command, Price's Mo. and Ark. brigades, Marmaduke's and Shelby's Cav. Losses: *Union*, 57 killed, 117 wounded, 32 missing; *Confed.*, 173 killed, 687 wounded, 776 missing.

—Surrender of Vicksburg to Maj.-Gen. U. S. Grant; end of the siege. Losses, during the campaign and including Port Gibson, Raymond, Jackson, Champion's Hill, Big Black River, assaults May 19th and 22d, siege operations and skirmishes: *Union*, 1514 killed, 1395 wounded, 453 missing; *Confed.* (Incomplete) 1260 killed, 3572 wounded, 4227 captured or missing in action, surrendered (including non-combatants attached to the army) 29941.

4 and 5.—Bolton and Birdsong Ferry, Miss. *Union*, Maj.-Gen. Sherman's forces; *Confed.*, Gen. Johnston's Command. Losses: *Confed.*, 2000 captured.

—Monterey Gap and Fairfield Pa., and Smithsburg, Md. *Union*, Kilpatrick Cav.; *Confed.*, Hampton's Cav. Losses: *Union*, 30 killed and wounded; *Confed.*, 30 killed and wounded, 100 captured.

5.—Lebanon, Ky. *Union*, 20th Ky.; *Confed.*, Morgan's Cav. Losses: *Union*, 9 killed, 15 wounded, 400 missing; *Confed.*, 3 killed, 6 wounded.

6.—Hagerstown and Williamsport, Md. *Union*, Buford's and Kilpatrick's Cav., *Confed.*, Stuart's Cav. Losses: *Union*, 33 killed, 87 wounded, 293 missing; *Confed.*, 125 killed, wounded, and missing.

7 to 9.—Boonsboro, Md. *Union*, Buford's and Kilpatrick's Cav.; *Confed.*, Gen. Fitzhugh Lee's Cav. Losses: *Union*, 9 killed, 45 wounded.

8.—Port Hudson, La. Surrendered by Confederates to Maj.-Gen. Banks. (See May 23.)

9 to 16.—Jackson, Miss., including engagements at Rienzi, Bolton Depot, Canton, and Clinton. *Union*, 9th, 13th, 15th, and part of 16th Corps; *Confed.*, Gen. Jos. E. Johnston's Army. Losses: *Union*, 100 killed, 800 wounded, 100 missing; *Confed.*, 71 killed, 504 wounded, 764 missing.

MISSOURI ARTILLERY IN SHERMAN'S RAID, FEBRUARY, 1864

Battery M, First Missouri Light Artillery, originally in Colonel Frank P. Blair's infantry regiment, marched with Sherman from Vicksburg through Mississippi to Meridian during February, 1864. Sherman, with twenty thousand men and sixty pieces of artillery, was to break up all the railroad communications, so that small Federal garrisons would be able to hold important positions along the Mississippi. The advance corps under the intrepid McPherson left Vicksburg on February 3d and arrived at Meridian on the 8th. It was a precursor of the famous "March to the Sea," but on a smaller scale. The troops destroyed whatever would be of service to the Confederates, who fell back before Sherman, burning provisions and laying waste the country. At Meridian, the great railway center of the Southwest at the time, Sherman accomplished "the most complete destruction of railroads ever beheld." Meantime, General W. S. Smith, with the Federal cavalry force from Memphis, was unable to reach Meridian. Escaping in the night from a dangerous predicament at Okolona on February 22d, he managed to return safely to Memphis by February 25th, after having destroyed a million bushels of corn and many miles of railroad.

10 to Sept. 6.—Siege of Fort Wagner, Morris Island, S. C. *Union,* Troops of the Department of the South, under command of Maj.-Gen. Gillmore, and U. S. Navy under Admiral Dahlgren; *Confed.,* Garrison commanded by Gen. W. B. Taliaferro. Losses: *Union,* 1757 killed, wounded, and missing; *Confed.,* 561 killed, wounded, and missing.

—Falling Waters, Md. *Union,* 3d Cav. Division Army of the Potomac; *Confed.,* Army of Northern Virginia, Gen. R. E. Lee. Losses: *Union,* 29 killed, 36 wounded; *Confed.,* 125 killed and wounded, 1500 prisoners. *Confed.,* Maj.-Gen. Pettigrew killed.

13.—Yazoo City, Miss. *Union,* Maj.-Gen. Herron's Division and three gunboats; *Confed.,* Detachments of Capt. I. N. Brown. Losses: *Confed.,* 250 captured.

—Jackson, Tenn. *Union,* 9th Ill., 3d Mich. Cav., 2d Iowa Cav., and 1st Tenn. Cav.; *Confed.,* Gen. N. B. Forrest's Cav. Losses: *Union,* 2 killed, 20 wounded; *Confed.,* 38 killed, 150 wounded.

—Donaldsonville, La. *Union,* Advance of Gen. Weitzel's command; *Confed.,* Gen. Green's brigade, Col. Taylor's Cav. Losses: *Union,* 465 killed, wounded, and missing; *Confed.,* 3 killed, 30 wounded.

13 to 15.—Draft riots in New York City, in which over 1000 rioters were killed.

14.—Elk River, Tenn. *Union,* Advance of the Fourteenth Corps Army of the Cumberland; *Confed.,* Rear Guard of Gen. Bragg's Army in retreat. Losses: *Union,* 10 killed, 30 wounded; *Confed.,* 60 killed, 24 wounded, 100 missing.

—Halltown, Va. *Union,* 16th Pa. and 1st Maine Cav.; *Confed.,* Gen. J. D. Imboden's command. Losses: *Union,* 25 killed and wounded; *Confed.,* 20 killed and wounded.

16.—Shepherdstown, Va. *Union,* 1st, 4th, and 16th Pa., 10th N. Y. and 1st Maine Cav.; *Confed.,* Stuart's Cav. Losses: *Confed.,* 25 killed, 75 wounded.

17.—Honey Springs, Ind. Ter. *Union,* 2d, 6th, and 9th Kan. Cav., 2d and 3d Kan. Batteries, 2d and 3d Kan. Indian Home Guards; *Confed.,* Col. Cooper's Indians and Tex. Cav. Losses: *Union,* 17 killed, 60 wounded; *Confed.,* 150 killed, 400 wounded.

—Wytheville, W. Va. Union, 34th Ohio, 1st and 2d W. Va. Cav.; *Confed.** Losses: *Union,* 17 killed, 61 wounded; *Confed.,* 75 killed, 125 missing.

21 to 23.—Manassas Gap and Chester Gap, Va. *Union,* Cavalry advance and Third Corps Army of the Potomac; *Confed.,* Stuart's Cav. Losses: *Union,* 35 killed, 102 wounded; *Confed.,* 300 killed and wounded.

AUGUST, 1863.

1 to 3.—Rappahannock Station, Brandy Station, and Kelly's Ford, Va. *Union,* Brig.-Gen. Buford's Cav.; *Confed.,* Stuart's Cav. Losses: *Union,* 16 killed, 134 wounded.

21.—Quantrill's plunder and massacre of Lawrence, Kan., in which 140 citizens were killed and 24 wounded. Quantrill's loss, 40 killed.

25 to 30.—Averell's Raid in W. Va. Losses: *Union,* 3 killed, 10 wounded, 60 missing.

25 to 31.—Brownsville, Bayou Metoe, and Austin, Ark. *Union,* Davidson's Cav.; *Confed.,* Marmaduke's Cav. Losses: *Union,* 13 killed, 72 wounded.

26 and 27.—Rocky Gap, near White Sulphur Springs, W. Va. *Union,* 3d and 8th W. Va., 2d and 3d W. Va. Cav., 14th Pa. Cav.; *Confed.,* Gen. Samuel Jones' command. Losses: *Union,* 16 killed, 113 wounded; *Confed.,* 156 killed and wounded.

SEPTEMBER, 1863.

1.—Devil's Back Bone, Ark. *Union,* 1st Ark. 6th Mo. Militia, 2d Kan. Cav., 2d Ind. Battery; *Confed.,* Part of Gen. Price's command. Losses: *Union,* 4 killed, 12 wounded; *Confed.,* 25 killed, 40 wounded.

8.—Night attack on Fort Sumter, S. C. *Union,* 413 marines and sailors from the South Atlantic Blockading Squadron, led by Commander Stevens, U. S. N. *Confed.,* Garrison of Fort Sumter. Losses: *Union,* 124 killed, wounded, and missing.

9.—Cumberland Gap, Tenn. *Union,* Shackleford's Cav.; *Confed.,* Gen. J. W. Frazer's brigade. Losses: *Confed.,* 2000 captured.

* No record found.

HOLDING THE WESTERN FRONTIER IN '63

Two regiments of fighting men from the Northwest that partici-
pated in the rough campaigning of the frontier across the Mississippi in Arkansas in 1863.   In the upper picture is the camp of
the Twenty-eighth Wisconsin Infantry at Little Rock, and in the
lower view the Third Minnesota Infantry, Colonel C. C. Andrews
commanding, is drawn up on dress parade in front of the State
Capitol.   Both organiza-
tions fought in the expedition which Major-General
Frederick Steele organized
at Helena, August 5, 1863,
to break up the Confeder-
ate army under Price in
Arkansas. On the very day
that Vicksburg surrendered,
July 4th, the Confederate
General T. H. Holmes ap-
peared before Helena with
a force of over eight thousand. He had telegraphed
to his superior, E. K. Smith,
on June 15th, "I believe we

THE THIRD MINNESOTA

can take Helena; please let me do it." To which Smith had replied,
"Most certainly do it."   Holmes hoped to make a new Vicksburg
to keep the Mississippi closed from the west bank. Helena was
garrisoned by a force less than half as great as that which came
against it.   Among the defenders were the Twenty-eighth
Wisconsin.   On the morning of July 4, 1863, under command
of Major-General B. M.
Prentiss, these Federals
repulsed two vigorous
assaults, and Holmes, giving up hope of success, returned to Little Rock.
This aroused the Federals
to the importance of holding Arkansas, and General
Frederick Steele collected
about twelve thousand men
at Helena early in August.
The troops left Helena on
August 10th, and pushed
back the Confederates
under General Marmaduke.

10.—Little Rock, Ark. Evacuation by Confederates under Gen. Price. *Union,* Maj.-Gen. .Steele's troops and Davidson's Cav.; *Confed.,* Price's Division, L. M. Walker's and J. S. Marmaduke's Cav.

13.—Culpeper, Va. *Union,* Cavalry Corps, Army of the Potomac; *Confed.,* Stuart's Cav. Losses: *Union,* 3 killed, 40 wounded; *Confed.,* 10 killed, 40 wounded, 75 missing.

—Leet's Tan Yard, near Chickamauga, Ga. *Union,* Wider's mounted brigade; *Confed.,* Outposts of Gen. Bragg's Army. Losses: *Union,* 50 killed and wounded; *Confed.,* 10 killed, 40 wounded.

19 and 20.—Chickamauga, Ga. Army of the Cumberland, Maj.-Gen. Rosecrans; Fourteenth Corps, Maj.-Gen. Thomas; Twentieth Corps, Maj.-Gen. McCook; Twenty-first Corps, Maj.-Gen. Critten-den; Reserve Corps, Maj.-Gen. Granger; *Confed.,* Army of Tennesseee, Gen. Braxton Bragg; Gen. Polk's Corps, Longstreet's Corps (Army of Northern Virginia); D. H. Hill's Corps, Buckner's Corps, Gen. W. H. T. Walker's Reserve Corps, Forrest's and Wheeler's Cav. Losses: *Union,* 1644 killed, 9262 wounded, 4945 missing; *Confed.,* 2389 killed, 13412 wounded, 2003 missing.

—Blountsville, Tenn. *Union,* Foster's 2d Brigade Cav.; *Confed.,* 1st Tenn. Cav. Losses: *Union,* 5 killed, 22 wounded; *C o n f e d.,* 15 killed, 50 wounded, 100 missing.

—Rockville, Md. *Union,* 11th N. Y. Cav.; *Confed.,* Stuart's Cav. Losses: *Confed.,* 34 killed and wounded.

OCTOBER, 1863.

3.—McMinnville, Tenn. *Union,* 4th Tenn.; *Confed.,* Detachment of Gen. Bragg's Army. Losses: *Union,* 7 killed, 31 wounded, 350 missing; *Confed.,* 23 killed and wounded.

7.—Near Farmington, Tenn. *Union,* 1st, 3d, and 4th Ohio Cav., 2d Ky. Cav., Long's 2d Cav. Division, and Wilder's Brigade Mounted Inft.; *Confed.,* Wheeler's Cav. Losses: *Union,* 15 killed, 60 wounded; *Confed.,* 10 killed, 60 wounded, 240 missing.

—Blue Springs, Tenn. *Union,* Ninth Corps, Army of the Ohio, and Shackleford's Cav.; *Confed.,* Gen. J. S. Williams' command. Losses: *Union,* 100 killed, wounded, and missing; *Confed.,* 66 killed and wounded, 150 missing.

12 and 13.—Ingham's Mills and Wyatts, Miss. *Union,* 2d Iowa Cav.; *Confed.,* Chalmers' Cav. Losses: *Union,* 45 killed and wounded; *Confed.,* 50 killed and wounded.

—Culpeper and White Sulphur Springs, Va. *Union,* Cavalry Corps Army of the Potomac; *Confed.,* Stuart's Cav. Losses: *Union,* 8 killed, 46 wounded.

—Merrill's Crossing on La Mine Bridge, Mo. *Union,* Mo. Enrolled Militia, 1st Mo. Militia Battery, 1st, 4th, and 7th Mo. Militia Cav.; *Confed.,* Shelby's Cav. Losses: *Union,* 16 killed; *Confed.,* 53 killed, 70 wounded.

14.—Bristoe Station, Va. *Union,* Second Corps, portion of Fifth Corps, 2d Cav. Division, Army of the Potomac; *Confed.,* Divisions of Heth, R. H. Anderson, and A. P. Hill. Losses: *Union,* 51 killed, 329 wounded; *Confed.,* 750 killed and wounded, 450 missing.

15.—McLean's Ford or Liberty Mills, Va. *Union,* 5th, 6th, 7th, and 8th N. J., 151st N. Y., 115th Pa., 4th Bat. Me. Art. and Bat. K. 4th U. S. Art. *Confed.,* Gen. L. L. Lomax's Cav. Brigade. Losses: *Union,* 2 killed, 25 wounded; *Confed.,* 60 killed and wounded.

15 to 18.—Canton, Brownsville, and Clinton, Miss. *Union,* Portion of Fifteenth and Seventeenth Corps; *Confed.,* Gen. W. H. Jackson's command. Losses: *Confed.,* 200 killed and wounded.

18.—Charleston, W. Va. *Union,* 9th Md.; *Confed.,* Gen. Imboden's command. Losses: *Union,* 12 killed, 13 wounded, 379 missing.

19.—Buckland Mills, Va. *Union,* 3d Division of Kilpatrick's Cav.; *Confed.,* Stuart's Cav. Losses: *Union,* 20 killed, 60 wounded, 100 missing; *Confed.,* 10 killed, 40 wounded.

20 and 22.—Philadelphia, T e n n. *Union,* 45th Ohio Mounted Inft., 1st, 11th, and 12th Ky. Cav., 24th Ind. Battery; *Confed.,* Gen. J. S. Williams' command. Losses: *Union,* 20 killed, 80 wounded, 354 missing; *Confed.,* 15 killed, 82 wounded, 111 missing.

THE MONTH BEFORE MINE RUN, OCTOBER, 1863

Meade's Headquarters at Culpeper, Virginia.   In the vicinity of Culpeper Court House, ten miles from the banks of the Rappahannock and thirty miles northwest of Fredericksburg, the Army of the Potomac was encamped after Gettysburg.   Meade had followed Lee southward throughout the summer in the hope of striking his army before it had recovered from the blow dealt it in Pennsylvania.   But Lee, in great depression and wishing to retire, remained on the defensive; the departure of Longstreet for Chickamauga in September had made him still more wary.   Meade's forces had been reduced also by the despatching of two corps, under Hooker, into Tennessee, so he in turn was urged to caution.   The fall of 1863 was spent in skilful maneuvers with the flash of battle at Bristoe Station, October 14th, where Warren worsted A. P. Hill, and at Rappahannock Station on November 7th, where the Sixth Corps distinguished itself. At Mine Run, near the old Chancellorsville battle-ground, Lee was strongly entrenched and here the opposing forces came near a general engagement on November 30th, but the moment passed and both sides went into winter quarters.   By March, 1864, all was activity at Culpeper; the army awaited its new commander, Grant, who was to lead it again toward Chancellorsville and The Wilderness.

25.—Pine Bluff, Ark. *Union,* 5th Kan. and 1st Ind. Cav.; *Confed.,* Gen. Price's command. Losses: *Union,* 11 killed, 27 wounded; *Confed.,* 53 killed, 164 wounded.

28 and 29.—Wauhatchie, Tenn. *Union,* Eleventh Corps and 2d Division of Twelfth Corps; *Confed.,* Gen. James Longstreet's Corps. Losses: *Union,* 78 killed, 327 wounded, 15 missing. *Confed.* (estimated) 300 killed, 1200 wounded.

NOVEMBER, 1863.

3.—Grand Coteau, La. *Union,* 3d and 4th Divisions, Thirteenth Corps; *Confed.,* Gen. Green's Cav. Division. Losses: *Union,* 26 killed, 124 wounded, 576 missing; *Confed.,* 60 killed, 320 wounded, 65 missing.

6.—Rogersville, Tenn. *Union,* 7th Ohio Cav., 2d Tenn. Mounted Inft., 2d Ill. Battery; *Confed.,* Gens. W. E. Jones and H. L. Giltner's Brigades. Losses: *Union,* 5 killed, 12 wounded, 650 missing; *Confed.,* 10 killed, 20 wounded.
—Droop Mountain, Va. *Union,* 10th W. Va., 28th Ohio, 14th Pa. Cav., 2d and 5th W. Va. Cav., Battery B, W. Va. Artil.; *Confed.,* Gen. Echol's Brigade. Losses: *Union,* 31 killed, 94 wounded; *Confed.,* 50 killed, 250 wounded, 100 missing.

7.—Rappahannock Station, Va. *Union,* 5th Wis., 5th, 6th Maine, 49th, 119th Pa., 121st N. Y.; *Confed.,* Two brigades of Gen. Jubal Early's command. Losses: *Union,* 419 killed and wounded; *Confed.,* 6 killed, 39 wounded, 1,629 captured or missing.
—Kelly's Ford, Va. *Union,* 1st U. S. Sharpshooters, 40th N. Y., 1st and 20th Ind., 3d and 5th Mich., 110th Pa., supported by remainder of Third Corps; *Confed.,* Stuart's Cav. Losses: *Union,* 70 killed and wounded; *Confed.,* 5 killed, 59 wounded, 295 missing.

14.—Huff's Ferry, Tenn. *Union,* 111th Ohio, 107th Ill., 11th and 13th Ky., 23d Mich., 24th Mich. Battery; *Confed.,* Wheeler's Cav. Losses: *Union,* 100 killed and wounded.

16.—Campbell's Station, Tenn. *U n i o n,* Ninth Corps, 2d Division of Twenty-third Corps, Sanders' Cav.; *Confed.,*

Longstreet's Corps. Losses: *Union,* 31 killed, 211 wounded, and 76 missing; *Confed.,* 570 killed and wounded.

17 to Dec. 4.—Siege of Knoxville, Tenn. *Union,* Army of the Ohio, commanded by Maj.-Gen. Burnside; *Confed.,* Gen. Longstreet's Corps, Alexander's Art., Wheeler's Cav. Losses: Complete casualties not recorded. *Union,* 94 killed, 394 wounded, and 207 missing; *Confed.,* (minus the cavalry *) 182 killed, 768 wounded, 192 missing.

23 to 25.—Chattanooga, Lookout Mountain, Orchard Knob and Missionary Ridge, Tenn. *Union,* Forces commanded by Maj.-Gen. U. S. Grant, as follows: Fourth and Fourteenth Corps, Army of the Cumberland; Maj.-Gen. Geo. H. Thomas, Eleventh Corps; Geary's Division of the Twelfth Corps; Fifteenth Corps; Smith's Division, Seventeenth Corps, Army of the Tennessee, Maj.-Gen. W. T. Sherman; *Confed.,* Gen. Bragg's command; W. J. Hardee's Corps; Breckinridge's Corps; Art. Reserve, detachments of Cav. Losses: *Union,* 757 killed, 4529 wounded, 330 missing; *Confed.,* 361 killed, 2181 wounded, 6142 missing.

26 to 28.—Operations at Mine Run, Va., including Raccoon Ford, New Hope, Robertson's Tavern, Bartlett's Mills, and Locust Grove. *Union,* First Corps, Second Corps, Third Corps, Fifth Corps, Sixth Corps, and 1st and 2d Cav. Divisions Army of the Potomac; *Confed.,* Army of Northern Virginia, Gen. Robert E. Lee. Losses: *Union,* 173 killed, 1099 wounded, 381 missing; *Confed.,* 98 killed, 610 wounded, 1104 missing.

27.—Ringgold and Taylor's Ridge, Ga. *Union,* Portions of Twelfth, Fourteenth, and Fifteenth Corps; *Confed.,* Rear Guard of Gen. Bragg's Army on retreat from Chattanooga. Losses: *Union,* 68 killed, 351 wounded; *Confed.,* 50 killed, 200 wounded, 230 missing.

DECEMBER, 1863.

1 to 4.—Ripley and Moscow Station, Miss., and Salisbury, Tenn. *U n i o n,* 2d Brigade Cav. Division of Sixteenth Corps; *Confed.,* Gen. S. D. Lee's command. Losses: *Union,* 175 killed and

* No record found.

[346]

THE ANCIENT SALLY PORT

Civil War Garrison at the Gate of Fort Marion, St. Augustine, Florida.   American guns were first turned against it when Oglethorpe led his expedition from South Carolina against St. Augustine in May, 1740.   Its style of architecture tells plainly of its origin and antiquity; it was called by the Spaniards "Castle St. Marcus."   When Commander Rodgers brought his flag of truce to St. Augustine, the mayor proposed to turn over the fort to him, but Rodgers instructed him to establish a patrol and guard at the fort and make careful inventories of what it contained.   Several good guns had been taken from it by the Confederates, but there still remained three fine army 32-pounders and two 8-inch seacoast howitzers, with a quantity of ammunition.   About a fifth of the inhabitants of St. Augustine had fled at the coming of the Federals, but of the 1,500 that remained Commander Rodgers reported that they were "many citizens who are earnestly attached to the Union, a large number who are silently opposed to it, and a still larger number who care very little about the matter."

wounded; *Confed.*, 15 killed, 40 wounded.

2.—Walker's Ford, Tenn. *Union*, 65th, 116th, and 118th Ind., 21st Ohio Battery, 5th Ind. Cav., 14th Ill. Cav.; *Confed.*, Wheeler's Cav. Losses: *Union*, 9 killed, 39 wounded; *Confed.*, 25 killed, 50 wounded.

8 to 21.—Averell's raid in South-western Va.; *Confed.*, Gen. Jno. D. Imboden's command. Losses: *Union*, 6 killed, 5 wounded; *Confed.*, 200 captured.

10 to 14.—Bean's Station and Morristown, Tenn. *Union*, Shackleford's Cav.; *Confed.*, Longstreet's Corps, Martin's Cav. Losses: *Union*, 700 killed and wounded; *Confed.*, 932 killed and wounded, 150 captured.

19.—Barren Fork, Ind. Ter. *Union*, 1st and 3d Kan., Indian Home Guards; *Confed.** Losses: *Confed.*, 50 killed.

28.—Charleston, Tenn. *Union*, Detachments of the 2d Mo. and 4th Ohio Cav. guarding wagon train; *Confed.*, Wheeler's Cav. Losses: *Union*, 2 killed, 15 wounded; *Confed.*, 8 killed, 89 wounded, 121 captured.

30.—St. Augustine, Fla. *Union*, 10th Conn., 24th Mass.; *Confed.*, 2d Fla. Cav. Losses: *Union*, 4 killed.

—Waldron, Ark. *Union*, 2d Kan. Cav.; *Confed.*, Maj. Gibson's command. Losses: *Union*, 2 killed, 6 wounded; *Confed.*, 1 killed, 8 wounded.

JANUARY, 1864.

1 to 10.—Rectortown and Loudon Heights, Va. *Union*, 1st Md. Cav., Potomac Home Brigade; *Confed.*, Col. J. S. Mosby's command. Losses: *Union*, 29 killed and wounded, 41 missing; *Confed.*, 4 killed, 10 wounded.

3.—Jonesville, Va. *Union*, Detachment 16th Ill. Cav., 22d Ohio Battery; *Confed.*, Jones' Cavalry. Losses: *Union*, 12 killed, 48 wounded, 300 missing; *Confed.*, 4 killed, 12 wounded.

16 and 17.—Dandridge, Tenn. *Union*, Fourth Corps and Cav. Division of Army of the Ohio; *Confed.*, Longstreet's command. Losses: *Union*, 150 wounded.

19 and 24.—Tazewell, Tenn. *Union*, 34th Ky., 116th and 118th Ind., 11th Tenn. Cav., 11th Mich. Bat'y.; *Confed.*, Longstreet's command. Losses: *Confed.*, 31 killed.

27.—Fair Gardens or Kelly's Ford, Tenn. *Union*, Sturgis's Cavalry; *Confed.*, Martin's and Morgan's Cavalry. Losses: *Union*, 100 killed and wounded; *Confed.*, 65 killed, 100 captured.

28.—Tunnel Hill, Ga. *Union*, part of Fourteenth Corps; *Confed.*, Outposts of the Army of the Tennessee. Losses: *Union*, 2 wounded; *Confed.*, 32 wounded.

31.—Smithfield, Va. *Union*, Detachments 99th N. Y., 21st Conn., 20th N. Y. Cav., 3d Pa. Artil., and marines from U. S. Gunboats *Minnesota* and *Smith Briggs*; *Confed.** Losses: *Union*, 90 missing.

29 to Feb. 1.—Medley, W. Va. *Union*, 1st and 14th W. Va., 23d Ill., 2d Md., Potomac Home Brigade, 4th W. Va. Cav., Ringgold (Pa.) Cav.; *Confed.*, Col. T. L. Rosser's Cav. Losses: *Union*, 10 killed, 70 wounded.

FEBRUARY, 1864.

1 to 3.—Bachelor Creek, Newport Barracks, and New Berne, N. C. *Union*, 132d N. Y., 9th Vt., 17th Mass., 2d N. C., 12th N. Y. Cav., 3d N. Y. Artil.; *Confed.*, Expedition commanded by Gen. Geo. E. Pickett. Losses: *Union*, 16 killed, 50 wounded, 280 missing; *Confed.*, 5 killed, 30 wounded.

1 to March 8.—Expedition up the Yazoo River, Miss. *Union*, 11th Ill., 47th U. S. Colored, 3d U. S. Colored Cav., and a portion of Porter's Fleet of gunboats; *Confed.*, Gen. J. E. Johnston's command. Losses: *Union*, 35 killed, 121 wounded. *Confed.*, 35 killed, 90 wounded.

3 to March 5.—Expedition from Vicksburg to Meridian, Miss. *Union*, Two Divisions of the Sixteenth and three of the Seventeenth Corps, with the 5th Ill., 4th Iowa, 10th Mo. and Foster's (Ohio) Cav.; *Confed.*, Gen. Polk's command; Loring's and French's divisions, Forrest's and Armstrong's Cav. Losses: *Union*, 56 killed, 138 wounded, 105 miss-

* No record found.

FIGHTING IN FLORIDA—DECEMBER, 1863

A Civil War skirmish took place at St. Augustine, Florida, December 30, 1863, before the quaint old bastions of Fort Marion —the oldest Spanish fort in the Western Hemisphere, and the oldest anywhere outside of Spain. St. Augustine, however, was not disturbed by the one serious attempt that was made to penetrate the interior of Florida. If this could be done, it was throught at Washington that many citizens of the State would flock to the Union cause and could be reconstructed into a State whose electoral vote would be extremely valuable in retaining the Lincoln Administration in power. On February 5, 1864, under orders from General Gillmore, an expedition left Hilton Head and, arriving at Jacksonville, Florida, pushed forward across the State. Rapidly collecting reënforcements from Savannah and Charleston, the Confederate General Finegan met the Federals at Clustee and sharply defeated them February 20, 1864. This put an end to the only effort to invade the State of Florida.

ARTILLERY INSIDE THE FORT

ing; *Confed.*, 503 killed and wounded, 212 captured.

5.—Quallatown, N. C. *Union*, Detachment of 14th Ill. Cav.; *Confed.*, 26th N. C. Losses: *Union*, 3 killed, 6 wounded; *Confed.*, 50 captured.

6.—Morton's Ford, Va. *Union*, Portion of Second Corps; *Confed.*, Wade Hampton's Cav. Losses: *Union*, 14 killed, 218 wounded, 391 missing; *Confed.*, 100 killed, wounded, and missing.

9 to 14.—Barber's Place, St. Mary's River, Lake City, and Gainesville, Fla. *Union*, 40th Mass. Mounted Inft. and Independent (Mass.) Cav.; *Confed.*, Gen. Joseph Finnegan's command. Losses: *Union*, 4 killed, 16 wounded; *Confed.*, 4 killed, 48 wounded.

10 to 25.—Gen. Wm. Sooy Smith's Raid from Memphis, Tenn., into Mississippi. *Union*, Smith's Division; *Confed.*, Forrest's Cav. Losses: *Union*, 47 killed, 152 wounded, 120 missing; *Confed.*, 50 wounded, 300 captured.

14 and 15.—Waterproof, La. *Union*, 49th U. S. Colored and U. S. Gunboat *Forest Rose; Confed.*, Col. Harrison's command. Losses: *Union*, 8 killed, 14 wounded; *Confed.*, 15 killed.

20.—Olustee or Silver Lake, Fla. *Union*, 47th, 48th, and 115th N. Y., 7th Conn., 7th N. H., 40th Mass., 8th and 54th U. S. Colored, 1st N. C. Colored, 1st Mass. Cav., 1st and 3d U. S. Artil., 3d R. I. Artil.; *Confed.*, Colquitt's and Harrison's brigades under Gen. Joseph Finnegan. Losses: *Union*, 193 killed, 1175 wounded, 460 missing; *Confed.*, 940 killed and wounded.

22.—Okolona, Miss. *Union*, Smith's Cav.; *Confed.*, Forrest's Cav. Losses: *Union*, 47 killed, 152 wounded, 120 missing; *Confed.**

25 to 27.—Buzzard Roost, Tunnel Hill, and Rocky Face, Ga. *Union*, Fourth and Fourteenth Corps and Cavalry Corps Army of the Cumberland; *Confed.*, Troops of Gen. Jos. E. Johnston's command. Losses: *Union*, 17 killed, 272 wounded; *Confed.*, 20 killed, 120 wounded.

28 to March 4.— Kilpatrick's and Dahlgren's Raid from Stevensburg, Va., to Richmond. *Union*, Kilpatrick's Cavalry; *Confed.*, Cavalry commanded by Gens. G. W. C. Lee, Bradley T. Johnson, and Wade Hampton and Home Guards. Losses: *Union*, 330 killed, wounded, and captured; *Confed.*, 308 killed, wounded, and captured.

MARCH, 1864.

14.—Fort De Russy, La. *Union*, Detachments of Sixteenth and Seventeenth Corps and Porter's Miss. Squadron; *Confed.*, Troops under Gen. Walker's command. Losses: *Union*, 7 killed, 41 wounded; *Confed.*, 5 killed, 4 wounded, 260 prisoners.

21.—Henderson Hills, La. *Union*, Detachments of Sixteenth Corps and Cavalry Division Nineteenth Corps; *Confed.*, 2d La. Cav. Losses: *Union*, 1 wounded; Confed., 8 killed, 250 captured.

24.—Union City, Tenn. *Union*, 7th Tenn. Cav.; *Confed.*, Forrest's Cav. Losses: *Union*, 450 captured.

25.—Fort Anderson, Paducah, Ky. *Union*, 122d Ill., 16th Ky. Cav., 8th U. S. Colored Artil.; *Confed.*, Forrest's Cav. Losses: *Union*, 14 killed, 46 wounded; *Confed.*, 10 killed, 40 wounded.

26 to 30.—Longview and Mt. Elba, Ark. *Union*, 28th Wis., 5th Kan. Cav., 7th Mo. Cav.; *Confed.*, Gen. Price's command. Losses: *Union*, 4 killed, 18 wounded; *Confed.*, 12 killed, 35 wounded, 300 captured.

30.—Snyder's Bluff, Miss. *Union*, 3d U. S. Colored Cav.; *Confed.*, 3d, 9th Tex. Cav. Losses: *Union*, 16 killed, 3 wounded; *Confed.*, 3 killed, 7 wounded.

April, 1864.

1.—Augusta, Ark. *Union*, 3d Minn., 8th Mo. Cav.; *Confed.*, Gen. Price's command. Losses: *Union*, 8 killed, 16 wounded; *Confed.*, 15 killed, 45 wounded.

—Crump's Hill or Piney Woods, La. *Union*, 14th N. Y. Cav., 2d La., 2d Ill., and 16th Mo. Cav., 5th U. S. Colored Artil.; *Confed.*, Gen. Richard Taylor's command. Losses: *Union*, 20 wounded; *Confed.*, 10 killed, 25 wounded.

* No record found.

THE BASTIONS OF FORT MARION

On one of the bastions of Fort Marion, St. Augustine, a white flag was raised on the evening of March 8, 1862, as Commander C. R. P. Rodgers sailed up the harbor. He had been detached from the expedition sent from the North under command of Flag-Officer Du Pont to recover control of the whole line of seacoast of Georgia, Florida, and Alabama. Florida troops had been the first to seize a Federal fortification, taking possession of Fort Barrancas and the navy yard at Pensacola, January 13, 1861, and Fort Marion, at St. Augustine, was the first fortification in Florida to be surrendered to Federal authority, Flag-Officer Du Pont having seized and garrisoned the abandoned Fort Clinch, at Fernandina, on March 4, 1862. The Confederate troops in Florida abandoned their fortifications as Du Pont's expedition approached, and at St. Augustine were found the first inhabitants who had remained in their homes.

The citizens of St. Augustine raised the white flag on Fort Marion in answer to the one which Commander Rodgers was bearing as he approached to assure them of pacific intentions. Landing at the wharf, he was soon joined by the mayor and conducted to the city hall, where the municipal authorities were assembled. Rodgers assured them that so long as St. Augustine respected the Federal authority its government would be left in the hands of its citizens, and recommended that the flag of the Union be at once displayed at the fort. The night before a party of women had assembled in front of the barracks in Fort Marion and cut down the flagstaff to prevent its being used to again support the old flag. By order of the mayor, however, the Stars and Stripes were at once hoisted over Fort Marion.

THE OLDEST CHURCH IN AMERICA, 1864

3.—Okalona, Ark. *Union,* 27th Wis., 40th Iowa, 77th Ohio, 43d Ill., 1st Mo. Cav., 13th Ill. Cav.; *Confed.,* Gen. Sterling Price's command. Losses: *Union,* 16 killed, 74 wounded; *Confed.,* 75 killed and wounded.

4.—Campti, La. 35th Iowa, 5th Minn., 2d and 18th N. Y. Cav., 3d R. I. Cav. Losses: *Union,* 10 killed, 18 wounded; *Confed.,* 3 killed, 12 wounded.

—Elkins' Ferry, Ark. *Union,* 43d Ind., 29th and 36th Iowa, 1st Iowa Cav., Battery E 2d Mo. Light Artil.; *Confed.,* Gen. Sterling Price's command. Losses: *Union,* 5 killed, 33 wounded; *Confed.,* 18 killed, 30 wounded.

5.—Roseville, Ark. Seventy-five men of 2d and 6th Kan. Cav. (*Union*) in engagement with guerrillas. Losses: *Union,* 4 killed, 10 wounded; *Confed.,* 6 killed, 20 wounded, 11 captured.

7.—Wilson's Farm, La. *Union,* Cavalry of Nineteenth Corps; *Confed.,* Gen. Richard Taylor's command. Losses: *Union,* 14 killed, 39 wounded; *Confed.,* 15 killed, 40 wounded, 100 captured.

8 and 9.—Sabine Cross Roads and Pleasant Hill, La. *Union,* Portions of Thirteenth, Sixteenth, and Nineteenth Corps and Cavalry Division of Gen. Banks; *Confed.,* Walker's, Mouton's, and Green's Divisions of Gen. Richard Taylor's command. Losses: *Union,* 300 killed, 1600 wounded, 2100 missing; *Confed.,* 600 killed, 2400 wounded, 500 missing. *Union,* Maj.-Gen. Franklin and Brig.-Gen. Ransom wounded. *Confed.,* Maj.-Gen. Mouton and Brig.-Gen. Parsons killed.

10 to 13.—Prairie D'Ann, Ark. *Union,* 3d Division Seventh Corps; *Confed.,* Gen. Price's command. Losses: *Union,* 100 killed and wounded; *Confed.,* 50 killed and wounded.

12.—Blair's Landing, La. *Union,* Gen. Kilby Smith's command, Gunboats *Osage* and *Lexington; Confed.,* Gen. Green's Division of Taylor's command. Losses: *Union,* 7 wounded; *Confed.,* 200 killed and wounded.

13.—Moscow, Ark. *Union,* 18th Iowa, 6th Kan. Cav., 2d Ind. Battery; *Confed.,* Gen. Price's command. Losses: *Union,*

5 killed, 17 wounded; *Confed.,* 30 killed and wounded.

13 and 14.—Paintsville and Half-Mountain, Ky. *Union,* Ky. Volunteers; *Confed.,* Johnson's brigade Ky. Cav. Losses: *Union,* 4 wounded; *Confed.,* 25 killed, 25 wounded.

15 and 16.—Liberty P. O., and occupation of Camden, Ark. *Union,* 29th Iowa, 50th Ind., 9th Wis.; *Confed.,* Gen. Sterling Price's command. Losses: *Union,* 255 killed and wounded.

17 to 20.—Plymouth, N. C. *Union,* 85th N. Y., 103d Pa., 16th Conn., Gunboats *Southfield* and *Miami; Confed.,* Gen. Hoke's command, iron-clad ram *Albe-marle.* Losses: *Union,* 20 killed, 80 wounded, 1500 missing; *Confed.,* 500 killed, wounded, and missing. *Union,* Lieut.-Com. Flusser killed.

18.—Poison Springs, eight miles from Camden, Ark. *Union,* 18th Iowa, 79th U. S. Colored, 6th Kan. Cav.; *Confed.,* Shelby's Cav. Losses: *Union,* 204 killed and missing, 97 wounded. *Confed.,* 16 killed, 88 wounded, 10 missing.

22 and 24.—Monette's Ferry, Cane River, and Cloutersville, La. *Union,* Portion of Thirteenth, Seventeenth, and Nineteenth Corps; *Confed.,* Gen. Richard Taylor's command. Losses: *Union* (estimate), 350 killed and wounded; *Confed.,* 400 killed and wounded.

25.—Marks' Mills, Ark. *Union,* 36th Iowa, 77th Ohio, 43d Ill., 1st Ind. Cav., 7th Mo. Cav., Battery E 2d Mo. Light Artil.; *Confed.,* Troops of Gen. Kirby Smith's command. Losses: *Union,* 100 killed, 250 wounded, 1100 captured; *Confed.,* 41 killed, 108 wounded, 44 missing.

26.—Moro Creek, Ark. *Union,* 33d and 40th Iowa, 5th Kan., 2d and 4th Mo., 1st Iowa Cav.; *Confed.,* Troops of Gen. Kirby Smith's command. Losses: *Union,* 5 killed, 14 wounded.

30.—Jenkins' Ferry, Saline River, Ark. *Union,* 3d Division of Seventeenth Corps; *Confed.,* Texas, Missouri, and Arkansas troops under Gens. Kirby Smith and Sterling Price. Losses: *Union,* 200 killed, 955 wounded; *Confed.,* 86 killed, 356 wounded.

THEATRE OF
WESTERN CAMPAIGNS

SCALE OF MILES

0   25   50   75